ABRAHAM

ALSO BY DAVID ROSENBERG

Dreams of Being Eaten Alive (2000)

The Book of David (1997)

The Lost Book of Paradise (1993)

A Poet's Bible (1991)

The Book of J (1990)

ABRAHAM

The First Historical Biography

DAVID ROSENBERG

A Member of the Perseus Books Group
New York

Published by Basic Books,
A Member of the Perseus Books Group

Grateful acknowledgment is made for use of the following works:
Selections from *The Epic of Gilgamesh: A New Translation*, translated by Andrew George (London: Allen Lane, The Penguin Press, 1999). Translation copyright © Andrew George, 1999. Reproduced by permission of Penguin Books Ltd.
Selections from *Inanna: Lady of Largest Heart: Poems of the Sumerian High Priestess Enheduanna*, by Betty De Shong Meador (Austin: University of Texas Press, 2000). Translation copyright © Betty De Shong Meador, 2000. Reproduced by permission of University of Texas Press.
Selections (revised) from *The Book of J*, translated by David Rosenberg (New York: Grove Press, 1990). Translation copyright © 1990 by David Rosenberg. Used by permission of Grove/Atlantic, Inc.

Designed by Brent Wilcox
Text set in 11.5-point Minion

Library of Congress Cataloging-in-Publication Data
Rosenberg, David, 1943-
Abraham : the first historical biography / David Rosenberg.
p. cm.
Includes author's English translation of Hebrew texts from the book of Genesis about Abraham.
Includes bibliographical references and index.
ISBN-13: 978-0-465-07094-7 (hardcover : alk. paper)
ISBN-10: 0-465-07094-9 (hardcover : alk. paper)
1. Abraham (Biblical patriarch) 2. Patriarchs (Bible)—Biography. 3. Sumer—Religion. 4. Middle Eastern literature—Relation to the Old Testament. 5. Bible. O.T. Genesis XI-XXV, 11—History of Biblical events. 6. J document (Biblical criticism) 7. E document (Biblical criticism) I. Title.
BS580.A3R634 2006
222'.11092—dc22

2006001687

06 07 08 / 10 9 8 7 6 5 4 3 2 1

To Rhonda,
my coauthor

And to the memory of
Abraham and Shifra
of Wynmoor

The great figures of the Old Testament are so much more fully developed, so much more fraught with their own biographical past, so much more distinct as individuals, than are the Homeric heroes. Achilles and Odysseus are splendidly described in many well-ordered words. . . but they have no development. . .

—Erich Auerbach, *Mimesis* (1946)

Contents

PROLOGUE

Man at the Crossroads

These days we commonly accept the idea that Jesus was a Jew, that like thousands of other Jewish revolutionaries he spent his life actively involved in a debate about what it was to be a Jew, preached his ideas on this subject to other Jews, and died in their midst, probably as a consequence of those ideas. However, this notion is surprisingly new. It is the result of the work of a rigorous band of nineteenth-century German academics, whose ideas took more than half a century to make their way into mainstream culture. Just imagining the pre-Christian Jesus as Yeshua would have seemed strange to most of us, but a steady diet of popular books and films, and a sweeping spirit of ecumenism have allowed this idea to flourish.

More recently, the same kind of light is being turned on a figure that takes us even farther back in history, nearly four thousand years ago, to the very dawn of the Judaism into which Jesus would later be born. That man is Abraham. His very name evokes powerful images: bearded patriarch; progenitor of the Jewish and Arab peoples through Isaac and Ishmael; wild-eyed ascetic who, having smashed his father's idols, wanders off into the desert, turning his back on the gods of his fathers to bring into being the monotheism we know so well. This is Abraham, first Jew among Jews.

But much of this popular image is far from the truth.

To begin with, Abraham was born into Sumerian culture, raised in the eighteenth century BCE in the ancient capital of Ur, which presided over fertile lands in a crescent bounded by the Euphrates River to the east and the Tigris to the west, in what is now southern Iraq. Abraham's famous journey out of the homeland of his fathers into Canaan was begun by his father, Terah, prompted by the decline of Sumerian culture at the hand of newly ascendant Babylon. Far from being the renegade spiritual wanderer of popular lore, Abraham was the scion of a prosperous and well-educated family; his family's success and his own ambitions to greatness were, in fact, distinctly Sumerian.

Abraham's ideas about his profession, his family, the afterlife, divinity and its impact on the seemingly capricious, fragile nature of life—concerns that form the backbone of any culture—all arose out of Sumer. They could have been discussed as animatedly at the base of a third millennium BCE ziggurat in Ur, its temple jutting into the sky, as they might be today over coffee at Starbucks, or in a monthly book group. Although Sumerians differed from us in their valuing many gods, they adhered to a set of public religious beliefs quite apart from their active secular lives and private lives at home. In fundamental ways we are all latter-day Sumerians, yet we are startlingly, profoundly unaware of it.

When the great king Hammurapi united Mesopotamia in the eighteenth century BCE, creating a kingdom centered in Babylon, Sumer's ancient capital Ur was destined to become a backwater. Although Sumerian ideas were still venerated even in Babylon, they were being codified and losing their vitality in the process. Sumer itself was becoming a dead civilization in Abraham's time, and Abraham's own mission was rooted in its fate. His westward journey and the new world that arose from it were not the consequence of a blind wandering in the desert. It was born of a specific ambition: to found a civilization that might survive the growing threats to the ancient culture of Sumer. Its death throes intensified his yearning for a future that could not be extinguished, and to create it he would be prepared to endure the unknown and grave hardship.

The powerful truth of Abraham's life and ideas has been obscured by the passage of time and by thousands of years of mythmaking. For instance, the story of Abraham's smashing his father's idols in Ur is not in the Bible. It is a cover story invented to convince us that Abraham rejected his father's religion. To reclaim that truth we will go back in time to Abraham's world, to the imposing libraries and soaring ziggurat of Ur, past the teeming bazaars of Harran, through the caravan trade towns and small enterprising kingdoms along the way to Canaan, down the Nile to potent Egypt, and then back to Abraham and Sarah's tent, pitched in the sweet grasses of the Promised Land. The Abraham who emerges from this odyssey is well equipped to negotiate a relationship with Yahweh, to forge the Covenant that will sculpt the future every bit as much as the signal achievements of Abraham's Sumerian ancestors, who gave us writing, the wheel, the plow, the sailboat, the vault, the dome, sophisticated art, and scores of other sudden innovations.

THE HISTORICAL ABRAHAM

The story of Abraham is embedded like ancient lapis in the history of Sumer and Akkad, provinces of Mesopotamia, that rich land cradled by the Tigris and Euphrates Rivers: Abraham's context of Sumerian culture and religion. Following the outline provided in Genesis, we add the textures of Abraham's world, with the help of original sources, especially Sumerian literature taught in the schools Abraham must have attended in Ur. However, the principal sites on Abraham's journey, fundamental to the Bible, are largely gone, buried in desert sands. It will be our task to bring this historical past to life by drawing on cuneiform writing deciphered for the first time in the twentieth century and still turning up in newly discovered clay tablets. This trove contains Sumerian texts being read for the first time in almost three thousand years. Just a few years ago, new texts from an ancient city-state in Turkey were decoded.

As we examine the connection between the pre-Abrahamic world of various gods and the religion of our ancestor, we see how, from a Sumerian pantheon of public and personal gods, a God can emerge who loves humanity. This affection will allow our human fear of death and annihilation to be transformed through a journey of personal exploration—

just as Abraham's was. As we embark on our detective work, some clues will come from Abraham's time, and others will require investigation into the period nearly a thousand years after Abraham's death, when his story would be recorded in the court of King Solomon.

In that later epoch, scholars and writers compared oral transmission with written literature and translations from cuneiform into Hebrew in order to create a history of humanity. This text would become the earliest known strand of the Jewish Torah, or the first five books of the Christian Old Testament. The motives and historical context of the first biblical writers would inevitably shape the image of Abraham that emerged in Hebrew. And this image in turn would become visible to the world only through layers of subsequent editing and writing, further complicated by the clutter of three thousand years of cultural projections. However, by understanding these creative forces, and the intimate relationship between Abraham and God that the original writers sought to weave out of their Sumerian sources, we gain new perspective on our subject. And we gain insight on our own sense of identity at the very time and place when it first comes into being.

THE WRITERS BEHIND THE SCENES

Although some readers may be confronting the notion of the authorship of the Bible here for the first time, it has been the subject of biblical scholarship for more than a century and is taught widely in universities and seminaries. In short, the biblical text has been acknowledged as the product of several recognizable hands. The earliest may be that of a woman, a writer labeled "J" after her name for the creator, Yahweh, pronounced "Jahweh" by the Germans. J brought extraordinary sophistication and literary art to her task. The core of her original sources were Sumerian writings and Akkadian adaptations (from the neighbor who conquered Sumer)—cuneiform carvings into tablets of clay and stone. These sources would find new expression through J's transformations. In this way, Sumerian and Akkadian histories and concepts became enfolded in the language of a later people, the Israelites of J's time, as they explored their own origins.

Understanding J's work, and the process of adding and editing by subsequent authors that yielded the Torah (or Five Books of Moses: the Pentateuch), is valuable not only for the text we can still read today; it is also profoundly revealing about its original audience some twenty-five hundred to three thousand years ago, and the assumptions this readership brought to the text. These educated readers knew the lands that Abraham traversed, and the history of conflict that had embroiled its peoples, as well as all the assumptions that the Sumerian Abraham would bring to every moment of his life's journey. J's reader was also alive to the nuances and ironies that J contributed to the narrative.

THE PROMISED LAND

The biblical writers' retelling of Abraham's journey was a recovery of the oldest human vision of sanctified land. The Sumerian story of a people springing from the clay in a sacred land is older than Sumer itself. Almost a thousand years after Abraham died, a writer of the Bible in Jerusalem tells us that Abraham's travels were a journey to a "Promised Land." But that is not the whole story of how Abraham encountered it. For Abraham himself, the new land promised instead a dialogue with the past greatness of Sumer. And for J, Sumerian stories such as the Creation and the Flood could now be reinterpreted themselves as steps on a journey to the Promised Land of a more complicated God, a God who became a synthesis of the one Abraham brought from Sumer and the one he met in Canaan—a God who becomes humanized in conversation with the man he has chosen. This face-to-face conversation in which we participate as audience is a technique borrowed directly from Sumerian literary and religious tradition.

FROM "MY GOD" TO "THE ONLY GOD"

Most important of all to our understanding of Abraham the Sumerian, and to those who followed him, is the religious context in which he lived. In Abraham's Ur there were two main forms of worship. The public form took place at the temple. Here statues of the gods and their families were arranged in moving tableaux, becoming dramatis personae in the temporal lives of the gods on Earth. Priests or priestesses would wake their gods in the morning, dress them, provide food and drink, take the gods for outings, and put the god to bed at night. Those Sumerians who could afford to do so commissioned votive statues of themselves to be placed in the temple so that they themselves could be represented observing the daily lives of the gods at all times, and in this way partake of divinity as a rapt audience. This made for a lively trade in statues, bringing prosperity to artists and artisans such as Abraham's father, Terah.

Privately, the Sumerian founder of a household also adopted a more personal god, sometimes after a dream or vision. This vision was usually a scene of mutual understanding between god and man, a symbol of a relationship that was close, often tender. This god became the household god, an intermediary who argued for its human family's well-being among the more powerful, more public gods. It is here in Sumerian culture, then, that we find the precedent for Abraham to be indulged on an equal footing, as when he reasons with Yahweh in Canaan, rather than being awe-struck and overwhelmed as he might have been in another tradition.

In Abraham's day, public gods, those for whom daily theater was being performed in the temples, were already losing their dramatic potency. Public institutions associated with the old order were waning, and as they did the personal household gods took on added importance. These were also "portable" gods, so that when Abraham set out from Harran for Canaan with a large entourage of animals and servants—and a considerable cache of silver and gold—his personal god would not be left behind.

Moreover, the laws and codes of ethics that Abraham brought with him to Canaan (such as the well-documented "Code of Hammurapi") would become the basis for biblical concepts and commandments. These would be refined by Judaism and Christianity in the centuries to come, first in the Mosaic tradition that would lead to Talmudic law, and later in the medieval philosophy that attempts to distinguish between what is fixed by divine law and what is subject to personal interpretation. Although these are some of the great cultural and philosophical developments of western civilization, their seeds are all there in Abraham's time. And we will watch them planted in new soil as we follow Abraham's journey.

One of the clichés of religious history has it that Christianity somehow humanized an otherwise one-dimensional Old Testament God. As we will see, it was Abraham, along with the authors of the Hebrew Bible, who achieved that life-altering perspective by translating the idea of God from the Sumerian to the Hebrew. The Sumerian personal god is transformed into the personal god of a people; a private household god of a man from Ur merges with a public creator-god of Canaan. And the God who emerges is newly humanized as a self-conscious being—supernatural and nonhuman, yet one who can also be a lonely being in need of an Abraham.

What is unique here is not simply monotheism, not just the "one" God as conventional wisdom has it, but rather his new relationship with humanity. That is the reason Abraham's God is still with us today—whereas another fledgling monotheism, that of the Egyptian Pharoah Akhenaton, for example, is not. Something new happened after Sumerian concepts were married with the deity Abraham met in Canaan, something never seen before, a manifestation of respect between man and creator that stands revealed by Abraham's history. In the chapter that lies ahead we will see what the Bible tells us of Abraham's journey, translated from the original Hebrew by this author. Then we will return with Abraham to Ur—to follow his footsteps out.

PART 1

THE OVERVIEW

CHAPTER 1

The History of Abraham

Until recently, when we began in the last century to decipher the clay tablets from Sumer, Akkad, and other ancient kingdoms, all that we knew of Abraham's history was contained in the Bible. However, there are numerous later legends and stories about Abraham, and even today accounts of Abraham's life continue to be based on them. It remains the supposition of most commentators that Abraham was always a legendary character, even in the Bible. But the aim of this book is to render that assumption itself a relic of the past. The biography that unfolds in the chapters ahead will show that a historical individual, Abraham, must have existed and that the earliest authors of the Bible relied upon written evidence of this.

In the narrative that follows, I present a new translation of the relevant passages by the original biblical authors. Later, we will examine why and how it was written to be a history. We'll see why members of the original audience in ancient times, for whom it was written, knew a great deal of history—of their people, their region, and the world—that we have unfortunately lost. But we are beginning to recover that earlier, pre-biblical history, and with it we can restore the context of how the Bible was first heard and understood.

As a translator, I generally favor a seamless translation that can be read without interruption, just like most Bible translations. Nevertheless, in this, the first translation of its kind, I have chosen to emphasize the styles of the different biblical authors. I look behind the late biblical Hebrew recension (which is all that has survived and dates back no earlier than the fifth century BCE) to deduce the early Hebrew language and original idiom in which each author would have actually written.

A great author known today as J, of whom we are about to discover a great deal more in these pages, wrote the major part of this translation as early as the tenth century BCE in Jerusalem. In her text, Yahweh and Abraham speak as intimately as would a man and his personal god in ancient Sumer, going as far back as the thirty-third century BCE.

The passage beginning "These are the days when the four kings" was translated by J from an author, designated as X by scholars, writing in Canaan very near to the time of Abraham in the eighteenth century BCE. The language of the original writing, Akkadian, would have been the same as spoken by Abraham.

The portion written by E, as early as the ninth century BCE in Samaria, the new capital of the divided kingdom of Israel, begins with a retelling of the problem of Sarah's being both a wife and a sister to Abraham. In E's version, the history is situated in Canaan rather than Egypt, as it was in J.

The passages written by E (culminating in the dream of Isaac's near sacrifice) have been translated in verse form. Since the value of the writing surface—whether clay, papyrus, or parchment—required that every available space be utilized, there were other ways to suggest verse form in this ancient period. Even the earliest Sumerian poetry was written down to look like prose.

Finally, there are brief passages by P that are attached to the others. P wrote in the seventh century BCE, in Jerusalem.

What follows, then, is all that most people knew about the historical Abraham until now. It begins in ancient Sumer (called Shinar in the Bible) with the building of a ziggurat in Babylon that the biblical author models upon one that Abraham may have visited in his own day.

THE AUTHOR'S TRANSLATION FROM THE ORIGINAL HEBREW

Now listen: all the earth uses one tongue, one and the same words. Watch: they journey from the east, arrive at a valley in the land of Sumer, settle there.

"We can bring ourselves together," they said, "like stone on stone, use brick for stone: bake it until hard." For mortar, they heated bitumen.

"If we bring ourselves together," they said, "we can build a city and tower, its top touching the sky—to arrive at fame. Without a name we're unbound, scattered over the face of the earth."

Yahweh came down to watch the city and tower the sons of man were bound to build. "They are one people, with the same tongue," said Yahweh. "They conceive this between them, and it leads up until no boundary exists to what they will touch. Between us, let's descend, baffle their tongue until each is scatter-brain to his friend."

From there Yahweh scattered them over the whole face of the earth; the city there came unbound.

That is why they named the place Bavel: their tongues were baffled there by Yahweh. Scattered by Yahweh from there, they arrived at the ends of the earth.

These are the records of Shem . . . Reu lived after his father Serug seven and two hundred years, and he fathered sons and daughters. Serug lived thirty years and he fathered Nahor. And Serug lived after his fathering Nahor two hundred years, and he fathered sons and daughters. Nahor lived twenty-nine years, when he fathered Terah. And Nahor lived after his fathering Terah nineteen and a hundred years, and he fathered sons and daughters. And Terah lived seventy years, when he fathered Abram, Nahor, and Haran.

These are the records of Terah: Terah had fathered Abram, Nahor, and Haran, and Haran had fathered Lot. Haran died in the lifetime of Terah, his father, in the land of his birth, Ur of the Chaldees. And Abram and Nahor took wives. Abram's wife was named Sarai, and Nahor's wife was named Milcah, daughter of Haran.

—

Now Sarah was barren, she had no child. Terah took his son Abraham, his grandson Lot, the son of Haran, and his daughter-in-law Sarah, the wife of his son Abraham, and they set out together from Ur of the Chaldeans for the land of Canaan; but when they had come as far as Harran, they settled there. The days of Terah came to 205 years and Terah died in Harran.

—

"Bring yourself out of your birthplace," Yahweh said to Abraham, "out of your father's house, your homeland—to a land I will bring you to see. I will make of you greatness, a nation and a blessing; of your name, fame—bliss brought out of you."

One who blesses you I will bless; curse those who curse you; bring all families of earth to see themselves blessed in you."

Now Abraham comes out, follows Yahweh's words to him. Lot went out with him.

—

Abraham crossed into the land, as far as the sanctuary of Shechem, the oak of Moreh; he found the Canaanites in the land, back then. Now Yahweh revealed himself to Abraham: "I will give this land to your seed." He built an altar there: to Yahweh, who appeared to him.

He rose, came to the hills east of Beth El, pitched his tent there—Beth El to the west, Ai to the east. It was there, building an altar to Yahweh, he called on him by name, Yahweh. Yet Abraham kept on, journeyed down toward the Negev.

Now look: a famine grips the land. Abraham went down further, toward Egypt, to live—starvation ruled the land.

At the point of entering Egypt, listen: "To look upon," he said to his wife, Sarah, "you are as lovely a woman as I have known. Imagine the Egyptians when they see you—'That one is his wife.' Now I am killed; you, kept alive.

"Say you are sister to—and for—me, for my good and on your behalf. As my flesh lives, it is because of you and with you."

So it was: Abraham crosses into Egypt; the Egyptians see the woman, how lovely. Pharaoh's officers see her, praise her to Pharaoh. Now the woman is taken away, into Pharoah's palace.

On her behalf, it was good for Abraham. Look: he had sheep and cattle, donkeys and asses, servants and maids, and camels. But Yahweh struck Pharaoh with disease as if with lightning—his whole house stricken—on behalf of Sarah, Abraham's wife.

Now Pharoah called for Abraham: "On whose behalf have you done this to me? Why not tell me this is your wife? Why say, 'This is my sister'—I would of course take her in, for my wife. Yet now, look: a wife that's yours—take her out of here, for life."

Now Abraham rose up from Egypt—wife, household, and Lot with him—up toward the Negev. He was surrounded with livestock, slowed with silver and gold.

His journey took him from the Negev to Beth El, to arrive at the very place he pitched his tent in the beginning, between Beth El and Ai. Here was the calling: the first altar made, he called the name Yahweh.

Lot who traveled with Abraham—he too was surrounded by many sheep, cattle, tents. Now look: argument breaks out between Abraham's shepherds and Lot's—this was when the Canaanites were settled on the land, along with the Perrizites, back then. "Please, hold off this quarreling between us, between our shepherds," Abraham said to Lot. "We are men who hold each other as brothers. You may let go of me and face the whole country, open before us. Please yourself, make your own way: left, and I'll go right; south, I'll go northward."

Now Lot lifted his gaze, drank in the whole Jordan valley—how moist the land was everywhere (this was before Yahweh destroyed Sodom and Gomorrah)—like Yahweh's own garden, like Egypt—gazing as far as Zoar.

Lot chose all the Jordan valley for himself; he set out toward the east—and so a man let go of his brother. Abraham settled in Canaan's land; Lot in the cities of the valley, his tents set beside Sodom.

Now the people of Sodom had gone bad, parading contempt in Yahweh's eyes.

"Open your eyes, and may it please you look around you," said Yahweh to Abraham after Lot had parted, "from the place you are standing to the north, then down to the Negev, to the sea and back, westward. The whole land you see I will give to you: to your seed for all time.

"I have planted that seed, made it true as the dust—like each grain of dust no man could ever count. Rise, walk around on this land—open and broad—it is to you I will give it."

Abraham folded his tents, moved on; he settled by the oaks of Mamre, beside Hebron, built there an altar to Yahweh.

These are the days when the four kings—Amraphel of Sumer, Arioch of Ellasar, Chederlaomer of Elam, and Tidal of Goiim—went to war with the five: King Bera of Sodom, Birsha of Gomorrah, Shinab of Admah, Shemeber of Zeboiim, and the king of Bela, *or Zoar as it now is called.* These last joined together in the Valley of Siddim, *or the Dead Sea.* Twelve years they had served Chederlaomer, but in the thirteenth they turned away. In the next year, Chederlaomer and his allied kings returned and conquered the Rephaim in Ashteroth-karnaim, and then the Zuzim in Ham, the Emim in Shaveh-kiriathaim, and the Horites in the hills of Seir, near El-paran, which borders the wilderness. After that, they turned around to En-mishpat, *now Kadesh,* overpowering the region of the Amalekites, including the Amorites, who inhabited Hazazon-tamar. At that point, the kings of Sodom, Gomorrah, Admah, Zeboiim, and Bela, *which has become Zoar,* who had joined together in the Valley of Siddim, were attacked there, five kings taken on by the four, Chederlaomer of Elam, Tidal of Goiim, Amraphel of Sumer, and Arioch of Ellasar.

One bitumen pit after another—that was the Valley of Siddim. They dove into them as they ran—the kings of Sodom and Gomorrah hiding there, the others escaping into the hills. The conquerors took all the goods of Sodom and Gomorrah, and all their food, and left. Also captured was Lot, Abraham's nephew, who had been living in Sodom; they took him and all that he owned.

An escapee brought the news to Abraham the Hebrew at the terebinths of Mamre the Amorite, who was related to the allies of Abraham, Eshkol and Aner. When Abraham heard that Lot his relative had been captured, he gathered his men—all those serving or born into his household, numbering 318—and pursued the captors as far as Dan. He positioned all his men around the others at night, overcame them, and stayed on their heels as far as Hobah, north of Damascus. All the goods were recovered, along with his relative Lot and all that he owned, including the women and others.

As Abraham came back from defeating Chedorlaomer and his allied kings, the king of Sodom came out to the Valley of Shaveh, known as the King's Valley, to receive him. There too Melchizedek, king of Shalem, came out with bread and wine. As priest of El-Elyon, he blessed him, saying "Honored is Abraham by El-Elyon, creator of heaven and earth. Honored is El-Elyon, who brought your enemies to you." So Abraham allotted to him a tenth of everything.

Then the king of Sodom said to him, "Give the people to me and you take the goods." Abraham demurred. "I have promised Yahweh, El Elyon, creator of heaven and earth, that not even one thread or a sandal strap would I take of what belongs to you, saving you from ever saying, 'I made Abraham rich.' For me, nothing but what my men used up, but for the allies who joined me, Aner, Eshkol, and Mamre, a fair portion."

These things had passed when Yahweh's word came to Abraham in a vision passing before him: "Have no fear Abraham, I am your shield and reward, a shield that prospers."

Lord Yahweh," said Abraham, "what good is prospering when I walk toward my death without children, my inheritance passed down to a son of Damascus, Eliezer, accountant of my house. Look at me," Abraham continued, "you have given me no seed; and look, a son not mine—though under my roof—inherits my household."

Now hear Yahweh's word that passed before him: "Not this one for your heir—only what passes between your legs may inherit from you." He drew him outside: "Look well, please, at heaven; count the stars—if you can count them. So will be your seed"—and so it was said to him. He trusted Yahweh, and it was accounted to him as strength.

"I am Yahweh, who drew you out from Ur, of the Chaldeans," he said to him, "to give you this land as heir."

"Lord Yahweh," he said, "how may I show it is mine to possess?"

"Bring me a heifer of three," he said to him, "a she-goat and ram, three-year-olds also, a turtledove and fledgling dove." All these he brought, cut down the middle, placed each one's half opposite the other; the birds he left unparted.

And the vultures descend on the carcasses, but Abraham scared them off. Now look: as the sun goes down, a deep sleep falls over Abraham—a covering darkness thrown over him: underneath he is plunged in fear.

"Know this within," he said to Abraham, "your seed will be strangers in a land not theirs; slavery will be their state—plunged in it for four hundred years. Yet the nation which enslaves them will also know judgment.

"After, they will come out prosperous, surrounded with it.

"You will come to your forefathers peacefully, when good and old be settled in your grave. They will be a fourth generation before they return: that long will Amorite contempt build, until the glass is full."

So it was: the sun gone, darkness reigns. Now look: a smoking kiln and its blazing torch pass between the parted bodies.

It was that day Yahweh cut a covenant with Abraham: "I give this land to your seed, from the river of Egypt to the great river, Euphrates—of the Kenite, the Kenizzite, the Kadmonite; of the Hittite, the Perizzite, the Rephaim; of the Amorite, the Canaanite, the Girgashite, the Jebusite."

—

Now Sarah, his wife, had no children with Abraham; she had an Egyptian maid, Hagar her name. "See how it is," Sarah is saying to Abraham, "Yahweh has held me back from having children. Please go into my maid now; maybe a child will come out of it." Abraham grasped Sarah's words; his wife Sarah had taken in Hagar the Egyptian, her maid (it was ten years since Abraham had settled in the land of Canaan), and hands her to Abraham to go into as a wife.

Now he came into Hagar so that she conceived; she saw that she was pregnant and looked down at her mistress with contempt in her eyes. "I have been hurt on behalf of you," said Sarah to Abraham. "I gave my maid into your grasp and now, seeing that she's pregnant, she looks down at me—may we know Yahweh's judgment between you and me."

"See how it is: your maid is in your hands," said Abraham to Sarah. "Do as you see best." Now Sarah punished her; she fled beneath her eyes.

Yahweh's angel found her by a watering hole: a spring in the desert on the track to Shur. "Hagar, maid of Sarah," he called, "from where have you come, where are you going?"

"I am escaping," she said, "the cold eyes of my lady, Sarah." "Go back to your lady," Yahweh's angel said to her, "hand yourself back to her desire."

Now Yahweh's angel said to her: "Your seed I will sow beyond a man's eyes to count." "Look," said Yahweh's angel again, "you have been made pregnant. You will give birth to a boy: Ishmael, you will name him. Yahweh heard your pun*ish*ment: you will hear a *male.*

"Impudent, he will be stubborn as wild donkeys, his guard up against everyone and theirs raised against him. The tents of his rebellion will rise before the eyes of his brothers."

Yahweh had spoken to her and the name she called him was, "You are the all-seeing God," having exclaimed, "You are the God I lived to see—and lived after seeing." That is why the hole was called "Well of Living Sight"—you can see it right here, between Kadesh and Bered.

—

When Abram was ninety-nine years old, the Lord appeared to Abram and said to him, "I am El Shaddai. Walk in my ways and be blameless. I will establish my covenant between me and you, and I will make you exceedingly numerous."

Abram threw himself on his face; and God spoke to him further, "As for me, this is my covenant with you: You shall be the father of a multitude of nations. And you shall no longer be called Abram, but your name shall be Abraham, for I make you the father of a multitude of nations. I will make you exceedingly fertile, and make nations of you; and kings shall come forth from you.

"I will maintain my covenant between me and you, and your offspring to come, as an everlasting covenant throughout the ages, to be God to you and to your offspring to come. I assign the land you sojourn in to you and your offspring to come, all the land of Canaan, as an everlasting holding. I will be their God."

God further said to Abraham, "As for you, you and your offspring to come throughout the ages shall keep my covenant. Such shall be the covenant between me and you and your offspring to follow, which you shall keep: every male among you shall be circumcised. You shall circumcise the flesh of your foreskin, and that shall be the sign of the covenant between me and you. And throughout the generations, every male among you shall be circumcised at the age of eight days. As for the homeborn slave and the one bought from an outsider who is not of your offspring, they must be circumcised, homeborn, and purchased alike. Thus shall my covenant be marked in your flesh as an everlasting pact. And if any male who is uncircumcised fails to circumcise the flesh of his foreskin, that person shall be cut off from his kin; he has broken my covenant."

And God said to Abraham, "As for your wife Sarai, you shall not call her Sarai, but her name shall be Sarah. I will bless her; indeed, I will give you a son by her. I will bless her so that she shall give rise to nations; rulers of peoples shall issue from her. Abraham threw himself on his face and laughed, as he said to himself, "Can a child be born to a man a hundred years old, or can Sarah bear a child at ninety?" And Abraham said to God, "O that Ishmael might live by your favor!" God said, "Nevertheless, Sarah your wife shall bear you a son, and you shall name him Isaac; and I will maintain my covenant with him as an everlasting covenant for his offspring to come. As for Ishmael, I have heeded you. I hereby bless him. I will make him fertile and exceedingly numerous. He shall be the father of twelve chieftains, and I will make of him a great nation. But my covenant I will maintain with Isaac, whom Sarah shall bear to you at this season next year." And when he was done speaking with him, God was gone from Abraham.

Then Abraham took his son Ishmael, and all his homeborn slaves and all those he had bought, every male in Abraham's household, and he circumcised the flesh of their foreskins on that very day, as God had spoken to him. Abraham was ninety-nine years old when he circumcised the flesh of his foreskin, and his son Ishmael was thirteen years old when he was circumcised in the flesh of his foreskin. Thus Abraham and his son Ishmael were circumcised on that very day; and all his household, his homeborn slaves and those that had been bought from outsiders, were circumcised with him.

Now Yahweh was seen by Abraham among the oaks of Mamre; he was napping by his tent opening in the midday heat.

He opened his eyes: three men were standing out there, plain as day. From the opening in the tent he rushed toward them, bent prostrate to the ground.

"My Lord," he said, "if your heart be warmed, please don't pass your servant, in front of his eyes. Take some water, please, for washing your feet; rest a moment under the tree. I will bring a piece of bread to give your hearts strength. Let your journey wait; let your passing warm your servant—to serve you."

"You may," they said, "make what you've said true."

—

Abraham rushed toward the tent, to Sarah. "Hurry, three measures of our richest flour, to roll into our finest rolls."

From there to the cattle he runs, chooses a tender calf—the best—gives it to the servant boy, who hurries to make it ready.

Now Abraham gathers curds, milk, and the tender meat he had prepared, sets it down for them under the tree, stands near, overseeing: they ate.

—

"Your wife—where is Sarah?" they asked of him. "Look, she is here," he said, "in the tent."

"I will appear again to you—in the time a life ripens and appears. Count on it and see: a son for Sarah, your wife." Sarah was listening by the tent opening—it was right behind them.

But Sarah and Abraham were old, many days were behind them; for Sarah the periods of women ceased to exist. So within her, Sarah's sides split: "Now that I'm used to groaning, I'm to groan with pleasure? My lord is also shriveled."

"Why is Sarah laughing," asked Yahweh of Abraham, "when she says, 'Now I can count on giving birth, when I'm elderly?' Is a thing too surprising for Yahweh? In the time a life ripens and appears I will appear to you—and to Sarah, a son."

Sarah hid her feeling: "No, I wasn't laughing"—she had been scared. "No," he said now, "your sides split, count on it."

—

The figures rose, starting down toward Sodom; from there they could see its upturned face. Abraham walks with them, showing the way.

"Do I hide from Abraham," said Yahweh within, "what I will do? Abraham will emerge a great nation, populous, until all nations of the earth see themselves blessed in him. I have known him within; he will fill his children, his household, with desire to follow Yahweh's way. Tolerance and justice will emerge—to allow what Yahweh says to be fulfilled."

Now Yahweh says: "The noise from Sodom and Gomorrah grows; as their contempt grows heavy, it rises.

"It weighs on me to go down, to see what contempt this disturbance signifies. If brought down to find offense, I will pull them down. If not, I will be pleased to know."

So the figures, leaving there, descend toward Sodom. Now Abraham stands aside, facing Yahweh.

—

Abraham drew close: "Will you wipe away the innocent beside those with contempt? What if there are fifty sincere men inside the city, will you also wipe the place away? Can you not hold back for the fifty innocent within it?

"Heaven forbid you bring this thing to light, to erase the innocent with the contemptuous—as if sincerity and contempt were the same thing. Can it be—heaven forbid—you, judge of all the earth, will not bring justice?"

"If I find fifty innocent inside the city," said Yahweh, "I will hold back from the whole place on their behalf."

"Listen please," said Abraham, pressing further, "I have imagined I may speak to Yahweh—I, mere dust and ashes. What if we have less than fifty sincere, five less—for these five will you wipe away an entire city?"

"I will not pull down," said Yahweh, "if I find forty-five there."

Yet he found more to say. "Consider," he pressed on, "you find forty there." And he said, "On behalf of these forty I will not act."

"Please, do not lose patience my lord," he continued, "if I speak further. Consider thirty are found there." And he said, "I will not act if I find thirty there."

"Listen please," said Abraham, pressing further. "I have imagined I may speak to Yahweh—I, made of mere dust and ashes. Consider twenty are found there." "I will not pull down," he said, "on behalf of these twenty."

"Please, do not lose patience my lord," he continued, "if I speak further—for the last time. Consider ten are found there." And he said, "I will not pull down on behalf of those ten."

Now Yahweh, having finished speaking to Abraham, went on. Abraham turned back, toward his place.

In the evening two angels arrived in Sodom. Lot was sitting in the courtyard of Sodom's gate. As he saw—then recognized—them, Lot rose, then bent prostrate, face to the ground. "Please hear me, my lords," he said, "and stop at the house of this humble servant. Stay the night, wash your feet, rise refreshed, then go on—the road will wait."

"No," they said, "we will lie by the broad road."

Then he begs them, until they stop, to go with him to his house. Now he makes them a feast, complete with fresh-baked matzah and drink: they ate.

Yet before they had fallen asleep, the townsfolk—Sodomites—press round the house, from boys to graybeards, the whole population from as far as the outskirts. "Where are the people who visited you tonight?" they call to Lot. "Bring them out for us," they ask. "We want to know their intimate ways."

Now Lot came to the door, closing it behind him. "Brothers, please don't act by showing contempt. Listen, I have two daughters who have not known a man intimately. Let me bring these out for you: handle them as you please. Only leave the visitors untouched, bring no hand to them: I have brought them under my roof's wing."

"Get out of my way," one said. "He comes here to share our shelter and already he hands down the law. Now you will know more than them, a touch of our contempt." They pressed against the man, against Lot, were ready to break down the door.

But from within a hand stretched out, brought Lot toward those visitors in the house. Now they shut him in. They blinded them with light:

the people at the door, boys as well as graybeards. They would grope for the door handle vainly.

The visitors with Lot said: "Are there others of yours—a son-in-law, sons, daughters—anywhere in the city, to be gathered from this place? The offense has risen to Yahweh's ear. Yahweh sends us—to bring down this loud violence."

Lot hurries to speak to his sons-in-law—those his daughters prepared to marry. "Pack up now, leave this place," Lot said. "Yahweh is prepared to overturn the city." Now watch: the sons-in-law see only—in him—a joke on them.

Now the sun began to rise; the angels pressed Lot on. "Get up," they said, "gather your wife, your two daughters that are left—or be gathered into the crush of citizens—in this city's sin." He wavered; the figures grasped his arm, his wife's, the hands of his two daughters—it was Yahweh reaching out to them. They brought him out, stopping only outside the city.

So it was: while being brought out, one said to them, "Pity your lot—run, don't look back, don't stop until the end of the valley. Escape to the mountain—or be crushed."

"My lord," Lot said to them, "please not so. Listen to me: if this servant has warmed your heart, evoked your tender pity—you have kept me alive—then see: I cannot survive in the mountains, where the hand of contempt brands me. Look instead at this town within my chosen lot, small enough to overlook. Let me fly there, please, it is small, insignificant—and so will I be there."

"Hear," he answered, "I pity your lot again, will not overturn this city you speak for. Hurry, run—I will do nothing until you're there." And this is how one came to call this city Smallah.

The sun rose above the earth as Lot came to Smallah.

Now Yahweh spilled on Sodom and Gomorrah a volcanic rain: fire from Yahweh, from the sky. These cities he overturned, with the whole valley, all the citizens in the cities and plants in the earth.

Behind him, Lot's wife stopped to look back—and crystallized into a statue of salt.

Abram arose that morning, hurried to the place he had last faced Yahweh, had stood there with him. Looking out over the upturned faces of Sodom and Gomorrah, over the whole face of the valley, he saw—so it was—a black incense over the earth climbing like smoke from a kiln.

But Lot went out from Smallah, toward the mountains, his two daughters with him—he grew afraid to stay in Smallah, settled in a cave alone with his daughters.

"Father is getting old," the firstborn said to the youngest. "There are no men left on earth to enter us—to follow the way of the earth.

"We'll pour drink for our father; with wine we will lie with him—life will follow from our father's seed."

On that night their wine poured out for their father. The eldest now comes, lies with her father; he recalls no sense of her lying there, nor when she rises.

Now listen: "I lay last night with my father," said the eldest to the youngest. "Follow me. We will have him drunk with wine tonight again, so you may have from him. At his side, we will give life to our father's seed."

The wine flows on this night also, for their father. The youngest rises, to lie with him; he senses nothing of having her, nor her rising.

So Lot's two daughters became pregnant by their father. The eldest gave birth to a son named Moab—"from father"—the father of the Moabites we see today. A son was born as well to the youngest, whom she called Ben Ami—"son of my kin"—the father down through today's sons of Ammon.

—

From there Abraham moved to the Negev
stopping between Kadesh and Shur
settling in Gerar.

"She is my sister," he said
of Sarah his wife.
When Abimelech, king of Gerar, heard

he took her. And God came too
that night in a dream
saying "Death is the price
for taking a man's wife."

Abimelech had not touched her
when he asked, "My Lord, will you kill
a man who is innocent?
I heard "She is my sister"
from him. And from her, "He
is my brother.

"My heart was innocent
my hands clean
when this happened."

And God answered in the dream
“Because I knew it was innocently done
I held you back from touching her
from committing contempt.

“Now return the wife to the man
and live
for he is a man who speaks up:
he can plead your cause.

“Or else die, if you hold on to her.
You and all who are attached to you.”

Abimelech summoned his servants next morning
retelling the conversation in the night
until the men were overcome with fear.

Abraham was called and heard this plea:
“Why did you do this to us?
How did I move you
to settle upon me
and my kingdom
this charge of contempt?
How have I handled you
that you would touch me with contempt?

“What did you foresee
happening
to cause this thing?”

“I said to myself,” Abraham began,
“‘There is no fear of God here;
they’ll kill me
to have my wife.’

"But she is also my sister
my father's daughter
yet not my mother's
and she became my wife.

"When heaven ordained I wander
far from my father's house
I said, 'Be my loyal wife
in whatever strange place we settle;
tell them this about me:
"He is my brother."'"

Abimelech took sheep and oxen
male and female servants
gave them to Abraham
and restored Sarah to him.

"Here, my land is yours to settle on"
Abimelech said to Abraham
"anyplace your eye prefers."

To Sarah he said
"Here, a thousand pieces of silver
for your brother
enough to cover the eyes
of everyone attached to you
to what has happened,
proof of innocence."

Abraham pleaded his cause to God
and Abimelech was restored
along with his wife
and his female servants:
children could now be born.

For God had closed the womb of everyone
attached to Abimelech
as in a protective dream—
for Sarah, wife of Abraham.

—

Now Yahweh conceived for Sarah what he had said.

Sarah became pregnant and, the time ripe, gave birth: a son appearing from Sarah, for Abraham in his ripe old age.

"Now who would conceive of Abraham having children at Sarah's breast? But I gave birth to a son—not to wisdom—for his old age."

—

And when his son Isaac was eight days old, Abraham circumcised him, as God had commanded him. Now Abraham was a hundred years old when his son Isaac was born to him.

Sarah said, "God has brought me laughter; everyone who hears will laugh with me."

—

The child grew
was weaned
and on that day a great feast
was made by Abraham
but Sarah saw the son of Hagar the Egyptian
the one carried by her for Abraham
laughing with her own son, Isaac
and she turned in protest to her husband

"Send away that servant and her son.
No son of hers can divide with Isaac

his inheritance." In Abraham's eyes
this was wrenching:
it was his son too.

Then God in the night said this:
"Do not be torn between boy and servant;
listen to Sarah's voice;
it is Isaac that continues your name.
But the servant's son too
will father a great nation
being your child."

Next morning, Abraham
got together bread and water
for Hagar, fixing a skin of water
to her back, sending her and the child away.
She wandered in the desert near Beer-sheva
Until the skin was dry, then sheltered
The child beneath a bush.

She walked away, far as an arrow flies
and sat opposite, weeping, saying to herself
"Let me not hear the child die"
and closed her eyes.

When God heard Ishmael's wail
his angel called to Hagar from heaven:
"What pains you, Hagar?
There is nothing to fear. God has heard
the child's cry, clear as day.
Arise, take the boy in your arms
soothe him, he will become
a great nation."
Then God opened her eyes:

a well of water was visible
before her. She walked over
filled the skin with water
let the boy drink.

God was with the boy
as he grew up
making the desert his home.
It was in Paran and he grew
skilled with arrow and bow.
It was his mother who got a wife
for him, from the land
of Egypt.

—

And some time later
after these things had happened
God tested Abraham
speaking to him
"Abraham"
"I am listening," he answered.

And God said
please take your son
whom you love
dear as an only son
that is, Isaac
and go out to the land of Moriah

There you will make of him a burnt offering
on a mountain of which I will tell you
when you approach

And Abraham rose early in the morning
saddled his donkey

took two of his young workers
to go with him and his son, Isaac
having already split the wood
for the burnt offering
and he started out for the place
of which God had spoken
to him

It was on the third day
Abraham looked out in the distance
and there, afar, was the place
and Abraham turned to his young men
you will wait here by yourselves
with the donkey
while the youth and I go on ahead
to worship and then
we will return here to you

Abraham took the wood for the burnt offering
laying it upon Isaac, his son
and in his own hands he took the flint
and the knife
then the two walked on together

At last Isaac spoke to his father, Abraham
"Father"
"I am listening, my son"
We have the flint and the wood
to make the fire, but where is the lamb
for a burnt offering?

Abraham answered
God will reveal his lamb, my son
for the burnt offering
and the two walked on together

And they approached the place
of which God had spoken
there Abraham prepared an altar
set the wood upon it
then bound his son, Isaac
and laid him there, on the altar
lying upon the wood

Abraham reached out
with his hand, taking
the knife, to slaughter
his son

But a voice was calling to him
an angel of the Lord, calling
from out of heaven
Abraham, Abraham
I am listening, he answered

Do not lay your hand upon the youth
you will not do anything to him
for now I know yours is an integrity
dedicated to God
not holding back your son
your dear one, from me

Then Abraham looked around and there
behind him
its horns tangled up in a thicket
a ram had appeared

And Abraham went over to it
carrying the ram to the wood
for a burnt offering
instead of his son

The name of that place
was given by Abraham, meaning
“The Lord reveals”
and today we still say
“The mountain of the Lord
is revelation”

The Lord’s angel spoke again
calling to Abraham from heaven
By myself I have sworn
says the Lord
as by yourself you have acted—
have not held back even your son
dear to you as an only one—
and for this thing you are immeasurably blessed
and your seed multiplied
immeasurable as the stars in the sky
and as the grains of sand by the sea

For this thing you have done
your descendants will walk freely
through the gates of their enemy
and all the nations of the earth
will feel themselves blessed
one day, knowing
that your descendants thrive
living among them—
for it was you who listened
and heard my voice

So Abraham returned to his young men
they turned and started out together
for Beersheba
and Abraham stayed there, in Beersheba.

And Sarah's life enfolded a hundred years and seven and twenty. Sarah died in Kiryat Arba—it is today Hebron—in the land of Canaan. Abraham mourned for Sarah, crying over her. Then Abraham stood and turned from the sight of his dead to the sons of Het, saying "I am a foreigner and an immigrant here. Allow me a plot for a tomb among you. May I bury my dead here, out of my sight . . . "

Abraham took the weight of money of which the sons of Het had heard him speak and counted it out for Ephron. It was four hundred shekels of silver, according to the current rate. So Ephron's field in Machpelah, opposite from Mamre, was purchased by Abraham before the witness of the sons of Het. It included the cave that was in the field and every tree, and testimony to it was given at the city gate.

So then Abraham buried Sarah, his wife, in the cave of the field of Machpelah, opposite Mamre—which today is Hebron—in the land of Canaan. So that the field and the cave within it were testified to, by the sons of Het, as passing in possession to Abraham.

These things had passed when Abraham would hear: "Listen carefully, Milcah too gave birth to children, for your brother, Nachor. Uz, the eldest; then Buz his brother, and Kemuel, father of Aram; then Chesed, Hazo, Pildash, Jidlaph, Bethuel." Bethuel fathered Rebecca—but these eight were mothered by Milcah for Nachor, Abraham's brother. His second wife also gave birth: Reumah mothered Tebah, Gaham, Tahash, and Maacah.

Now Abraham was very old, his better days—thoroughly blessed by Yahweh—behind him.

“Please put your hand under my thigh,” said Abraham to the senior servant, head of all under his roof. “Swear for me, by Yahweh, God of sky and earth, that you will choose no wife for my son from Canaanite daughters, though I’m settled among them. Instead, visit my homeland, my birthplace, bring out a wife for Isaac, my son.”

“What if the woman won’t come, following me back to this land?” the servant asked him. “Do I then bring out your son—from here, back to the land you left behind?”

“Watch yourself,” Abraham said to him. “Don’t turn to returning, especially my son. Yahweh, God in the skies, who took me out of my father’s house, my homeland, who spoke to me, giving his word—‘I will give this land to your seed’—will place his angel by your side, until you choose a wife from there, for my son. If she won’t follow, won’t be beside you, be cleansed of this vow—so long as my son doesn’t settle there.”

CHAPTER 2

Out of Sumer

Let the ways of Sumer
which have been destroyed
*be restored for you!**

By the year 5 of the kingship of Hammurapi, more than a millennium had passed since the art of writing, invented in Sumer, inspired huge archives of clay tablets and the construction of libraries to house them. Now, as the transfer of archives from the ancient, defeated Sumerian capital of Ur to the new, southern Mesopotamian center of Babylon was being completed, a man of Ur conceived a plan to set out in the opposite direction, beyond his civilization's borders. His name was Terah. His family could be traced back through several generations to the founding of the third dynasty of Ur—that last flowering of glorious Sumer coinciding with the migration of Amorites, or Semitic people in the north, toward Canaan, the land that Terah's son, Abram, would one day call home.

HERITAGE

Where was Terah going, and why? "Now these are the generations of Terah: Terah begat Abram, Nahor, and Haran . . ." We are not told

*From "Lament for Ur," a city in southern Mesopotamia destroyed (and later rebuilt) at the end of the twentieth century BCE.

much more than Terah's name here, and that he set out from Ur with his family "for the land of Canaan; but when they had come as far as Harran they settled there." We are not told what Terah looked like, what he did for a living, why he left Ur and was called to Canaan, or exactly when. We are, however, provided with an ending to his story: "The days of Terah came to 205 years and Terah died in Harran."

Yet we can be fairly certain of several things surrounding the life of Terah and his son Abram (he has not yet changed his name to Abraham, which will signify his founding of a people). We know that Abram must have been an educated man, the first-born son in a prosperous family. Thus Terah was not likely a poor wanderer forced to roam from place to place in order to scratch out a living for his family. Why then would he have picked up and moved his family from the former center of civilization, Ur, to a distant outpost of the Sumerian culture?

Speculation cannot replace history, but it can serve as its proxy until the borders of the unknown are pushed back. Until recently, most of the details of Abram's cities lay on the far side of that boundary. However, historians are now making substantial inroads. In Ur, Abram's birthplace, Sir Leonard Woolley excavated half a million clay tablets in the 1920s. Covered with cuneiform, the first form of syllabic writing, invented by Sumerians in c.3700 BCE, these tablets bring to light the culture, education, and religion that Terah and his sons lived and breathed as citizens of Ur. Based on this evidence we can use speculation as a tool for building on what we know to be true.

In Terah's day the passage of time was marked not strictly in linear fashion but according to important events, such as "the year 5 of the kingship of Hammurapi." Contrary to what many scholars have thought, the Sumerian tradition was both historically authentic and preoccupied with accuracy. The historical mindset of the Sumerian tradition is neatly organized, but in terms of spheres of influence, measured in eras rather than merely in years. Why have we thought otherwise? Because the years ascribed to the older kings on the famous Sumerian King-lists seem absurd to us: some were said to have lived for hundreds of years, especially those before the Flood. In the same way, the ages ascribed to the early human figures in the Bible—from Noah at 900 years old to Terah, 205 years, Sarah, 160 years, and Abraham, 180 years—seem to suggest exaggeration at best.

What we are only beginning to understand is that these ascribed ages were never intended to be literal, but rather to accurately circumscribe historical periods, some of which, by necessity, overlapped. The foundation records and foundation boxes of Sumerian buildings and monuments that have recently been recovered bear out how crucial was written record-keeping, the foundation of history, in this cultural tradition—exactly the opposite of the impression originally given by these dates.

THE WRITTEN WORD

By 3300 BCE, long before Terah and Abraham lived, the city of Uruk—called Erech in biblical Hebrew—had a population of 55,000. Sumer was enjoying a flowering of technology, architecture, social and political structures, sculpture, and literature, like no civilization before. And the linchpin of all these achievements was writing. Some scholars suggest that Sumer's wedge-shaped cuneiform script evolved from the temple's desire to preserve its ritual literature. Others believe it derived from the need to keep track of the growing number of complex economic transactions; a revolution in transportation, brought on by the visionary ideas of creating canals for navigation and attaching wheels to boards, had opened up new trade routes, and business was booming.

No matter why the first writer put stylus to clay, the ability to record ideas, contracts, and inventions—and thereby to create history—was the spark igniting every element of what we call civilization. It was the Sumerians who classified and catalogued the most crucial elements of human society. They developed a class of scholars and translators to write and authenticate historical literature. They built museums and libraries to preserve history, schools and textbooks to preserve knowledge and the skill of writing itself, and codified law to preserve order among loosely connected, liberally ruled city-states. They also created a formal system of government that for a time preserved the balance of church and state.

In modern-day excavations of Mari, Ur, and other cities of ancient Sumer, writing is found inscribed on the surface of nearly everything. Tablets with the "blueprints" of buildings were mortared into their foundations; praise was engraved on the statues of city gods. In the libraries, archaeologists have found the first cookbooks, the first farmers' almanac, and the first pharmacopoeia. A treasure trove for historians, written tablets neatly catalogued in Sumerian libraries reveal even more than expected about the culture at the time: colophons (what we think of as copyright pages today) included a tablet's title, its first line of the text, the names of the patron, author, scribe and/or translator, the tablet's owner, and the date for the provenance of the original text copied by the scribe. In keeping with Sumer's dating system a book's colophon might read, "The year that the wall of Kazallu was destroyed," or "The year of the golden statues of Utu and Shenirda."

As a spoken language Sumerian was no longer widely used in Abraham's world. It had died out with the fall of the third dynasty of Ur, to be replaced by Akkadian, the language of the conquering people from the north. But if Sumerian was studied and heard only in the temple and the *edubba* (school), it was carved everywhere—on buildings, monuments, and statues; more importantly, the values embodied by Sumerian culture, with its unique way of looking at the world and understanding one's place in the universe—these things were written not only in stone but in the hearts of generations long after the fall of Ur.

A LIKENESS OF THE GODS

Statues provide another invaluable set of keyholes into Sumerian life. Making statues had once been a big business in Ur. Terah was likely a tradesman, a man of certain means and stature who could and would have educated his son. If his workshop had, for example, fashioned statues of clay, wood, and stone, there were certainly strong economic forces pushing men like him away from the old capital, now a city in decline, toward places providing new opportunities. And statues, as we shall see, will prove integral to the past and future of his son Abram.

Terah's workshop might well have turned out more than a dozen stone statues a year, including life-sized gods and statues of kings and civic figures, purchased by temples and courts. Smaller figures of the gods and votive statues of individuals made of less expensive clay and wood were bought by private households. Every family in the former provinces of Sumer and Akkad had need of votive statues to place in the temples, as well as household gods, and there were several workshops in Ur to make and sell them. Of these, perhaps a dozen were licensed to produce the civic statues, imposing figures of kings and courtiers, scribes and musicians, brought to life as if rescued from their original blocks of stone.

The city's temples, which provided its principal public architecture, also required sacred images of Ur's city god, the moon god Nanna, and his family. Terah's workshop would have produced one such statue every few months. Once such work would have been much in demand for its classic, lifelike vigor, but now Babylonian tastes had shifted toward more formal and ritualized images of the ancient Sumerian gods that Babylon had adopted as its own. Despite shrinking demand, emotional accuracy would still have been seen in the statues of Terah's family, as it was in other figures uncovered from this period, for workshops such as this had been founded upon the inspiration to restore what was great in Sumerian culture. A subtle tension in the poses of their figures reflected the anxiety and loss that followed in Ur for centuries as the glory of the Third Dynasty faded.

So why would Terah have decided "in the year 5 of the kingship of Hammurapi" to leave Ur with his family? Economics would have been one pressure. Another was a shift in power. The Akkadians, the northern neighbor who had once overrun and absorbed the Sumerians, were now themselves absorbed among the Semitic inheritors of Babylon. In the new kingdom of Hammurapi, great cities such as Mari, based upon classical Sumerian-Akkadian culture, were being conquered and sacked. Hammurapi had hauled off the statues and artworks from Mari's temple and palace to Babylon, where they were used as models for making copies. Copying was the art that Hammurabi's Babylon preferred to originality; quantity and monumental scale represented the Babylonian imaginative thrust. This inspiration to copy was extended into collecting and codifying. The scholarly work of gathering and assembling a vast, pre-existing history of laws, judgments, and actual case records resulted in what archaeologists have called the "Code of Hammurapi," a written archive famous for an originality it never possessed.

Hammurapi's intent was to make the city of Babylon the modern center of his empire, and in this endeavor the city of Ur was to be leached of both its art and its libraries. The Babylonians were not interested in the high level of original works characteristic of Sumer in the Third Millennium. Instead, endless copies adorned with extravagant ornaments were becoming the fashion. Terah and his family were surely under pressure to shift their workshop to Hammurapi's new capital, to increase production, and to place new emphasis on uniformity.

In Abram's Ur, on the other hand, breathing life into statues was still considered more than merely a matter of artistry. The votive statue, which represented an individual in the temple, was clearly representational, as were statues of kings. But the sacred statues—the gods in their temples—were something else again. Not only were they rendered by artisans in the most lifelike manner, they were literally treated as such, with their daily meals and outings borne by the temple priests. Were these sacred statues literally considered alive? Did the original Sumerian audience in the temple distinguish between the drama that brought the gods alive—as if they were characters in a play—and the statues themselves?

If statues of the gods were considered to exert power on their own, it would be easy to say that Terah or his son Abram represent the first people in history to express their dissatisfaction with such supernatural things by setting out to find a new way to be in the world without monitoring the lives of the gods on Earth. We might then have cause to agree with the popular image of Abraham smashing his father's "idols." But what if the gods were alive in their drama the way King Oedipus is alive as a character in Sophocles' plays? Where would such characters go when the play was over? The answer to this question may change our entire mindset about the sophistication of this first great civilization and its influence on history. Because where the gods in their cosmic drama went when the temples of Sumer—and to a lesser extent in its successor cultures of Akkad, Babylon, and Assyria—closed their doors at night was to sleep. Just like the citizens of the city around them, the gods were put to bed at night and in the morning the cosmic drama began again when the gods received their morning meal.

This is not to suggest that the gods were just like human beings, even though they went through the same daily routines of living that we do; rather, what is implied is that they share with us the attributes of being alive, of genuine existence. Whether or not the Sumerians saw themselves as dependent upon the gods for their own lives is a complicated question that we can set aside for now. The important question is, were the Sumerians aware that the gods were dependent upon them not just to create and sculpt and adorn their statues but also to give them life by creating a theater of the temple, on which the workings of the cosmos are brought to life by elaborate ritual-scenes and texts—what we would call plays? And if it is Sumerian culture that thereby "gave life" to the gods, to what extent did a person educated in classical Sumerian culture view this as theater?

COSMIC DRAMA

What we are required to face in order to answer these questions can be disorienting to the twenty-first-century mind. An educated citizen of Ur in eighteenth century BCE is aware that the aliveness of the gods, which means the reality of the entire cosmos, visible and invisible, physical and immaterial, is maintained by a human theater. Perhaps the gods could destroy us and live perfectly well without us, as they did before we human beings came into existence. Yet even this presumption cannot go unchallenged, for the gods in Abram's time are dependent on being part of the human theater. They must be bathed and fed and dressed, read to, carried about, and have poems written for them, if possible great poems. So it would have been perfectly clear to a person at the time that it is the drama that creates their aliveness—and were it not for their convincing roles in this drama these would be only lifeless statues.

If our contemporary monotheistic religions of Judaism, Christianity, Islam, and others were viewed as a cosmic theater, would we not admit that our participation is absolutely necessary? For the original monotheism of Abraham was based upon a covenant, a dramatic compact between a human being and the Canaanite god known as Yahweh, filled with ritual scenes and elaborate words "given" by God but provided for by humans in spoken and written language. And yet, the convulsive origins of this monotheism are based upon an assertion that earlier civilizations and religions were inferior in their knowledge of the cosmos. That they believed in "statues" or in multiple "gods" was proof of their fallacious knowledge of the world, and that they wrote hymns and poems in which these gods appeared real was proof of their moral subordination. Could it be true that our own texts, the poems and narratives of monotheism, the laws and prophecies, remain a form of the same cosmic drama that was authored in Sumer and studied by Abraham during his youth and later life in Ur?

Within the drama of their stories and testaments, the Sumerian gods came alive in a prototypical cosmic theater that involved all the human arts, from sculpture and poetry to music and choreography. The science of the day was also involved with astronomers determining the times for certain actions, and mathematicians establishing the scale of Sumer's ziggurats, on top of which sat yet another stage for the cosmic drama. In Ur, the largest such stage contained the little one-room house of the moon-god, and all the vast architecture below served to raise up this humble abode to Nanna—which was named Heaven.

The ziggurat was a human artifact intended to remind us of a natural one, a mountain (of which there were none in Sumer). (The Bible quotes the people of Sumer as saying, "If we bring ourselves together, we can build a city and tower, its top touching the sky, to arrive at fame.") A complex staging of gods and humans took place on its terraces and stairs, but this was human theater, as opposed to what took place in the temple, where gods and their retinues dwelt in an ongoing visitation from heaven. In short, the ziggurat was a civic project, more like our Empire State Building or former World Trade Center, if we consider them as monuments representing communal inspiration, rising out of the society that made them possible. The scale of these buildings rivals a natural landscape of mountain and canyon, and the art and science enfolded in their shape and physics remind us of our reach: not to the cosmic heaven but to the earthly embodiment of it in a human world woven of trade and commerce.

We might think that our civic buildings, unlike ziggurats, have no pretension to mediate heaven and earth—other than the aesthetic awe of their work and our perspective. And in that way, we are superior to earlier civilizations in being able to separate the physical world from the infinite cosmos. However, confronted with a new understanding of how the ziggurats looked, we must think again, because the aesthetic claim of the ziggurat was perhaps more powerful than any architecture we currently envision. In other words, the combination of secular and spiritual vision embodied in a ziggurat is more complex even than the inspiration behind a church or cathedral. The ziggurat was really a faux mountain, and more significantly, it resembled something more physically complicated, as if both the inside and outside of a mountain were present at the same time. The contemporary reconstruction of the ziggurat at Ur is actually just a skeleton of its former presence, a mere scaffolding for what it contained. Originally it was hung with terraces and staircases that were covered with soil and planted with trees, so that it gave the appearance of wooded hills.

In recent years archaeologists have discovered that in the architecture of the ziggurat not a single straight line existed. All was composed of calculated curves, the walls bending slightly inward so that we look not only upwards but also inwards to the center, past the skin of burnt brick suggesting a rock face. Upwards we are drawn to the summit of a mountain to which the illusion of forests on the terraces, with trees and hanging gardens clothing every terrace and stair, gave the uncanny sensation of the Mountain of God. The genius of Sumer is a striving for origins—of the restoration of origins—and it seems that this people, who likely originated in the Indus Valley and set out on a journey toward the mountains of the northeast, instead fell in love with the pristine, lush lands that they would call Sumer, which seemed like paradise to them, yet the mountain remained an icon of their deepest longings.

BOUNDARIES

Two thousand years later, Babylon would take over Sumerian culture and make it its own. What was once myth would become literal, as if it was the plain truth, rather than the high drama of the Sumerians. The stirring encounters of an individual with gods both public and personal were lost. But for Abram it was possible to leave Babylon behind. In Canaan, where he migrated, Abram revived the drama of daily encounters with the cosmic realm beyond time and space, and beyond the humanly unknowable boundary established by death.

Four thousand years after that, polls show that a majority of citizens in the Americas and Europe hold the irrational belief that human beings are not primates. Does that mean our civilization is not rational? On the contrary, it confirms that the realm of the irrational or unknowable has a secure place in our reasoning—just as it did in Abraham's Sumer. Knowing the difference is the key. When world-renowned astrophysicist Stephen Hawking contemplates "the mind of God," he is marking a border at which human knowledge faces the unknowable.

In the first civilization of Sumer the known world pushed back the boundary of the unknowable, but allowed religion to be active in its own realm. Eventually a man came along who represented the boundary itself by representing it as a negotiated covenant between man and God. And the culture of Sumer was translated onto the stage of Israel, is represented in the presence of the name Abram within Abraham. Abram was a Sumerian name, and Abraham a name of much later vintage, but both contain an originating principle in the syllable *Ab*, meaning father, or author. Abram, or Abraham, confronted what was possible in an encounter beyond temporal power and empire—beyond the merely human. Sometime during the past century Abraham became the "father of the three great monotheistic religions." Transformed into a historical poster-boy by our need to anchor the progress of Western civilization in the flight from mythology, Abraham came to be seen as a peacemaker, a go-between for God and man.

In fact, myth had long been gone from the world by Abraham's day. For almost fifteen hundred years before him, the world of myth had been appropriated as poetic text and used for temple dramas. There, as we now know, the statues of both gods and the human representatives who esteemed them were moved about by handlers, enacting encounters between gods, as well as their everyday domestic activities. These handlers were intended to be invisible to their audience, just like the actors who wore masks in the Greek theater, where only the masks were intended to be seen. Even though Sumerian civilization preceded ancient Greece by two thousand years, already the gods had become symbols; ritual and liturgy in the temple had become high art and drama. With the aid of their invisible handlers, the statues dramatized their own meaning. In the temples the Sumerians created a stage on which the relationship between the knowable, natural world and the unknowable cosmos could be acted out. How can we know with certainty that we will rise from our beds tomorrow? No scientific advancement will eliminate the uncertainties posed by death, yet the interplay between the gods can be instructive.

These statues stand at the origin of our beliefs, at the source of our great religions. Indeed, if we consider the Sumerian statue in terms of the Catholic Eucharist, where the consecrated wafer *becomes* the body of Christ (through transubstantiation), then the statue *becomes* the body of a god in a drama more elaborate, for it took place in a temple that was turned into a cosmic home. The drama went on twenty-four hours a day, 365 days a year. Since a Sumerian citizen could only be present intermittently, additional statues of himself and his family, votive statues, were placed there in constant symbolic witness of this drama. And we have every indication that this, in fact, is how it was. Some interpreters have imagined that the hands held together by the votive statues were clasped in prayer; it is more likely, however, that the hands were held in a clapping position, for these representatives of Sumerian citizenry were a perpetual audience in this, their great invention, the cosmic theater.

It was this same cosmic theater—once throbbing and vital at the heart of Sumerian society, and which had become lackluster by Abraham's time—that he strove to recreate. It was the living boundary between this world and the divine; between the rational and the irrational; between ancient Sumer and his own epoch, that impelled him to move on. Not toward the source of that degeneration, Babylon, but in the very opposite direction, to Canaan. Here he would restore the old by forging something new, a profoundly new cosmic theater with Yahweh at its heart.

CHAPTER 3

The Original Audience in Jerusalem

By the sixth century BCE the history of Abraham in the Hebrew Bible, along with commentary, had completely taken over as the founding story of the Israelites. It will be many centuries before Christianity absorbs these Hebrew sources, and many centuries beyond that before Islamic scholars would reinterpret these same Jewish sources, which by then had been translated into many languages, including Greek and Arabic. Buried and forgotten to these later religions, however, are the origins of the Hebraic culture that produced the text of these first five books of the Hebrew Bible, and later the Christian Old Testament. But it is precisely this period, coupled with the history of ancient Sumer, that will give us the true insight into our subject, Abraham.

But how did Abraham first become the object of a literary rendering? This question is rarely asked yet crucial to our understanding of what he stands for. Today, popular accounts all begin by denying history: "Nothing can be known for sure about the historical Abraham. . . ." What is being buried in this way, however, are not the bones of Abraham, which would tell us little of what we need to know anyway; what has been lost to us are the authors and the Hebraic culture that bound Abraham into history. Especially vague are the first authors of the Hebrew Bible in which Abraham's life unfolds.

Many authorities are reluctant to face the issue of the original authors, fearing that Abraham might have been an imagined character, that his whole history may be the mythical stuff of campfire tales. Some historians believe Abraham was invented at a later stage of ancient Israel's existence, in order to claim political right to the land. But there is now an abundance of fresh evidence that allows us to ask new questions about when the writers who brought Abraham to the written page lived, how they were educated, and what they knew about their subject. Some of these crucial questions can also be asked about Abraham himself. That is, how was he educated in Ur, the ancient cultural capital in which he lived until his mature years? What can we know today about his time and place in history? What did he know and how did he pass it on?

Unfortunately, history pays scant attention to the creative era of Hebraic culture, which would have provided answers to these questions. Instead, historians tend to ask, what was the agenda of the original biblical narrative? But why must we think of great literature as needing an agenda? What was the political program of "*Oedipus Rex*" or "*Hamlet*"—and is that all we need to know? How much does it matter in appreciating and understanding the work? Typically, the modern view of J and the later biblical authors suggests that they manipulated their stories to the advantage of Judah or Israel, which were rival kingdoms after the fall of Rehoboam, King Solomon's son. The problem with such explanations is that they fail to imagine the renaissance of Hebraic culture that began almost a century earlier with King David.

Physical evidence of this renaissance can be found in *bullae,* discovered in recent digs at the ancient City of David. In the 920s BCE, at the court of King Rehoboam, the cylinder seals invented in Sumer thousands of years earlier were still being applied—not to clay tablets, but rather to papyrus scrolls. These *bullae* are the impressions made by the seals, akin to wax seals on an envelope, which were proof of the royal provenance of palace scrolls of papyrus. The scrolls and wrappings themselves have long since disintegrated, but knowledge of how they were used yields a picture of the writer's art.

Papyrus sheets were pressed plant stems, held together with a flour paste made from grain to form rolls that were portable and often of great length. The writing instrument was still the reed, but used now with a medium of dyed water that painted the surface with letters rather than etching the incisions of cuneiform. And the Hebrew letters that were inscribed formed a new language—just as the Sumerian cuneiform had once been new—which, coupled with holding the reed and writing in a new way, held out the promise for unanticipated thought once again.

J

For the writer who set down the history of Abraham on the papyrus scroll, no seal or reed ownership has been found. We know this person only as "J," an identity given by modern textual analysis. Yet much can be put together about J's background from what we know of the time. Undoubtedly this person was well educated, steeped in a written historical tradition. (Even the very small kingdom of Ugarit, a city-state Abraham probably visited on his journey from Harran to Canaan, has been found to have had a court life of historians, writers, scribes, and translators who produced a unique written culture that predated Jerusalem.) Solomon's royal household is described as being composed of hundreds of wives, and there is no reason to doubt the claim, since it was common for the royal court to cement civil and international treaties by means of political marriages. This would mean many more hundreds of princes, princesses, cousins, and in-laws, all of whom would be highly cultured. Their children would be educated in the new Hebraic culture, and many would become translators and scribes. The early biblical authors, including J, were very likely of this class.

What kind of career would J have had, given her talents? Most likely she was a youthful prodigy, trained in various languages by the best scholars, implying she was a member of Solomon's family. All court writers would have been translators, as the work of absorbing older written traditions into the new alphabet required knowledge of cuneiform, perhaps even of pictograms. Using the Phoenician-derived Hebrew alphabet that had only recently surpassed cuneiform as a vehicle for literature, J and her colleagues worked in a language experiencing its first flowering. For Hebrew, this period at the court of Solomon and his son was a time comparable to the Elizabethan age and the blossoming of English. Renown as a translator and poet-scholar led to J's commission for a historical document, and so it is that we possess a coherent portion of that work, embedded within the Torah.

Of course, that an author must also have a gender is not just a matter of historical curiosity. Depending on whether the writer is male or female, he or she may have recourse to a particular range of emotions, of passion and restraint toward the characters and situations to be depicted. So, for example, when Yahweh hears Sarah's laugh from within the tent, after he has suggested to Abraham that in her advanced age she will become pregnant, God responds to her as a man who has been disarmed, possibly even offended. Sarah is then given a chance to apologize, and while it is not altogether clear whether she does so, by focusing upon her the text has given her a stubborn presence.

This is only one of many instances where female characters are made to seem more interesting in their words and actions than men. There are others that give us indications that the author of these stories is a woman. For example, wouldn't it be most likely that a woman rather than a man would make the entire covenant between man and God revolve around Sarah's conceiving a child when she was impossibly old? Finally, because all of these passages are written in the same style, a manner quite different from that of the second significant early author, it seems likely that they were the work of a single hand.

Not surprisingly, then, the females in J's narrative, from Eve to Zipporah, the wife of Moses, tend to exhibit more character than the males (her Joseph, whose charismatic life resembles that of King David, is a moving exception). Her point of view toward men is ironically nuanced, or implied, which is why we are unsure of Abraham's emotions on the journey to Canaan.

J TRANSFORMS

The second primary author, whose style is quite different from J's, has been designated as E, after his frequent references to God as *Elohim.* E is responsible for writing down the story of Isaac's brush with death at the hands of his own father. Interestingly, it is an episode in which we do not hear anything of Isaac's mother. The same arm's-length approach to women holds true for the other passages written by this second author: females in these episodes do not act and speak with particular insight, or in ways that surprise us.

It makes sense, then, to begin to imagine the first author as a woman, and the second as a man. But at Rehoboam's court it was to be expected that only a princess, or the daughter of a scholar, or perhaps a widow of Solomon, would take up such work as writing and translating, and later become esteemed for the vitality of the narratives she produced.

Long before either of these biblical authors began to write, however, there had already been a history of Abraham. Although they did not merely record what was known but infused it with a great deal of interpretation, neither did either author simply invent the tale. It may have begun with Abraham's diaries, or with those of his children. It may even have originated with Isaac writing down the story of his father, which could be the reason there are so few details about Isaac himself—like the person missing in a family photo because he himself is taking the picture. It's easy to speculate here because it matters little who is the original source. What is important is that this story became sufficiently interesting to be read and retold among later generations. At some point in the retelling, material was added or changed or removed, though not in a significant way. We know this because of the enduring Mesopotamian emphasis on history that began in Sumer, a value given to history both for its own sake and for its value to a lineage and a culture.

Still, it's natural to assume that the conversations between Abraham and Yahweh were re-imagined by the biblical author, and much else besides, because the author at the Jerusalem court was more than a mere narrator. This author was a translator but not just from one language to another, given that the task required reinterpreting older material into an altogether new language and culture. She was a literary stylist whose fidelity was to making history active and vital in the present—in short, making it a work of high art. To do that, J had to convey a sense of loss. Even as we read the conversation between man and God, we are made aware that it took place in the irretrievable past. The original audience in Jerusalem was conscious of this, even in the tenth century BCE. And in this same way the Jerusalem audience was also aware of the loss involved in Abraham's leave-taking of the classical Sumerian culture. If nothing else, they understood it as the loss of a city, and the city was a stand-in for civilization in Jerusalem, just as it had been in ancient Sumer.

> *"Bring yourself out of your birthplace," Yahweh said to Abraham, "out of your father's house, your homeland—to a land I will bring you to see. I will make of you greatness, a nation and a blessing; of your name, fame—bliss brought out of you."*
>
> *"One who blesses you I will bless; curse those who curse you; bring all families of earth to see themselves blessed in you."*
>
> *Now Abraham comes out, follows Yahweh's words to him. Lot went out with him.*

When Abraham responds to Yahweh's call, we can read little into his response. It is matter-of-fact. Once arrived in Canaan, contending with an unknown emotional future, he does the expected things. I'll build an altar here, what else can I do? That's the obvious thing to do next, like a mother putting the food on the table. But for the audience of the Jerusalem court, this Sumerian gesture would be seen as redolent with significance. For in the wilds of Canaan the religious ritual no longer has the meaning it would have had in Sumer: Abraham's loss is deep and multi-layered, including a loss of meaning in the things he used to do. In emphasizing the deed, now empty of any specific content or ritual, the biblical author underscores for readers the difference between this act and the public spectacle of worship in the Sumer left behind, where the cosmic theater was filled with gods, persons, servants, and drama.

Although we have the words, that is, the text that in its very being renders the biblical author historical, what we really need is the context. For this we must bring the *author* to life—and in this case there are two to start with. For both—Abraham and his author—what is required is the same: a re-imagining of the culture in which they lived. We would expect it to be easier today for a creative writer, a poet or novelist, to intuit and express the way sources are taken up and transformed from cliché and overused rhetoric into innovative forms. Yet radar for what constitutes a cliché is only the first requirement of a poet; next comes the capacity to transform worn-out rhetoric. So we may ask of J, who was also a poet in her time, the following question. How did a conventional encounter between Abraham and his personal god in Ur, as it may have been represented in a Sumerian form, become an intimate negotiation during a walk downhill toward Sodom—such as was undertaken by Abraham and the God he came upon in Canaan? For that is how J, the primary biblical author, wrote it.

One goal that has remained constant from Abraham's time to the present is to make tangible the boundary between the knowable world, as human knowledge has claimed it, and the unknowable cosmos that lies outside of time and space. The Covenant was established between Abraham and his God in order to keep that boundary clear. Even before that, the same boundary was rendered sacred in Ur and dramatized in the temples of Sumer. And today, our science pushes back the unknown, yet the boundary of what lies beyond time and space—what came before the Big Bang and before there was a before—remains in question, both for science and religion. A poet and translator today, confronting the boundary of our human future, is pretty much in the same position as J found herself. She took the historical source of the Covenant and fleshed out its rhetoric into a visionary drama between Abraham and his God that brought the boundary into focus.

A MATTER OF CONTEXT

As a translator, especially one in an age charged with embodying a culture, J also had to risk mistakes. It may not have been strictly accurate then that Abraham first heard the words of Yahweh in Harran, rather than in Canaan, but by this assertion J has forced us to acknowledge the depth of Abraham's commitment, a more important assertion.

Likewise, as readers translating J's culture into our own, we must risk certain mistakes. We can't be absolutely certain that J was a secular woman, for example, however much the literary evidence points to it. By risking this mistake, however, we gain the knowledge that the author was unique in her uncanny gift for exposing the interior life of her characters, that she resisted the stereotypes that other authors accepted, that she found rare character traits in women, that she approached the character of Yahweh without a son's obeisance, and most important, that she was a person with irreplaceable talents and point of view.

Her most obvious point of view was her Hebraic culture, which did not begin with a blank slate any more than Abraham was born in Canaan. Unlike the monkish scribes of medieval monasteries, Hebraic authors were trained in other literatures and languages allowing them to embody their translations, to re-tell and re-phrase the cuneiform Sumerian and Akkadian tablets and early Hebraic scrolls in their archive. It would be a mistake then to assume that J was preserving the exact words that God and Abraham spoke (anymore than those who came before her had). The educated audience of this author expected to relive the past through the sensibility of its new culture, and not by rote transmission. Words, for the Hebraic authors, were their stage—not clay icons of the past but the very ground upon which a cosmic theater as powerful as the old one in Sumer could be restored. This new one in Jerusalem, however, takes the stage out of the temple and the heavens and places it in a natural, earthly landscape, Canaan.

For a reader of the Hebrew Bible today, a question immediately arises: Where did this God come from? Just as Christianity could not have existed without Judaism, or Buddhism without the preceding Hindu culture, Judaism had to have a precursor. It was, of course, Sumerian. Had it not been for the dynamic strength of Sumer and its persistence in Akkadian culture, no Judaism would have been possible. More specifically, Judaism came from a translation, a restoration of older cultures in which Abraham's role was crucial.

Western history as it is taught today designates Abraham as Hebraic because that is the culture in which his history was set down. Nevertheless, the biblical text states more than once that Abraham came from Ur, and since Ur was not a nomadic site but rather a seat of ancient Sumerian and Akkadian civilization, we can be reasonably confident that the Bible is making a historical point about Abraham's background and culture.

During his education in Ur, Abraham would have encountered the Sumerian devotion to history, stretching back in documented form for more than two millenniums. This was a secular form of history, divided from the mythological by talented Sumerian authors who established new forms of expression by bringing to older, oral forms the written media of clay, much as J and her colleagues had done with papyrus. Writing thousands of years before J, these poets continually reinvented the old Sumerian mythology, playing with the roles of the gods, while the historical records were treated differently, maintained with great fidelity. In his scribal school, Abraham would have been trained in both sides of the cultural equation: the inventive poetry of religion and the painstaking logic of recorded history.

J'S AUDIENCE

These insights into Abraham's education that we are only just discovering were already known to the Hebraic audience for the original writers of the Bible. Their authors did not need to explain to the audience of educated Jerusalemites in the tenth century BCE that Ur was a place of great sophistication. This would have been assumed much the way we would expect a certain worldliness from Roman poets.

After slowly deciphering the thousands of ancient tablets dug up each year, we are coming closer to the original text of what would one day become the Bible, beginning to imagine more closely the original audience in Jerusalem as it listened to the Hebrew telling of world history.

Now listen: all the earth uses one tongue, one and the same words.

It sounds as if we are going back to the childhood of *Homo sapiens,* to a version of early man that can be found in many cultures. Back to a primitive state when we lived in the forest, hunting and gathering.

Watch: they journey from the east, arrive at a valley in the land of Sumer, settle there.

Suddenly, time collapses and we arrive at the point of earliest historical memory, to the founding of civilization, of Sumer. Would the Jerusalem audience for this biblical text in the tenth century BCE have known that the first Sumerians came from an earlier civilization in the Indus Valley? Certainly they knew of venerable civilizations in India at the time. As they are listening to this story, in their new language and newly unified culture, they are reminded that this was something quite old in the world, having been experienced not only by ancient Sumerians but by an even earlier civilization.

In only three sentences the expectations of the audience have already been set back three times: We are not in a primitive time, not in another world; instead, we are in a kind of dream that has never been told before.

"We can bring ourselves together," they said, "like stone on stone, use brick for stone: bake it until hard." For mortar, they heated bitumen.

"If we bring ourselves together," they said, "we can build a city and tower, its top touching the sky—to arrive at fame. Without a name we're unbound, scattered over the face of the earth."

Until the libraries of Mesopotamia were unearthed, biblical commentators had little idea of what sources the Bible's writers possessed. It was assumed the biblical authors were provincial, and for this reason the stories of Babylon (Babel) and the Flood, Eden and Sodom, and even the cutting of the Covenant with God, have been described as forceful and even ironic, but still naïve, unaware of earlier history.

Now we know something different. We know that the biblical writers sat among archives that contained cuneiform tablets, including some that told about the restoration of ziggurats. They might even have visited those sites in what was known as the Babylonia and Assyria of their day. They would have known, for instance, that the ziggurat or tower in Babylon was named "Linking Earth and Heaven." When the author has the people of Babylon saying, "we can build a city and tower, its top touching the sky—to arrive at fame," the cosmic drama of Babylon's religion is satirized by being taken literally.

But satire of Babylon is not at the heart of what the biblical writer is after. It is the origin of Babylon that is being focused upon, the time of Hammurapi and Abraham, and the biblical writer knew very well that this was not a mythical time when "all the earth uses one tongue, one and the same words."

In the Bible's next sentence, the writer takes us back to the founding of Sumer, the origin of known human civilization, a time more than two millenniums before Hammurapi, and proceeds to tell a story of "innocence," of human naïveté as it reached for godlike power. But what power is this, in fact? "To arrive at fame" is all that the Sumerians are actually proposing. The same fame that Babylon achieved.

The Bible's tale of Babylon concludes with Yahweh coming down "to baffle their tongue" until "the city there came unbound." An unbound city is exactly how a decaying Mesopotamian site from an earlier era might have appeared to a tourist in biblical times. Our tourist would also have encountered the ruins of earlier ziggurats, prompting the question, "What had happened to these grand projects, these cities that are the mark of civilization?" Like every other human endeavor, they would be unbound by time. The lasting contribution of Sumer would be artistic and spiritual, the stage it created for interactions between man and the unknowable, which would prove invaluable as Abraham confronted Yahweh.

Expecting to be in a primitive state of the world, we find ourselves instead in a civilization with architectural and engineering sophistication. Already we are building a city, the foundation of civilization. The gods have immortal names, and so the human creative drive is also to make a name, and through its fame to achieve immortality. Here is the dream of civilization: a name that will outlive us, a culture that may live forever. It was a dream uneasily shared by this early biblical audience, their hope and expectation linked to the realm bound together by King Solomon perhaps only a few decades before these words were written in Jerusalem, and eroding under the far less capable leadership of his son, King Rehoboam.

> *Yahweh came down to watch the city and tower the sons of man were bound to build. "They are one people, with the same tongue," said Yahweh. "They conceive this between them, and it leads up until no boundary exists to what they will touch. Between us, let's descend, baffle their tongue until each is scatter-brain to his friend."*

"Us?" Is Yahweh not alone in heaven? It is as if the world of gods, the civilization of Sumer, is still alive. The Sumerian cosmos of the gods is mirrored by the city: they have their homes there, the city temples, and their dramas are tended by the human world. And yet here the gods, including Yahweh, are content to destroy the city and dismantle its population—in other words, eradicate civilization as we know it. Why?

What is crucial in this passage is the boundary between human and God: Yahweh is telling his colleagues in heaven that humans have lost their place on the stage of the cosmic theater. The unity of human tongue and purpose, ironically, confuses them about their roles in the drama—for it is the gods who have one language. The scatter-braining of civilization is a way of imposing the need for translation and interpretation. Far from destroying civilization, it is this very necessity for interpretation, of complication, that will impel cultures to progress.

From there Yahweh scattered them over the whole face of the earth; the city there came unbound.

Is this an explanation for the demise of Sumer or for the monumentalism of Hammurapi's Babylon in Abraham's day? At first glance it would seem the former, but the emphasis here is on the scattering, the migration of peoples. It is also, of course, foretelling that of Terah and Abraham. Under pressure to go along with the unification imposed by Hammurapi's empire, father and son moved in the opposite direction, toward a new beginning.

That is why they named the place Bavel: their tongues were baffled there by Yahweh. Scattered by Yahweh from there, they arrived at the ends of the earth.

Here is an anti-climax that is normally mistaken for the climactic moral of the story. They did get to name their city, at least, and the result was a long run of fame. The fame defeats them only because civilization is complex, and just as there was a scattering of tongues, words too have come unbound and have more than one meaning. The fame of Babel is undone by complexity, by an alternate meaning, one that this Hebraic author of the Bible interprets from the sound of the Hebrew word for Babylon, Bavel.

Meanwhile, the audience in Jerusalem, the original readers of this story, were aware of the diversity of sources and history that were being reinterpreted in their new Hebraic culture. They would have understood the spirit of Sumer and its cosmic drama—except that the stage for their cosmic theater is the written text itself.

The sources for the Babel story could be found in the Sumerian poems of the tablet library at Solomon's court. There we find that Enki,

The lord of wisdom, who scans the land,
The leader of the gods,
Changed the speech in their mouths, put contention into it,
Into the speech of man that had been one.

So we can see how the Bible writer not only translated but transformed Babylonian history in the Babel story. As the cosmic drama becomes the human family drama of Terah, Abraham, and Abraham's progeny, a new history begins, one in which we read our own lives as modern translations of the ancient family tale.

Why is it still so difficult to imagine ourselves living in a fully civilized world that existed long before the Jews? It may be that we are used to a history centered upon historical figures in a family, of whom Abraham is the first. (Kings Gilgamesh and Shulgi were among older historical figures in Sumerian civilization, but their histories don't take place in the context of family life.) The Sumerian cosmic theater especially seems remote to us now, though it was mirrored by the personal theater of the household or personal gods. We still feel the echoes of the sacred in the family drama, but after Abraham's journey we've lost the intimacy of the Sumerian family house. Yet were we to step through the doorway of Terah's house in Ur, we might feel at home again.

We might feel that what is lost about our historical past is that we cannot identify with the founding and renewal of a culture, but only identify with families and individuals. We've lost not only Terah's house in Ur, but also the court in Jerusalem where the biblical authors and their audience were housed. Yet by recreating their context, and what they knew, we can come, in turn, to know them.

CHAPTER 4

What Will History Be Now?

In the year c.1740 BCE, after Abraham has arrived in Canaan, he makes an altar. There is nothing particularly religious about this act, it's what any Sumerian immigrant would do.

He built an altar there: to Yahweh, who appeared to him.

It's stated simply. Abraham's life and acts are not religious but cultural, historical. He was born in Ur, he lived in Harran, he worked and married, he was childless, his father had set out for Canaan before him: these and other events in the text do not mark the life of a religious man. He does not pray; he does not observe rituals; he does not have visions: unless, of course, hearing and speaking and walking with God is a vision. But even these encounters are noted by the J writer as the most natural of conversations, with no great degree of piety.

THE SURVIVOR

For J then, Abraham is a historical person whose profession is transformed into that of a witness, the first professional witness. It does not change him though. His earlier profession in Ur and Harran is also related to being a witness, for that is what you get if you strip the scribal profession down to its bare essentials. The scribe was the eye of the culture, recording everything, bearing witness to civilization as it unfolded.

Abraham has no mission, no religious teaching, no message, exactly what we should expect of a proper witness. A tradition grew up many centuries later, having little to do with J's words, which made of Abraham a mystic and a patriarch, and eventually a religious icon. Yet nothing could be further from the plausible. The Bible is an artifact of history that we are fortunate to possess. It is a survivor when so many books and artifacts of other cultures have disappeared. There is nothing mystical about this, however: It survived because a culture existed to carry it on. The Hebrew Bible is a survivor, and the salient fact of Abraham's character is that he too is a survivor.

How has Abraham survived? The crucial first hurdle is noted in the Bible: he survived childlessness and founded a family. The other experience Abraham survived is the intimacy of his relationship with God. Obviously there is no proof for the historical God other than the testimony of witnesses. But Abraham was one such witness, and for the generations that followed it was enough to attest to his own existence—he who saw God and survived. This is not an incidental point. It was crucially important to the audience of what would become the Bible that what they were reading was history, accurate in its every detail. For the civilizations around them were already old by their time, and unbroken tablets or complete papyrus rolls were by then rare. Time was already deep for these witnesses to Abraham's history, and they were sensitive to its losses.

Certainly Abraham had been witness to the expectation that everything would be restored. Ur had been recreated from its early destruction, and Babylon was in the midst of ongoing reconstruction under Hammurapi. The imperative for restoration even triggered neurotic behavior in the kings of Sumer and Akkad, most notably in Gudea, who literally dreamed about his restorations. In one city, in which he restored fifteen temples, he not only recorded the details of the work on each building but also recounted the dreams that led to his results.

In the dream, a man told me to build a temple, though he did not explain his desire. And then a woman appeared, holding in her hand a stylus of flaming metal, immersed in her thoughts. The woman, I understood, was Nisaba, the goddess of writing and science. She said the plan of the temple will be revealed to me. It was so, and I brought craftsmen from afar. Magan collected timber from its mountains and I made a path into the cedar forests of the mountains that had never before been entered. The cedars were cut with enormous axes, and like giant snakes, cedars were floating down the river. The stones of quarries never before entered were delivered in large blocks, along with many precious metals, copper and silver mined from the mountains, and red stone from Meluhha. Nisaba, patron also of the edubba schools for the scribes, directed the building in accordance with the placement of the stars, and the patron of architecture, Nindub, held the temple plan on a tablet of lapis lazuli. The brick mold for the sacred brick was placed in the carrying basket that I would bear, and the male donkey pawed the ground impatiently. The donkey was myself, Gudea, who is eager to carry out the task.

Temples and cities were also reconstructed by later Sumerians and Akkadians who never claimed to build from their dreams or their own inspiration. They always noted that their works were restorations, and when they could not finish something they left a plea for the next king to do so. They made careful records of their restoration plans, inscribed on tablets, to be found by those who would follow. In most cases, these records were buried in the foundation of the restoration or built into the wall itself, made purposely invisible. Addressed to an unknown king of the future, they would only be found if the temple or edifice had once again been destroyed. This is the profound sense of history with which Abraham was imbued: loss and restoration were its substance, built into the literal bricks of the city.

RESTORATION

In 1250 BCE, a foundation record was incised in stone in great detail and then buried in the foundation of a restored gateway:

I cleared away its debris, reconstructed the weakened portions, and rebuilt the ruined section from top to bottom. I deposited my stelas. May a later prince restore the dilapidated gate and return my inscribed name to its place.

This stone was inscribed for Shalmaneser I (1273–1244 BCE) and contains much more about the king, including his political and war records, and most importantly, a description of the design of the building or edifice. This king in Middle Babylonia, three centuries before the J writer began the Hebrew Bible in Jerusalem and five centuries after Abraham died, follows an ancient Sumerian tradition of obsession with the restoration of very old buildings. The gate may have been two thousand years old at the time—and the king was thinking another two thousand years into the future, when "a later prince" would follow the design on the foundation stone.

Why this obsession with restoration? It comes from a desire not only to keep an objective record but to show respect for history. Mesopotamians were far more respectful of history than we are. We have our own tradition of cultural preservation and historical landmarks, but our leaders are not scouring the land for Native American fortifications to restore from a thousand years ago. To the Babylonian king looking out over his palace walls, the obligation to keep history alive and honor the Sumerian legacy was stronger than any other duty.

Along with the Mesopotamian attachment to history came the obsessive record keeping we've seen at play in Sumer and copied in Babylon. In this kind of culture, what would make such a man as Abraham embrace a contract with Yahweh that was unwritten, *unrecorded* for posterity? He was asked—and he himself wanted—to leave Babylon behind, but certainly he was not enchanted with the nomadic way of life, to which the typical Sumerian attitude can be found in this poem:

A wanderer blown in the wind and rain
He knows no barley
Digs up truffles in the steppe
Eats raw meat
He knows not to bend the knee
Knows not prayers
Has no house in his lifetime
Is not brought to burial when he dies.

Did Abraham find something, then, in the cultures of Canaan that helped him to make a leap of faith? Not likely. However idiosyncratic were the civilized cities of Canaan, they were still derivative of Mesopotamian culture, and it is difficult to imagine that they might have offered anything new to his educated mind. As a man trained in classical Sumerian, Abraham was steeped in a religion that already allowed for leaps of faith, expressed theatrically. Still, the covenant between Yahweh and Abraham was an unlikely leap because Sumerian culture was so grounded in *written* laws and contracts. In his scribal training, Abraham would have become especially well versed in the language and certification of contracts. How unique, then, is this unwritten covenant with Yahweh, whose wording is so imprecise and poetic.

> *"Bring yourself out of your birthplace, out of your father's house, your homeland—to a land I will bring you to see. I will make of you greatness, a nation and a blessing; of your name, fame—bliss brought out of you.*
>
> *"One who blesses you I will bless; curse those who curse you; bring all families of earth to see themselves blessed in you."*

A real contract would be signed and literally "sealed," a historical document. As a historical person, then, how would Abraham have attested to this contract with his family and children? How to prove it? This may seem a trivial question to twenty-first century minds, yet it would be anything but trivial for those involved, as well as for J's audience, since issues of inheritance form the foundation of the Bible. Abraham's conversations with God are about just this, and even the story of Sodom is about Abraham's nephew, Lot, and Lot's daughters. Yet the most crucial element in establishing inheritance consists of establishing the historical facts.

And J? What did these notions mean to her and her readers? First, it's important to remember that what the Temple religion considered important were the tablets of the Ten Commandments and the bones of Jacob. J's narrative was not yet considered essential. The Temple already had its sacred proof of those who had gone before. It is only later, when these artifacts are lost, that J's narrative takes their place. Yet J's work is something different from the objects it replaces; it is a translation of history. What kind of history was this? In part, it was Abraham's *sense* of history, a history of loss transformed into a new epic of land and family. The Sumerian creativity left behind in Ur was already drying up, turning into mere copies in Babylon, which wanted to freeze Sumer in time. In this new land, Abraham would both restore and transform what had been lost to him.

As the civilized survivor of Sumer and its culture, Abraham holds the essential knowledge of that time and inevitably carries with him the question, what will history be now? The future, of course, lies in the answer to that question. In Sumer, history existed within the cosmic theater and in the way it marked and sanctified the days and epochs of a people, which survived in translation. But that, too, was losing its power in Abraham's time. He knew only too well that the life of civilizations can come to a halt—everywhere there was evidence of this in ruined cities.

The survivor knows better than anyone that life—a whole civilization even—can be snuffed out, and that even the invisible realm of inspiration can be lost with it. In such times, the question of inheritance becomes the crucial one, and for later generations it requires more than legend and myth by way of answer. Religion will supply the legends afterward, when the historical evidence is lost. But the drive to recover the true history is essential to Abraham's spirit.

Later Jewish tradition is always a struggle between supernatural faith and the survival of historical Jewish culture. The Babylonian Talmud is a record of such an energizing struggle. It allows the culture to survive beyond disaster and domination, and to translate itself into new forms and places. Yet the crucial inheritance remains basic: the covenant with the land of Israel. When Jews were forbidden to live there, they traveled as a Sumerian travels—if you don't have a city, you carry your civilization with you. Abraham, when he traveled in what is Israel today, carried with him the formative civilization of history, the Sumerian.

PART II

THE EDUCATION

CHAPTER 5

A Portable Culture

The early Bible did what no religion alone could do: it established a culture, the Hebraic, that was outside the conventions to which civilization had long adhered. Clearly, the God of Abraham was not going to be accepted or even known in Babylon; Yahweh would remain the God of the Hebrews only. Yet while neighboring Semitic peoples did not recognize Abraham's God, they were understood by the Hebrews to be historically related, descended from Abraham. So Abraham embodied—for Israel at least—the assumption of a common ancestor, and he also represented a common origin in Sumer, the original seat of civilization. Thus during the time of J, the Bible was being written as if it were a "portable pantheon." Portable because copies could be dispersed and hidden, even when Israel was later threatened with destruction, portable because it supplanted the fixed pantheon of the gods of Sumerian origin with Abraham and his portable God.

The idea of civilized origins was so pervasive in J's time that a biography of Abraham's life and education in Ur and Harran was hardly necessary. The Sumerian pantheon and culture were still extant in contemporary Babylonia and were widely known—why should Abraham's education have been different than what was available to a cultured Babylonian? Moreover, there was no reason to expect that the Sumerian pantheon *would ever end.* And since it would not grow obsolete, there was no need to write about it. The circumstances of Abraham's life, if not known precisely, were commonly understood.

Today the Sumerian culture that underpinned Akkad and Babylon has been lost and forgotten, and that is all the more reason we must recover what the early biblical writers knew. Yet what they knew can't be separated from how they knew it. In other words, we need more than history, we need the *sensibilities* of Abraham and his authors as only a biography can embody them. The sensibility of J, for instance, can be found in her complex feelings about her historical characters. J must have depended on there having been—long before she was born—a presumption about Abraham as a complicated man. The episodes in his life that J records are many-sided and would have been anchored in the written sources that came down to the royal court of Solomon. In addition to this, J imparted her own sensibility as a gifted writer, so that each biblical character became capable of unexpected behavior and ideas.

If we examine the dimensions of J's sensibility—the range of her feelings and thought—we suddenly come face to face with the loyalty to history that was ingrained in Hebraic culture. For example, Abraham's son, Isaac, would have to marry a woman from Harran, Rebecca, in order to make up for lost origins. Or, as in this more specific instance, where J remains true to linguistic origins as she explains the derivation of a site in Israel of her day:

> *Yahweh had spoken to her [Hagar] and the name she called him was, "You are the all-seeing God," having exclaimed, "You are the God I lived to see—and lived after seeing." That is why the hole was called "Well of Living Sight"—you can see it right here, between Kadesh and Bered.*

Citing a Canaanite attribution for Yahweh, as the Egyptian-born Hagar would have known it, "the all-seeing God," we are shown how the term is transformed into Hebraic history—and then, as direct evidence to the original reader in Jerusalem, we are brought to literally "see" it.

The Hebraic culture is also evident in the way that J wrote about Abraham and Yahweh. Before we witness Abraham in action, his sensibility is already divided between mind and heart. He will seem to act from the heart, responding without question to Yahweh, and though we do not see aspects of his mind we see the results: a complex and seemingly enigmatic way of encountering events. By referring to "his mind" we invoke his education, his personal and cultural history in Ur and Harran. It is as if they are seeds he is carrying to begin a new history, one whose unfolding is part of the cosmic narrative. History is now more than a reporting; it is a journey, and Abraham's journey begins it. Everything he needs has come with him, it seems. It is all portable because it lies within: it is in his education.

In J's nuanced style, the narrative action presents Abraham's strengths mixed together with his weaknesses. (This complexity mirrors his predicament: he is in exile from his native culture yet at home in the new history he is founding.) It would be counted as a weakness, for example, that Abraham takes no interest in his own parents and does not even inquire about them once he has left home. Driven by circumstance, in many cases he dissembles, as before an Egyptian pharaoh and a Canaanite king—claiming his wife, Sarah, is his sister. Later, Abraham shrinks when his wife makes her feelings known about Hagar and her son, Ishmael:

> *"I have been hurt on behalf of you," said Sarah to Abraham. "I gave my maid into your grasp and now, seeing that she's pregnant, she looks down at me—may we know Yahweh's judgment between you and me."*

Yet in the same breath, J credits Abraham with the strength to allow autonomy to his wife.

> *"See how it is: your maid is in your hands," said Abraham to Sarah. "Do as you see best."*

It is this kind of human complexity that allows J's audience to appreciate how Abraham could negotiate a new culture deriving from his Sumerian past and his Canaanite present. It was understood that he educated his children in this new culture, that it even became the inspiration for a new language—the very one, early Hebrew, in which J was now writing and the audience listening and reading.

And apart from Abraham's sensibility, which is bound up with his journey, J also presents *Yahweh*'s sensibility in contrast to Abraham's. Abraham, for example, never thinks of the future at all, except when he questions Yahweh's pronouncements. Yahweh knows everything about the future, of course, and yet permits himself to forget it and to act like a human.

> *"Why is Sarah laughing," asked Yahweh of Abraham, "when she says, 'Now I can count on giving birth, when I'm elderly?' Is a thing too surprising for Yahweh?"*

Yahweh is especially careful not to break the natural order, not to forget the boundary between natural and supernatural realms. When he asks, "Is a thing too surprising for Yahweh?" he is creating a bond with humans by almost laughing at himself. He has crossed the boundary into the natural world and takes on its limitations. Why this humbling? Yahweh wishes an intimacy that can persuade his human subjects to think of themselves as created beings and thus have a purpose in partnership with him—a meaning that will become known through the negotiation of Yahweh's covenant. By virtue of the covenant, we humans are granted full freedom to explore *our* side of the boundary, the *natural* world. The same drama of recognition between human and divine was established in the Sumerian cosmic theater, and an explosion of human inventions ensued. But the Creator's direct involvement in founding the cosmic theater of the Hebrews reveals a new purpose to history: the more we understand it, the clearer becomes the boundary between human and God, knowable and unknowable. The human bond with Yahweh, which includes entering into a drama of origins together, persuades us to feel jointly responsible for civilization. And it gives J the artistic license to place Yahweh's sensibility beside Abraham's. This bond will hold even in a future that involves Israel's exile, because Yahweh has become part of Abraham's journey—and that journey is now contained in a portable, written narrative.

Once we have understood that Hebraic authors are at work in a later era, we can uncover a new depth to Abraham's sensibility by distinguishing J's Jerusalem from Abraham's Ur and Canaan. And in this manner of acute perspective, the biography of Abraham must move forward and back from Abraham's time in the eighteenth century BCE to the writing of J's historical account in the tenth century BCE. For in J's Jerusalem Abraham's covenant is being fulfilled: his descendants have become a nation that is writing as well as embodying his history.

When we near the end of Abraham's life, we arrive at a climactic scene that poses the betrayal of both his history and his future. In order for Abraham to sacrifice his son Isaac, he would have to betray *his* father, Terah. For if Isaac were cut off from inheriting the covenant, the reason for Abraham leaving his family history in Ur and Harran behind would be nullified. And yet that going "out of your father's house" became the overarching history that led to the covenant in the first place: the start of a new kind of history. Thus the survival of Isaac in the unfolding narrative now implies that his education includes his father's past in Ur and Harran together with his father's God in Canaan—and although this was evident to J and her audience, it can only come clear for us today in a historical biography, as we shall see.

Not only did Abraham leave his parents behind, he never thought of them again or sought to help them. As readers today, we tend to overlook the art of what the words imply. Yet it must have been a tremendous loss to Abraham, Sarah, and all their relatives and household. But consolation came in the unexpected birth of a child, Isaac. This child would receive a new kind of inheritance, a unique education from his father.

Probably it was Isaac who first inscribed his father's history (it is not an insignificant fact that we hear little about Isaac's own life). But in this new cosmic theater of Abraham's God, it is the individual consciousness rather than family tradition that comes to the fore. We see this when Abraham leaves behind his own parents but also in his covenant-making with Yahweh, who appears focused upon making

Abraham aware of new possibilities. Yet it all began in Abraham's family history, in the changing culture in which his own father, Terah, would have found himself in eighteenth-century BCE Babylon. It was a culture that would have pinched Terah's spirit.

A SCENE FROM LIFE

In the year 5 of the Kingship of Hammurapi, Terah was pressed to move from Ur to the new capital, Babylon. Babylon was a boon to the business in statuary; new temples were being planned, older ones were to be renovated. The government offered promissory notes to expand Terah's workshop and to subsidize the move, but the offers contained regulations impinging on Terah's civic freedom. Owners of Amorite Semitic origin, which included Terah's family, would now be required to hire an equal number of Babylonian Semitic artists and artisans, scribes and translators.

The additional stipulation that sacred scribes had to be Babylonian cut deeply. Terah's statues were renowned for their rich and highly wrought inscriptions, due largely to the gifts of his son, Abraham, who had been educated as a scribe and translator in Ur, engraving and painting the statues from an early age.

There was much talk among Terah's family about trading the business or selling it, and perhaps moving out from Ur. The future of Ur being problematic, the idea to pull up stakes was broached in serious tones, a grave decision with implications for future generations that resembled the ancestral family's first decision—to put down roots in Ur—many generations ago. Taking place more than two centuries earlier, the family migration to Ur was retold every year in vivid detail, including the Sumerian proverb that went to the root of Terah's fear:

How lowly is the poor man!
A mill for him is the edge of the oven;
His ripped garment will not be mended;
What he has lost will not be sought for!

The family story told of the risky migration from the north where the family was poor, coming down to the province of Akkad with no provisions, no stake for a new life. Harmonizing with the last line of the proverb, the family history before that was lost. This last line also held a special poignancy for Abraham as he remembered being told how old was the proverb, a thousand years old, and yet something in it kept it from being lost itself while the family stories of countless generations were gone with no one caring to look for them. However, the proverb now occasioned a further reflection in Abraham: when the last line is translated into New Babylonian it seems to mean something different: Instead of sadness the proverb now sounds like a heaping of scorn on the poor, almost as if they deserved it. The Babylonians were no longer capable of imagining themselves trading places with the poor. And this failure of sympathy would have held little regard for a man like Abraham, whose sense of place itself would become portable. That may explain why we find no one like Abraham in later Babylonian literature. The verse reverberates:

What he has lost will not be sought for!

Abraham had first learned this Sumerian proverb in its original language, part of his early school curriculum. The way of learning to write cuneiform was to copy out the classic Sumerian literature as well as the popular literature of proverbs. "Did the young girl fart in her husband's lap? No, impossible, it has never happened." These plays on manners and convention, emerging from the fourth millennium BCE, can also turn grave and wise, as in

You don't speak of that
Which you have found.
You speak of that which you
Have lost.

In contrast to this ancient Sumerian, the New Babylonian of Hammurapi sounded to Abraham like a language of the victors—as if history began at Babylon, though Babylon was in fact a small town barely a hundred years before. In the New Babylonian language, the Sumerian classics, both high and low, encompassing almost two thousand years of cultural pursuits and writing, sound distorted. The Babylonians speak only of what they have found, or pretend they have founded; they ignore where it came from in the Sumerian tablets. Soon they will believe all wisdom is theirs—thoughts not uncommon to an educated person in Ur. Can a creative spirit survive in Babylon, where they speak only of founding and avoid the truth of finding?

CHAPTER 6

The Meaning of Journeys

When we arrive in the days of the Bible's first audience in Jerusalem, history will come in the form of story so that characters can be examined within their families, in private life, as well as without, in public. The individual sensibility was valued by the educated class at the royal court in Jerusalem. They needed to know that their culture would allow the individual to gain access to the full meaning of life—to the unknown as well as the unknowable. It is precisely the sensibility of Abraham that makes possible a new cosmic theater for this audience. Whether talking with his wife or an angel, his God or a foreign king, Abraham acts and reacts independently, based upon his educated Sumerian judgment.

We witness the interaction with Abraham's God in a realistic story: God's divine intervention only appears so—it is actually a storytelling convention, evoking a trance or dream state in which God can speak as an equal. What transpires, however, is entirely natural: a king's disease suddenly goes away, as if it were psychosomatic; what God has said can turn out to be realistic good advice and what Abraham has said can change God's mind; dreams oscillate into nightmares but ultimately the subject awakes in the same natural world in which he went to sleep (as when Abraham and Isaac return intact from their hallucinatory encounter with child sacrifice).

Although we have lost the thread of the original sources used by J and other biblical writers, we can begin to recover it by restoring the history of the authors themselves. This enlarging story of the origins of the Bible makes us aware of surrounding cultures and the reliance on the past by the authors. And like the biblical narrative, the story of the authors becomes part of our history. The rituals of religion can lose the thread of history—and with it, the legitimacy of historical knowledge. But when the biblical authors referred to *Shinar*, that ancient Hebrew word for Sumer carried the poignancy of lost greatness.

The hardest part to recover is the household religion of Sumer, which was not directly recorded. Among other sources, we have to infer it from the public religion that it mirrored, and from re-imagining J's audience. Yet the Abraham of real history had taken his household god with him while he journeyed and that simple act kept the basis for the Sumerian cosmic theater alive. This portability can be witnessed again in J's later account of Rachel, the daughter of Laban in Harran.

When we move ahead in J's narrative, to the story of Rachel, granddaughter of Abraham's brother Nahor, we find ourselves once again in Harran and Mesopotamian culture, for Nahor had not left Harran. Now his son's daughter will marry Jacob, who is Abraham's grandson and who has returned from Canaan—as Abraham never had. Jacob and Rachel (who, like him, would have been versed in the ancestral Sumerian culture) labored in Harran but eventually fled from Laban's control. And as they do, Rachel takes her family idols with her. Laban pursues, until

> *. . . he enters Rachel's tent. But Rachel had gathered up the idols, stowed them under the [camel's] saddle cushions—now she sits upon them while Laban searches through the tent, finding nothing. "Let it not inflame my lord if I do not appear beside you," she said to her father, "but I am in the way of women: my period is with me."*

This possessiveness toward personal gods is described by J with a Sumerian playfulness toward divinity that is also displayed in Abraham and Sarah's encounters with Yahweh. Thus Abraham may have brought with him from Harran his family god, though the family itself was left behind. It goes without saying that his own relations with his parents were cut; from the moment he left Harran and Terah stayed behind, his whole Mesopotamian family is an afterthought, except for those who have come to Canaan with him. And now his need to re-create his lost family origins within the new cosmic theater of Yahweh will take over the story of one family's epic struggle: how to pass down a cultural inheritance to future generations. To fully appreciate this history, we must return to Sumer and witness Abraham's growth as an individual. Abraham was the last biblical witness of Ur, center of Sumerian culture; we remain in his debt for what he brought with him.

INDIVIDUAL

In the temples of Sumer the first stage was created upon which the life of the gods and their interaction with humans could play out before the perfect audience. It was a civilized audience, one that could tolerate ambiguity and *neither innocently believe nor disbelieve.* Since the individual has been allowed to suspend disbelief, his or her faith is bound up with the entire cosmic theater itself—that is, a sacred space in which boundaries are acknowledged. Poets of Sumer wrote liturgical texts for this theater, exploring the boundary of temporal life. Neither the gods themselves nor the minds of human kings and priests were the primary concern; instead, it is a delving into the nature of existence that is center stage, a quest for the limits of mortality. The boundary between human and deity was tested and found to be parallel to the boundary between the natural world and the ineffable inner life in each individual.

It was with these cultural attitudes that Abraham was brought up to be a Sumerian individual. As he witnesses the interaction of god and man on the stage of the Sumerian temple, he partakes of both sides: mortal man and the inner life that still wishes for immortality and cannot believe in its own death. Today, we call that inner life the immortal soul. For the Sumerians, the soul was a medium, a sacred inner space where time and timelessness interacted. The public audience in the temple observed the timeless aspect of humanity in service to the gods, yet they also witnessed the dependence of the gods on having a house on Earth built by humans, a temple theater. So there was a relation between the gods' dependency and human mortality, a mutual awareness of boundaries.

In Abraham's family home, a mirror image of this theater was created, where each household was attended to by a personal god. The personal god acted as a medium between natural and supernatural worlds, and through this medium god and human conversed. This medium, too, is what religion today calls the soul in each individual. So while we no longer honor the Sumerian theater of personal gods, Abraham brought this concept into our Western consciousness when his personal god from Ur became linked to the public Creator-god he found in Canaan. It was all there in his classical Sumerian education.

Looking into this distant past from the vantage of J in Jerusalem, we can envision with her Abraham as having created the theater of what we now call Abraham's God. It is also a sacred space in which the covenant could be negotiated. In place of the Sumerian temple's stage, there is now the entire land; in place of a personal god, there is individual conscience. Much later, when the Jews will return from destruction and exile in Babylon, in the sixth century BCE, this conscience will be elaborated into the concept of what we call a soul. It is as if the soul has become the invisible inner character of each individual—and the source of an ancient drama.

But in the beginning, in Sumer, the audience in the temple and in the home understood they were responsible for sustaining the cosmic theater. As Sumer's culture withered away during the early rise of Babylon, this theater will fall apart and the worship of men and gods becomes interchangeable. Then, in a unique historical moment, Abraham begins to restore what had been lost in the new drama of the covenant. And J's narrative preserved it. It will be a new cosmic theater in which the individual is two things simultaneously: public witness in the temple King Solomon built and also audience to the theater of J's written words. Instead of personal gods, the narrative of history flowed into the life of each individual, as if the covenant with Yahweh was renewed in the reading of it.

With a personal god no longer essential, Yahweh has developed from a Canaanite creator-god into the one Creator: the God of Abraham. The Canaanite origin of Yahweh remains a subject for further exploration—as does his transformation into Abraham's God, which lies in Abraham's Mesopotamian background. We will meet there the Sumerian personal god named Kulla, a probable source, when we return to explore Abraham's education. First, we must probe further into the nature of consciousness in the age that shaped Abraham and its influence upon his biographer, J.

SOUL: A MEDIUM FOR DIALOGUE

Most of what we commonly know about Abraham today comes from a much later time in history. However, even taken as a whole, the legends about Abraham that were written down after the Hebrew Bible do not add up to a human life. They lack the compelling biographical questions about success, trouble, and loss, and thus reduce the story of his coming into maturity by presenting a one-dimensional figure.

The more we appreciate Abraham's Sumerian background, the more we need not depend upon miraculous interpretation to account for a crucial aspect of his life: his communication with God. The Sumerian temple drama of the daily life of the gods and the daily witness of humans came first; the conversations with one's personal or family god followed; and then came the literary conventions of trance or dream communication.

The Sumerians did not believe in a significant afterlife; for them, the soul was a medium that allowed humans to ask a question about what was unknowable and—in lieu of a reply—to dramatize the dialogue. When Abraham eventually hears the dramatic imperative to leave his home ("'Bring yourself out of your birthplace,' Yahweh said to Abraham"), this is the initial dialogue with a Sumerian personal god that would have been dramatized as advice—just as his father had received before him, advising him to leave Ur. The inner dialogue took place via the soul, a mediating concept for Sumerians. It represented the aspect of human consciousness that allows us to envision imaginatively what humans cannot know.

The mind has difficulty in maintaining the boundary between the unknown and the unknowable, even today, and questions about the soul continue to be addressed at many levels—in philosophy and modern psychoanalysis, for example. What is vital for us to know is that it was already an open question for Abraham and remained so in the later narrative of the Bible written by J. E, the major biblical author who followed J a century later, represented the soul more simplistically as a dream medium. The dramatic scenes of intimate dialogue elucidated by J dissolve into straight dream-dictation in E.

But when we return to Abraham and his family's immediate problem of survival, in the eighteenth century BCE, the individual and his or her soul are becoming overshadowed by the new empire of Babylon.

TCHOTCHKES

With the rise to power of King Hammurapi, his god of Babylon, called Marduk, ascended higher in the pantheon. This once small city god was inflated into the highest god, exchanging his name for Enlil, the oldest of Sumerian deities. The new literature commissioned in his name was pretentious to the point of sounding like a parody of distinguished literature, while the great literature of the past was now appropriated as if it *prefigured* Marduk or was actually meant to be about him. Heaven is described as if the gods are in need of hotel lodgings in his city, as in this hymn:

> In time past Marduk meant only "the beloved son," but now he is king indeed, this is so!
>
> *They shouted together,*
> *"GREAT LORD OF THE UNIVERSE!*
> *This is his name, in him we trust."*

When it was done, when they had made Marduk their king, they pronounced peace and happiness for him,
"Over our houses you keep unceasing watch, and all you wish from us, that will be done."

Marduk considered and began to speak to the gods assembled in his presence. This is what he said,
"In the former time you inhabited the void above, the abyss, but I have made Earth as the mirror of Heaven, I have consolidated the soil for the foundations, and there I will build my city, my beloved home.

"A holy precinct shall be established with sacred halls for the presence of the king. When you come up from the deep to join the Synod you will find lodging and sleep by night.

"When others from heaven descend to the Assembly, you too will find lodging and sleep by night. It shall be
BABYLON
'The home of the gods.' The masters of all the crafts shall build it according to my plan.'"

In the emerging empire of Babylon, the great myths are made pompously literal. Marduk re-invites the gods to earth and into the grandiose temple that is planned for him; more than that, the whole city of Babylon is envisioned as if it were to become a temple. The result is that the public will necessarily be reduced to an audience more isolated and distant from their divine figures, vicarious spectators to spectacle rather than enchanted participants in the cosmic theater.

In the original Sumerian drama, the statues were dependent on their makers much as a rapt young Abraham with his toy soldiers or Sarah with her doll house. The boy and girl are not passive watchers; they animate the drama. In the heroic days of Sumerian King Gilgamesh, more than a millennium previous, humans acted on the same stage as the gods: a statue was already a great wonder of collaboration between the artist and god. But in the Babylon of Hammurapi statue-making had been turned into an industry of making copies from an original—like the cheap replicas the poor could purchase. Soon a plaster-like Marduk will be in every bedroom in Babylon (and that era's dwellings have been found by archaeologists to be filled with such tchotchkes).

The original Sumerian statues and their votive watchers were envisioned as if alive, like the boy commanding his soldiers; at the same time, as spectator-participants in the drama we understand they are not alive, but rather mediators, like the household gods. The ascendance of mediating gods to public status, after thousands of years of acting as a private refuge, was the result of Marduk's having been set so far above the other gods that he was inaccessible. Meanwhile, every family would still have its own god. This would be a personal god taking the name of its owner, such as "the God of Abraham" (as we will find later in the Bible when it is applied to Yahweh). This personal god would act both as family guardian and also as intermediary with Marduk and other city gods. In return, it would receive a more intimate devotion. Indeed, most houses that have been excavated from this era contain a room for a private altar to the personal gods.

A SCENE FROM LIFE

Although the personal god may speak to us and for us, the temple god was more active in the cosmic theater that Abraham often witnessed. The whole drama began with the precious wood brought into the temple workshop, just two squares from his father's personal workshop. At his father's, stone statues of god-families as well as kings and watchers were made, and when a block of granite for a king was brought in, it was a day of excitement but no special ceremonial. All was ceremony, however, when the precious wood arrived in the temple workshop: it was treated as if the god had chosen it.

After the statue of a god was finished in the temple workshop, invitations for a ceremony for the "dressing" were sent out. At times, Terah would have been summoned to be among the token representation of artists or craftsmen in the audience. The clothing for this event took many months to make, with elaborate gold and silver ornamentation sewn in for the inauguration. First, the statue would begin a series of theatrical rituals to make it come alive. Then it could participate in many other dramas, such as the night procession to the riverbank where the stars and constellations were reflected in the metal ornamentation in a form of heavenly conversation.

In ancient Greek theater, which developed almost a thousand years after Abraham, the gods were represented by masks worn and manipulated by actors. But in Sumer and Akkad, actors manipulated complete, life-size embodiments of the gods fashioned by artists. To Terah and Abraham in Ur, trained in Sumerian culture, the statues they made were representations, models: exquisite, otherworldly, life-size dolls or works of art. And yet Abraham still would have trembled when recalling the most recent temple visit, only a week after Terah received the official request to move to Babylon. It was a mouth-opening ceremony for a new statue of Marduk, the high god of Babylon. What was always first revealed of the invisible realm of the cosmos were words and music, an overhearing of the gods, speaking in sacred text, in poems, and accompanied by musicians. On this occasion, a new *Lamentation for the Destruction of Ur* was being read by a chorus of voices, accompanied by harp and lute.

> *Your city has become a strange city; how can you now exist?*
> *Your house has become a house of tears . . .*
> *Ur, like the child of a street which has been destroyed,*
> *searches for you,*
> *The house, like a man who has lost everything, is empty like a*
> *hand stretching out to you.*
> *Your brickwork, like a human being, cries out, "Where have you*
> *gone?"*

A NEW LAMENT

Although the last dynasty of Ur had been overturned almost two centuries earlier, long before Abraham was born, a revival of Sumerian culture preceded Hammurapi's reign in Babylon. Hammurapi even commissioned poets to compose a new lament in the same Sumerian language as the older "*Lament for the Destruction of Sumer and Akkad*" (the one which authentically dated from the actual event).

Both laments have been found although no proof exists as to who authored them. This is a common situation when it comes to making later copies because adding a "signature" would have been considered vulgar, a scar on the perfect illusion of a work composed purely by inspiration or, more often, by inspired translation. Would a god put his signature on a natural creation, such as a tree or a bush?

Let us suppose, then, that Abraham was one of the scribes in Ur commissioned to contribute stanzas to the new lament. Of the commissioning, at least, we are sure; and of Abraham's professional education we can reflect on with considerable accuracy. The new composition, in its depths of grief and loss, was to be a tribute to Marduk. But how did Marduk earn this grief? By means of his elevation, and thus through the elevation of Babylon, the loss of Sumer was now being marked as a restoration—and it was Marduk's elevation to the high god that was being honored by this present Sumerian revival. In other words, grief and loss were transformed into celebration in an egregious example of Hammurapi's distortion of the arts of Sumer. How uncomfortable would Abraham, like his father, have been with the results?

JOURNEYING

After his family left Ur, the household god of Terah and his ancestors grew more precious. Finally, it became much more than a family god when Abraham migrated to Canaan. The family god, merging with the Canaanite creator god, Yahweh, created a new cosmic theater around Abraham. Yet it did not seem so unexpected to the original audience in Jerusalem many centuries later. For them, and for J, Abraham in fact was restoring the fundamental spirit of civilization in Ur. Thus, rather than a break with the past, the journey of Abraham to Canaan represented a restoration of Jewish roots in the original great civilization of Sumer. Even the Hebraic covenant was restoring the enlightened awe of Sumerian cultural and religious invention.

As J writes the history of Abraham's history, it is also a story of the growth of individual consciousness, as it inherits civilization anew. The central question on this journey becomes how is the new awareness to be passed on and inherited by future generations. The answer lies in the written tradition itself. As the audience in Jerusalem listens or reads, each person takes part as an individual, reliving several journeys: Abraham's migration to Canaan is one, and Israel's renewal of the origin of civilization is another.

That origin is found in an observance of the boundary between natural and supernatural worlds. The Sumerian invention of a cosmic theater came first, in which the boundary is dramatized in the temples. Throughout history—and here we sum up a core understanding in this chapter—there have been basically two ways to ignore this crucial boundary. One is to confuse the two realms, so that supernatural miracles intrude upon and determine our natural world. The other way of distorting civilization is subtler, and King Hammurapi's Babylon was a major example. It incorporated the Sumerian system but worshipped the gods themselves and neglected the theater. As a result, Babylonian culture became one of endless copies and enlargements, missing the creative tension that drove Sumer.

CHAPTER 7

The Call

In the tenth century BCE, at the court of Solomon's son, Rehoboam, a great biblical author began a translation of earlier stories about Abraham with God's call to him to leave both the ancestral "house" of his father's line and the literal two-story, substantial family house of his youth in Ur. How literal was this call in the mind of the author and the original audience in Jerusalem? How did the exact words come to be?

> *"Bring yourself out of your birthplace," Yahweh said to Abraham, "out of your father's house, your homeland—to a land I will bring you to see. I will make of you greatness, a nation and a blessing; of your name, fame—bliss brought out of you."*

It is plain to see that God's famous words to Abraham play upon the words just written by the same biblical author, J, as in the previous chapter of the narrative, about the men in Babel arriving at fame and making a name for themselves. The promise to Abraham involves the bliss of a blessing—in essence, what the Babel men forgot about in their emphasis on material fame. In light of these echoes of greatness and fame, our next question ought to be: Who is the audience for this play on words that runs from Babel to Harran, where Abraham has migrated with his father, Terah?

We might miss the connection today, but if we imagine the original audience in Jerusalem we see that Bavel, the Hebrew for Babylon, is a living reminder of Abraham's journey, for Abraham passed it by on the way from nearby Ur, heading past the city of Babylon for Harran, Ur's sister city. We know that the Babylonians kept scrupulous records of citizens who traveled and, in what seems likely for Terah, his summons from Hammurapi to move to Babylon would have been recorded. Yet it makes sense too that Terah would have been allowed to go to Harran, where he could continue his service to King Hammurapi at this outpost of empire, and now we can supply Terah's motivation for stopping there. It was a fear of being cut off from his ancestral culture that held him in Harran; that is why he did not follow his original plan to migrate all the way to Canaan with his son. When the biblical author first tells us that Terah intended to go to Canaan, the audience in Jerusalem (a city formerly included in the land of Canaan) would have understood why he stopped. They knew that the family coming from Ur was highly civilized, and that he would have been reluctant to leave this culture behind.

Since the author and audience in Jerusalem were far from nomads themselves, they could identify with the anxiety of losing touch with civilization that Abraham's journey evoked. They were members of the educated class at the king's court, numbering in the several thousands. They were sculptors and poets, musicians and dancers, architects and mathematicians, horticulturists and translators. They were part of a new Hebraic culture becoming established there, but with roots in the older Canaan, and of course in the origins of civilization in Sumer. The Abraham that they are focused upon is a founder of culture and is not particularly religious. He doesn't pray. His journey is *not* a nomadic one, with nothing to leave behind. Nor is Abraham's journey the first classic journey known to the biblical court, for they had read—and perhaps even translated into their own language—the *Epic of Gilgamesh* (aware that the Akkadian translation was Abraham's mother tongue). Gilgamesh journeyed into a future more human than mythic and god-centered, a coming to grips with mortality and the limitations of the gods. Thus Abraham's journey too is centered upon the issue of inheritance and clarifying the boundary of mortality with his God.

A SUCCESSFUL LOVEMAKING

The journey of Gilgamesh to the land at the end of the earth is a quest for the last hope of immortality. This is the secret of Ziusudra—the Sumerian Noah—who has survived the Flood and was granted eternal life. It is a journey that succeeds in its goal of arriving in Ziusudra's presence, yet therein lies disenchantment, for there is no magic, no recourse to the supernatural. Having internalized the knowledge of death, King Gilgamesh will return to his city and achieve fame for his civic works, his city gate especially. He settles for the fame of immortalizing one's name in time.

So too did the court poet of King Shulgi of Ur, who translated into Akkadian the Sumerian version of *Gilgamesh* that Abraham would have read. We have lost this poet's name, but like Abraham he was a man who was educated in Ur, and the spirit of winning fame by literary means would also be close to Abraham's heart. These types of fame—literary and civic, culture-founding—underlie the biblical history. We will see that Abraham's encounters in Canaan are not so much public events but touchstones of origin for Hebraic culture.

The call to Abraham promises this type of fame—literary and cultural—into the far future ("I will make of you greatness, a nation and a blessing; of your name, fame") and it also requires his acceptance of mortality: a reliance on his son, Isaac. In fact, this theme of inheritance is so ancient already that the biblical authors turn it on its head to illustrate the covenant: Everything depends on the *anxiety* of something so commonplace as a successful lovemaking between husband and wife. And the anti-heroic role of fatherhood is made tragicomically heroic because Abraham and Sarah are "beyond the years of childbearing." The new contract between man and the supernatural will rest upon an unlikely but natural pregnancy.

We can imagine the surprise and delight of the biblical author's audience upon first hearing this oddly domestic turn of events, so unlike the classical epics yet now put in a classic setting by a great writer of their own. Even the journey of Abraham to Canaan was surprising but precisely because it too was so uncannily domestic and Sumerian in spirit. The mind-stretching invention of a daily life for the statues of the gods, resulting in the need to put them to sleep each night—this Sumerian drama had been as commonplace as Abraham and Sarah's parenting problems. The moment of closing the eyes comes to everyone, but the moment of reckoning what it means, how it could come to something beyond a daily routine (lining up the god-statues all over again the next day)—that question was left suspended, unasked. Until the question was asked and answered many centuries later in Solomonic Jerusalem by the biblical authors of Abraham's life. For in the call to Abraham was an awareness of not just what was to be gained but what also was to be lost. Abraham's initial loss of civilization and home complicates his acceptance of a natural death and its maddening problems of inheritance. Had he remained in Harran or returned to Ur, there would have been a family lineage, a culture all around him to make up for his childlessness. But now his death would mean the death of all that came before him—a cultural inheritance and future, as well as a family legacy. All this would resonate in the Hebraic culture Abraham founded, for the biblical audience in Jerusalem was also attuned to the difficulty of their small nation's survival and how all could be lost. And the cosmic questions about the routine of daily life, vital in classical Sumerian culture, are answered in the telling of Abraham's journey and its struggles with inheritance.

But when we return to the time of Hammurapi's monumentalizing trend, the cosmic drama of Sumer was turning to lead, constricting the theater of the public gods of temple and ziggurat that had been the basis of Abraham's classical education. The creative spirit of civilization was in danger of vanishing, and remaining in Ur held out small hope of keeping it alive. Leaving Ur, however, Abraham would lose his intimacy with this serious playfulness, lose his place in the cosmic drama. As he tried to regain it in Harran, with a new emphasis on the personal god, a call that changes his world is heard. It is a call that would require a new domestic drama in a natural landscape seemingly without walls, in Canaan.

REDUCTIVE VERSIONS

After many years in Harran then, Terah's son, Abraham, gets his own summons as his father had earlier—not from a king but from Yahweh. Unlike his father though, the issue before him is not about obeying or disobeying. Yahweh promises him an almost exact replacement to the life he was losing, in which ordinary, daily things, as represented by the gods in their temples—meals and family visits and travels—would be transformed into his own domestic and cosmic drama. Abraham's literal journey to Canaan was no doubt eventful, full of experiences and encounters, as in Damascus, hinted at by the position in the story of Eliezer of Damascus, Abraham's designated heir in lieu of a son. But for the biblical audience in Jerusalem, Abraham no sooner embarks than he arrives in Canaan—as if he walked right up on a new stage, instantaneously.

The actual house in Ur that Abraham first lost; the education rooted in the classical civilization of Sumer; the cemetery of his ancestors—all that was left behind was known to the original author and audience of the Hebrew Bible. It would not have occurred to them that we, today, would be reading their words in another language and culture, and that we would have little idea of the importance of what Abraham left behind. The intervening centuries have offered cartoonish versions of "idol worship" that increasingly deny the reality of the sophisticated culture behind Abraham, and indeed, behind the Bible, and replace it with supernatural legend and a reduction of secular history. Nothing could be further from the inspiration at the origin of the Bible itself, which faces history with all the resources at its disposal. The audience in Jerusalem understood the history that we must now recover: Abraham once lived in a real house, in a real neighborhood, and even the "tents" in Canaan (the word merely suggesting their temporary nature) were on a scale commensurate with the elaborate housing of a well-born traveler.

HOME

In the year c.1750 BCE, the ancient city of Ur was built up along rational lines, in rectangular blocks, with suburbs extending in all directions. Buildings contained bathrooms and drains, as did the streets, drained by covered sewers. The main street was broad and paved. There were drain pipes made of pottery and water pipes in private houses, supplying kitchen and bathroom, along with water flushing arrangements for the toilets.

Terah's family would have lived in the inner city, near the palace and temple complexes, and a few blocks from the ziggurat surrounded by a huge plaza. The Temple of Nanna and its considerable courtyard were anchored across from it. In the neighborhoods to the south, between the temple and the king's palace, lived the professional classes who served both government and religion. That's where Terah's house would have stood near the West Harbor, the smaller of the two harbors within the walls of the central city. West Harbor was primarily used for smaller craft, government and passenger vessels, while the larger harbor to the north brought in the city's provisions.

The house itself was built around a central, enclosed courtyard. When entering, one stepped into a small vestibule that led to the courtyard. The rooms of the house opened onto the courtyard, from which life and light entered—there were no outside windows, no outside access. The rooms were quite small, and they were used sparingly in the daylight hours, except when the weather was inclement of course. The altar room, one of the largest, contained not only the household gods but "the Watchers," votive statues that had belonged to deceased members of the family, including those of some significant ancestors that had been handed down over the generations. These statues, two- to three-foot-high replicas of their human counterparts, once stood in the temple when their owners were alive. The huge eyes, however, echoed the temple statues, representing an openness and attention to the gods that they were crafted to watch—in perpetual attendance of the daily cosmic theater.

Abraham had his own room since early youth. After his marriage to Sarah, the couple continued to live in the family house in a new bedroom and sitting room that were built out of what had previously been a storage area and pantry, the latter necessities relocated into a new addition. This was a common type of renovation, found in recent excavations at the ancient site of Ur.

The graveyard of Abraham's family consisted of an abandoned house, built after the migration and inhabited for two centuries near the wharf: Ancestors had first been buried beneath the floor, as in a basement, and nowadays in the courtyard. The house itself had become a warehouse for Terah's collection of "decommissioned" statues, which, because they were no longer properly attended to and had been rescued from fallen temples, now served as models. Some defective or unfinished statues were also in the collection. When temples had fallen, the owners consigned them to Terah's warehouse for safekeeping because there was no room for these statues in a private home. They were all antiques, in a way, or more properly artifacts in the family museum—just as it was common for scribes and scholars to have their own private libraries.

The history of Terah's family before the migration to Ur recedes into the mists of the northern province (where an archaic Amorite culture continues to exist). Some ancient remnants of the family, called "distant cousins," lived in the Northern city of Harran, and once in every generation or so Terah's family would be invited to a feast there to reestablish old ties. (There was no question of these "poor relations" coming to Ur. Some were still semi-nomadic, living in mud-covered huts, involved in the caravan trade.)

COPYING

Terah and his ancestors in Ur collected things in the Sumerian manner: as models for possible transformation rather than mere evocations of the past. Historical sources, even archaic sayings, were modernized in the process of being translated. For the Hebraic authors of a later time, in Jerusalem, the writing of the Bible also was often an imaginative translation of historical sources—going back to Sumer and in the *spirit* of Sumer.

The kingdom of Akkad, a neighbor that eventually overtook Sumer, translated Sumerian literature into Akkadian in a different spirit altogether and with an eye to fidelity. It was inherently an acknowledgment that their culture was a latecomer and dependent upon the genius of Sumer. It's true that Akkad enlarged on the original Sumerian compositions at times, adding bridging material and weaving in transitions for the *Epic of Gilgamesh,* but by their spellbound loyalty to Sumerian culture, the Akkadians kept the spirit of Sumer alive. Thus it took hold of Abraham in his youth as it had most craftsmen of his period.

Eventually however, with the rise of King Hammurapi in Babylon, the new emphasis on rapid copying, combined with inflated proportions, cast a chill over original artistic expression.

MOUTH-WASHING

Sumerian culture had been most interested in changing the shapes of things. A statue of a god was not an abstract being but a transformation of stone into another order of being: a life hidden within it, lit from within.

As the solid stone was house for the spirit, so the soul was the hidden life in the solid body. The statue as a work of art was the embodiment of what we call soul music: an intuition of what lies behind the appearances of things. How else to explain the world if not by the confrontation with its hidden truths? The latter was understood by the Sumerians in the form of lifelike, albeit imagined, beings beyond time, come from a hidden heaven, and inhabiting the sculptures of the cosmic drama.

But first the statues had to be brought to life. It was in Terah's workshop that the ritual of coming alive would begin. When a statue was finished, its mouth was washed in preparation to eat. A more elaborate mouth-washing would follow in the secret riverbank ceremony that was part of the god's complex installation in the temple. It is natural to imagine that one day, during his school days as a scribe, Abraham's teacher showed him descriptions of this mouth-washing ceremony and told him of the much larger collection of tablets in the temple archives, recorded by each generation according to the details of the ceremony considered important in their day. In encountering these temple tablets, the descriptions on them would seem to Abraham more real even than the times he had witnessed the processions themselves, accompanying his father.

When he grew older and studied the Sumerian literature in detail in the *edubba,* or tablet-house, something similar took place. The words that described the theater of daily life for the gods in the old temples seemed more vivid to Abraham than witnessing the drama itself. The drama had become distorted by the elevation of Marduk, injecting an awkward pomposity into the ceremony while the tablets in the library preserved the record of an enthralling historical grace. Still, even in Abraham's day, the cosmic theater was astonishing to watch from its daily beginnings as the god-statues were roused from their sleep and made ready to open their eyes and to eat. It was only rarely that Terah and Abraham were allowed in though as witnesses: the gods can't have people regularly visiting or traipsing through their house.

When Terah and Abraham visited the temple, it was usually to repair a detail of a statue or to compare information with a new statue in progress or to examine statue placements and pediments. Such visits took place in the hours before the statues had awakened to their first meal, or later, when they were napping. But Terah and Abraham saw enough to enliven their sense of how the gods formed a household in which they slept, ate, listened to performed music, were addressed in poetry, and were dressed and re-dressed. Included in the household were the gods' or goddesses' consorts and group of lesser gods who served them and made up a kind of extended family. Complex staffs of human workers, ranging from priests to water carriers, not only waited upon the gods but were supervised by the lesser gods. In fact, they stage-managed the entire "estate." And far more than the average Sumerian, Terah and Abraham would observe a whole commerce that was created for the gods, in which the temple was an estate unto itself with functioning kitchens, reception areas, dining and living rooms, and bedrooms. There were accoutrements for transport, because statues that once sat in Terah's workshop needed carriages and boats to convey them on visits to other gods. On these ritual visits they would, among other things, help to settle disputes, oversee harvests and dairy festivals, and take the occasional vacation.

What this cosmic theater revealed about its original Sumerian audience was the unconditional commitment to live in the presence of another species of being: as if the gods were a higher species of humans, though superior in their powers and longevity. Even though they had fashioned them to look like humans, once the god-statues had become theatrically alive they were as different and on a higher plane from Terah and Abraham as humans were to donkeys. The god-statues were a projection of what the Sumerians knew to be their own limited domain within the animal and plant kingdoms. In some ways, their world-view might be said to have contained inklings of evolutionary knowledge, of a prehistory.

It was one thing for the Sumerians to know that humans had written the speeches of the gods, their hymns and myths, but it was even more of an advance to have understood that what animated the statues—an imitation of magical thinking—came from human desire and artfulness as well. But this self-awareness became lost under the influence of Hammurapi's new empire. Comparing the intimacy of the earlier Sumerian laments to the recent poetry from Babylon, Abraham would have found the latter had reverted to the confusion of magical thinking, as in supplications, entreaties, and other wishes for supernatural help. There was little ability to personally identify with the emotions of the gods, except in rare instances, as when the human side to the goddess Ishtar appears, and then it was only because the author lifted a few words from Sumerian poems about Inanna, the original model for Ishtar in the Akkadian and Babylonian translations.

"Say 'a pity!' about me, and let your mood be eased.
'A pity!' about my wretched body

that is full of disorders and troubles,
'A pity!' about my sore heart
that is full of tears and sobbings,
'A pity!' about my wretched, disordered,
and troubled portents . . ."

Yet this is still a god speaking in a cosmic drama, the goddess Ishtar to her peers. There is hardly a trace left of the earlier Sumerian poet's speaking for himself and the citizens of the city.

A GOD MADE PERSONAL

In marked contrast to literature in Hammurapi's Babylon, the earlier Sumerian lament, *Oh Angry Sea,* addressed the high god as father in a personal way throughout. As if he were a real father, we do not expect anything magical from him, such as making good our losses. Unlike the goddess Ishtar in the Babylonian lament, who is implored to do something, the high god Enlil in *Oh Angry Sea* is asked only for sympathy. He is spoken to like a real father, the poet expressing his helplessness in the face of grief without expectation of any supernatural act. Both poet and the reader of the Sumerian lament identify with the intractability of the god's emotional life and do not appear as supplicants. In this prototype of speaking to a god made personal, there is a hope for something new to happen, something unexpected, but not a thing specifically asked for, as there is in supernatural wishes and rituals of supplication.

Much evidence of unmediated magical thinking, and in particular divination, has been found nevertheless throughout the history of ancient Mesopotamia. It served a desire to predict the future likelihood of bad times and good, and at the popular level especially, the prediction of good and bad decisions. In classical Sumerian and Akkadian culture, this kind of lottery-playing with the future was held in check by the high civilization of the cosmic theater, and examples of this art are found in the great Sumerian laments in which magical thinking is suppressed.

Oh Angry Sea is a great Sumerian lament in which the heart of the creator god is directly addressed as a metaphor for the sea. The poet speaks to a father-god who embraces the full range of human memory, back to the catastrophe of the great flood.

Oh, you dwelling in anger, father, your angry heart, until
when will it not be pacified?

Abraham would have come to know this Sumerian lament as classic literature, not as sacred liturgy; he would have studied it in the library as if a secular work appreciated for literary values. It was among the texts all scholars studied and practiced translating, from Sumerian into Akkadian and the new Babylonian dialect. The Babylonian liturgy that was current, however, was full of clichéd ritual repetitions. It was recited at ceremonies marking the building or rebuilding of any temple—exactly what was happening at an unprecedented rate in King Hammurapi's Babylon. There would be nothing in the newly composed liturgy as poignant as the Sumerian identification with all living beings:

The bird pours out a wailing from its throat,
The girgilu-bird pours out a wailing from its throat,
Bitter crying, bitter tears, wailing from its throat it
pours out

Since the Master turned away from the nation,
And from the Black-headed, the head lolls lifeless on
the shoulder.

The Sumerian poet embraces the natural world without mythologizing it. His nature is already demystified, and the bird's cry of abandonment stands in stark contrast to the over-simplifications of the flood story referred to in the new liturgy commissioned by Hammurapi, where the catastrophe of the flood stands for purposeful punishment of human beings—and indifference to the suffering of the natural world that is swept away with it.

Unlike the later distortions produced in Babylon, the Sumerian author of *The Lamentation of the Destruction of Ur* does not feel punished by the gods; rather, he confronts his feelings as if he and his city had been abandoned by a real father for reasons unknown.

You, who take counsel only with yourself, you are exalted!
You, who covered your heart as one covers a basket,
Dignitary, you leaned your ear on your lap

The effect of Enlil's turning his back is felt by the writer as if he were an abandoned child. Yet in the following passage, here is an Enlil, the creator god, who is also king over human history and destiny, centuries before the Babylonian Marduk, and long before the Canaanite Yahweh, who will also become both creator god and father to a people.

In heaven, who is exalted? It is you who are exalted!
On the earth, who is exalted? It is you who are exalted!
Lord of all heaven, lord of the entire earth,
From the country of sunrise to the country of sunset,
In no country is there a king; only you exercise kingship,

The author goes on to call up all the endearing appellations of the god—and the irony of all these endearments lies in what the poet is asking for: simply that his father turn around.

"Shepherd of the Black-headed, turn around and look at your city!" let me say;
"The One Inspecting for Himself, turn around and look at your city!" let me say;
"The Warrior Who Leads the Troops, turn around and look at your city!" let me say;
"The One Who Feigns Sleep, turn around and look at your city!" let me say.
Enki, turn around and look at your city!

The creator being addressed as a father is also creator of water, for water is the life-giving element in which the wetlands of Sumer are nourished, and the following passage ends in the image of anger like a drowning storm:

In Nippur, young and old are raging,
In Babylon, young and old are raging,
In Isin, young and old are raging.
Those standing in the streets were being chased away,
Their genitals, the dogs carried hanging from their mouths,
Their scattered remains are set aflame,
The playgrounds of the young have filled with storms

The imagery and tone of the *Lament for the Destruction of Ur* approach a concreteness that outlasts the statues in the temple, and this kind of emotional speaking before the high god Enlil will become a model for how a person speaks to his own personal god.

THE NEPHEW

In the year 5 of Hammurapi, the king received a call from the gods and recorded it in the Prologue to the *Code of Hammurapi:* "Anu and Bel called me, Hammurapi, the exalted prince, the worshipper of the gods, to cause justice to prevail in the land, to destroy the wicked and the evil, to prevent the strong from oppressing the weak, to enlighten the land, and to further the welfare of the people."

Worthy endeavors, perhaps, yet they seem like bureaucratic rhetoric compared with the weight of the call to Abraham. Abraham is called, simply, to leave the domain of all that wordiness.

The great stele with Hammurapi's Prologue and Code was still an artifact of renown at the time of the biblical writer, and it was presumed by Israel that he was king at the time of Abraham's journey to Canaan. So when the writer at the Jerusalem court tells her audience (and us) that Abraham is asked to go "out of your father's house," namely Terah's house, they would have been aware that at the ascent of Hammurapi to the throne of Babylon, it was said that he "entered the house of his father." The play upon Hammurapi's words is unmistakable.

> *Now Abraham comes out, follows Yahweh's words to him. Lot went out with him.*

Let us consider for a moment, the momentous occasion of this straightforward passage where Abraham follows words, Yahweh's words, as if they were tracks leading out of his homeland. Abraham is a man of means, a man who would travel with servants and household staff and probably a herd of prize donkeys for eventual sale to the caravan trade. Yet in place of a description of Abraham's retinue there is only, "Lot went with him." Not even a family, with sons and daughters, but instead this casual identification of a single nephew, Lot, whose name, like that of Abraham, is Sumerian in origin (in its original "Abram").

Nothing is said here about Terah, nor Abraham's mother. It is as if the god who speaks to Abraham in the intimacy of a personal god, the God of Abraham, wants to join these two descendants of Sumer, Abraham and Lot—as if three came out, Abraham, Yahweh, and Lot. Lot keeps the implications of leave-taking at a cultural level and not a strictly personal one with Abraham. This is more than just one man's leaving home: it is leaving a homeland, and the beginning of a new culture.

KULLA

Now Yahweh has broken the family unity, taken the place of the father. The nature of this change is still being revealed in our time. In some of the houses excavated in Sumer, private chapel rooms for the personal gods of the family have been uncovered, and beside these, closets in which quantities of tablets were found, representing the family archive. The unity of the family, its past and future, is in evidence here. The father, when he died, was buried beneath it, never forgotten, as if he were the former high priest of the house, a role now inherited by his son.

Now, with Abraham uprooted, we must ask how he came to replace the family's personal god and where had he learned of Yahweh? This is the logical question, since Abraham has nothing himself to ask concerning God's identity. That is, the biblical text refers to Yahweh speaking, but he neither introduces himself to Abraham nor does Abraham even ask his name. Yet there was no deity in Mesopotamia by that name, so it would not be already familiar to him. From the outset, the original audience for the story in Jerusalem would have assumed that it was Abraham's personal Sumerian god who advised him to leave Harran; only later would Abraham be made aware of Yahweh's Canaanite identity. Indeed, that is the way the biblical author wrote it down: only after time has passed and Abraham has traveled in Canaan does the text state that Abraham called upon Yahweh for the first time by name.

Is it possible then that the Jerusalem author knew who the family god of Terah had been? Vast numbers of personal clay documents from the era are being found—letters, household documents, receipts, even notes to the gods—surely the household gods were named in several contexts. It would make sense that histories of the family available to the original author in the court archive named the god. Even the family's cuneiform tablets themselves, describing their ancestral history, eventually would have been brought from Harran to Canaan at a later date. Today we can only speculate about the name of this god, but we may find a higher degree of accuracy in imagining what the biblical authors knew.

One of the classic Sumerian epics known to an educated person at the Jerusalem court was "The World Order," a poem that one could consult for knowledge about Sumerian gods. In it, the god Enki tours the pantheon and comes to Ur, the capital of Sumer at the time of this poem, to foretell its significance,

"O city, well-supplied, washed by much water . . .
green like the mountain."

This green mountain becomes the ziggurat of Ur, planted with trees and hanging gardens. The significance of the ziggurat is described as the "neck to heaven," intimate with the moon and the moon-god Nanna, who is the city-god of Ur.

"O thou shrine Ur, neck to heaven mayest thou rise."

The first biblical author of Genesis consulting this Sumerian poem for knowledge of Abraham and the god of Ur would not have found a clue to Abraham's personal god until the work of the lesser gods is described. Then, suddenly, a particular god is evoked who fits the background of Terah's family:

Kulla, the brick-maker and tablet-maker . . .

—who was also the inspiration behind the making of houses, temples, and the ziggurat, as well as the clay tablets for writing.

If it is Kulla who became the family god for Terah and Abraham in the mind of the biblical author—Kulla, whose domain centered on the house—Abraham would have heard the voice of Kulla advising him to come "out of your father's house." This exhortation would have carried with it the further implication of leaving temple and ziggurat as well, the cosmic houses of his birthplace; it would have carried special weight. Yet by the time Abraham arrives in Canaan, Kulla is also left behind. The author has been playing with the pantheon of Sumer, familiar to her audience, in the same way as in the story of Babel.

Thus, in the antithesis to a builder-god lies the origin of the houseless Abraham, who will never live in a house again until his death. (There is no house for Yahweh either for a long time to come.) But if there is no house, then where does the personal god now reside? For in the Sumerian culture of Ur and Harran, the personal god has a home and is known also as the household god. The Canaanite creator god, Yahweh, has no need of a house until his people Israel established a kingdom in the future. So this critical juncture of houseless gods presents a new possibility.

This is the natural point at which the author, merging Abraham's personal god into Abraham's God, will place Yahweh in the house of words itself, in the Hebrew Bible, and thereby allow the creator god to enter into human history. The mythic history that began with Adam and Eve, which held sway until the preceding Tower of Babel story, is now opening into historical time. That history, in which Yahweh came down to inspect his creation from time to time, has now become a narrative where he is an engaged participant, actively making a covenant with his people.

CHAPTER 8

The Education of Abraham

In c.1790 BCE, in the city of Ur, the neighboring city-states of Isin and Larsa were the two most powerful ones in a period when central rule had declined. The Semitic kings of these city-states still described themselves as "King of Sumer and Akkad" with ambitions to control Nippur and Ur, the latter especially important as the spiritual capital and seat of Nannna (or Sin, in Akkadian) the moon-god. It had been almost two centuries since the downfall of the third and last dynasty of Ur, occasioning what would be the last *Lament for the Destruction of Ur,* but this lament was still vital to the classical Sumerian culture taught there, a city that had not been totally destroyed. In the years since the fall of Ur as a political power, the city was slowly restored, and more significantly, it became a center of restoration of Sumerian culture. The old tablets were re-translated into Akkadian and new statues were commissioned to replace those lost, a boost to the business of Terah's workshop.

We know this history because the city of Mari, seat of legendary Sumerian scholarly activity, was utterly smashed by Hammurapi a few decades later, after his city-state of Babylon had ascended in military power and defeated the kings of Isin and Larsa. Even though Mari was burned to the ground, confirming our knowledge of Hammurapi's cruel campaign, the tablets of its library were preserved, baked by the fire into a hardened state of preservation and found—more than fifteen thousand of them—in legible condition by archaeologists in the twentieth century.

From excavations, we also know that Mesopotamian cities were delineated by walls, most often imparting a rectangular shape. But Ur was distinctive. It was nearly a symmetrical oval, defined by a moat, suspended like an island between a canal and the Euphrates—a port city, a city whose ascendance rested not on the durability of walls but on its connections with the sea and the multicultural riches that defy physical might, resting instead on craft and exchange. Ur's cosmopolitan history was already millennial, and the most imposing walls were those inscribed for posterity by the first scribes, the Sumerians.

The city had a reputation of being rebuilt haphazardly, but those who lived in Ur or came through on the trade caravans or cargo boats had a very different impression. And those who had stood on the upper terraces of the central temple knew its secret. Abraham had stood at those vantage points, accompanying his father for the installation of the god-statues. From this view, even a child could understand that he was surveying a complex culture, full of intention and attention to detail.

Ur was a city that a child could rejoice in. Abraham would inevitably be drawn to the gates, the massive, sometimes ornate entrances to the city, huge doors that pivoted on stones, which were inscribed by a foreshadowing of a story or stamps of kingship or emblems of godship for the city. The pivot stones were masses of black rock, often diorite, brought down the river from the north, too heavy for donkeys. On the exterior of the gate sockets would be the Sumerian cuneiform inscriptions, which could be briefly glimpsed as the gates would open. Thus, the invisible would become visible, the classical past fully in view for a moment, adding to the excitement of entering the city.

Just inside the gates were the notaries. Temporary stands were set up each day by such scribes, who would sit awaiting those transacting business or exchanges. Nearly all transactions were recorded, and the records were inscribed on clay in cuneiform, a script that could embrace any language or culture. Text and texture were mixed in infinite ways, according to the training of the scribe and whatever art he possessed. In Abraham's eyes, this was a kind of inscribed sculpture of the street, away from the enclosed workshop and tablet house, and happening in the midst of everyone.

Abraham could watch one of these notaries for even longer than he could watch his father. At first there would be the wet lump of clay, which the scribe would mold into an oval or rectangular tablet that could be cradled in his hand. In the other hand would be the stylus made from a reed. Clay and reed went together, found in the slow-moving, knee-deep water where the large birds would fish. The raw cut reed would be trimmed to create an endpoint that could open the clay into wedge-like cuts and impressions. In this way, the clay would be turned into a document, the stylus moving across and up and down by a hand choreographed by the script of the scribes. This script was called cuneiform by the Assyriologists of the nineteenth century.

The parties to a contract were rarely as schooled in writing as the scribe was. They would impress their signatures with the small stone cylinders hung around their necks. Signatures were seals, and the intricate engraved pictures upon these stones would be perfectly captured for all time on the clay tablet that had now become a contract. The engravings were often comprised of scenes or symbols of special meaning from the individual's life, and we can be sure that Terah and Abraham wore their own. Underneath the cylinder seal impression, the scribe would write the name of the owner.

What came next was perhaps the most remarkable thing of all, the making of an envelope. A thin sheet of clay was molded, and upon it the tablet was placed and folded within; the scribe pinched off the excess as a breadmaker might. This was the magic part because the outer casing of clay never stuck to what was inside. This scribal secret was almost more revered than the writing, perhaps because it was invisible—until the document was released from its casing.

A scribal notary had once explained the secret of the contract's immortality. He said it was inherent in the god of the marshes, Enki, who held dominion over the movement of the clay. "The clay is ever alive until it sleeps. Wet clay can take any form, but as it dries it gets smaller until it moves no more. When there are two clays, including the document's envelope, wetness must be matched by wetness for the drying to be neat. The last to dry would crack and crumble if it housed the first to dry, for the first was now dormant and could no longer move with the movements of the outer." The later impression of Abraham's covenant with God would echo back to these contractual scenes. The envelope of his own movements had begun to set. Once the writing was done, the aliveness of the clay was soon to pass into sleep. But knowing this—how the language fixed in clay outlives its author—never kept him from the tablet-house. He needed the wetness of the clay, the changes made by the stylus in his hand, the possibility of new kinds of understandings, new words being said.

THE TEACHER

Before he'd been outside the city, Abraham would ask those who spoke of their travels, "How does Ur appear?" Always he would be told that Ur was a magic city for the traveler. There would be days of nothing but the sound of donkey hoofs tamping the endless flatness all around or wagon wheels grating or squishing the earth depending on the season, and then suddenly the city would be before them. The walls seemed to cut through the earth, and all would wake as if from a dream to find themselves surrounded by fields of barley, punctuated by plows moving. The men doing the plowing would be seen last. Or the wise men who tended the date palms of the groves, renowned for their knowledge of the secret origin of the trees and how new plants came from old.

The story was different for those who came into Ur on the Euphrates River and continued through its canals. The water placed the image of Ur constantly in their minds, and the anticipation of floating into the city was always within them. Many said they needed days of sleep afterwards to recover from the looking and watching. For them, Ur was a city with streets of water. To be sure, there were many more streets than canals, but this is what it felt like to float through the mouths of the high walls of Ur.

When he repeated these traveler's tales at school, the "big brother," the teacher's assistant, overheard. Surely the work of your father, Terah, has taken you outside the city? Yes, Abraham said, but never had he come into Ur from a far distance. Surely that held a truth he couldn't know. Impatiently, the big brother pulled him into the school archives, and then the "school father" appeared. Everyone in this school called him teacher. He said, "There is a difference between sight and vision, between sound and voice, between surveyor and architect, harpist and writer." He pulled out one of his copies of the Kings List, the measure of the long history of Sumer and Akkad. "I have never known a man to live as long as this king, but the writer says so. Was it true or false?" asked the teacher. A vigorous debate ensued but the teacher refused to supply the answer. He said simply that the answer had been in the question. "The writer has his reasons; a reader must interpret it as from a far distance."

Abraham's teacher had seen a tablet made of iron once, in a room of antiquities under the protection of a palace princess, now the priestess of the temple where the teacher had studied. It was inscribed with the last lines of the great *Epic of Gilgamesh.* This was an extraordinary thing, for iron was rare and no metalworker in Ur knew how to handle it, much less write upon it. It had come from the north, close to the mountain source of the water that filled the rivers. A miniature clay tablet affixed beside it on the wall attributed it to Nineveh and described the iron as coming from even deeper in the mountains of the west.

The teacher then recited the lines on the iron tablet from memory, winking when he was finished:

> *There is no permanence. Do we build a house to stand forever; do we seal a contract to hold for all time? Do brothers divide an inheritance to keep forever; does the flood-time of rivers endure? It is only the nymph of the dragon-fly who sheds her larva and sees the sun in his glory.*

At each of the four corners of the iron tablet, added the teacher, there was an inlaid rendering of a dragonfly made from lapis lazuli.

Abraham understood that his teacher winked because the mastery of the artist had undone the seeming permanence of his material with the wisdom of the story. That the tablet had been collected by the priestess had forever earned his teacher's respect.

TABLET MAKING

Abraham did not go to the school that had trained his teacher. By now the temple had lost its hold on the training of the scribes, and there were different schools throughout the city (the most important official school was attached to the palace). It was already unusual to have a teacher who had been fully educated within the temple; his knowledge was superior. When he became old, this teacher took the riches and reputation earned during his time of service and made part of his two-story home a tablet-house. This is where Terah sent his son, and it was a typical school for the time, except for the teacher.

The maze of streets to walk through to Abraham's teacher's house revealed nothing of its distinction. One would have to know the city and the district in which he were walking to know it was mostly comprised of those tied to the palace administration. The eye was propelled forward by the continuous ridges of the mud-brick walls, which seemed to undulate as one passed by. But they were perfectly still and blank. No windows faced outward, except perhaps on a second floor, though these would always be shuttered by their reed coverings. An occasional shop front would break through, though rarely, since most shops were in the bazaars. What caught the eye almost exclusively were the endless rows of bricks.

Brick defined the city. It was often inscribed, marking it as part of a king's résumé or under a god's protection, and this allowed writing and drawing to underlie everything. Composed of clay, tempered with straw, sand, or pebbles, bricks were usually made during summer, shaped by a mold and left to dry out in the sun, sometimes in as many rows as the cultivated fields. However, when used at the bottom of structures and most especially for the building of courtyards, drains, or anything exposed, they were usually baked for added durability.

When the bricks were laid, joined with mud mortar, and a wall was finished, it was plastered with additional mud and washed with white.

When he first attended school, Abraham had been asked, "What is your profession?" His only instruction from Terah had been to reply, "Inscriber of stone." That was why he had gained the privilege of attending school, and, in fact, this particular one. His teacher was an expert in the scribal needs of both temple and palace, and the statues made by his father were destined for both.

In the scribal school, Abraham would be seated with two others on a bench made of baked brick, cushioned with reed matting. There were several rows of these benches—every space filled. Above was the sky: classes were held in the courtyard of the home, which had been closed off from rooms dedicated to the running of the household. Living rooms and sleeping quarters for members of the teacher's family were on the second floor. When necessary, classes were held in a room off the courtyard, adjacent to his teacher's office.

The teacher had several assistants, one of whom acted as the everyday teacher, preparing new tablets for students to copy, checking their work, and hearing their recitations. This assistant, "big brother," also instructed them in the making of tablets and other objects used for inscription. This was an important part of the day, and it distinguished his teacher's school from others. Like Terah, who kept a collection in his workshop of all the materials from which a statue might be fashioned, Abraham's teacher kept a specimen of every object or surface that might be used for writing. These specimens, with not a letter or mark inscribed upon them, were displayed in the inside classroom.

First, there was the typical schoolboy's tablet, round and made of clay; it was rough with bits of straw, grit, and pebbles marking the surface. There was also a rectangular tablet, almost shimmering with the silky smoothness of the purity of its clay. There was a bronze tablet no bigger than his teacher's thumb. A clay cone—a kind of decorative nail—was paired with a bronze one. There were tablet specimens of gold and silver and hinged ivory and wood writing boards. The most unusual of all, a waxed board called the *tablet of life,* was hinged in several layers. And there were two bullae carved and polished from the seeds of a date palm. Papyrus and leather skins were also used, but it was painstaking work, since these surfaces did not yield easily to the delicacy of cuneiform inscription.

Not only were the students given instruction in the making of different kinds of tablets, but also in the gathering of raw materials. They were led by their teacher to an area outside the city gates, which was kept as it had been found by the Sumerian founders of Ur. It was set aside from all the other commerce of the city, so the reeds and clay could accrue as they had from the beginning. Here, the best reeds were said to grow, and the strongest cane for reinforcing the canals. Here, the students would learn how to cut the reeds with hand blade and clay sickle, and how to distinguish different qualities of clay.

We are able to follow Abraham's education because these historical details have recently come to light in archaeological investigations, helping us to understand how his mind may have been formed. The materials and process of writing, we learn, were a spur to critical thinking for a student like Abraham. As we noted in Abraham's scribal training, the medium of clay united countryside earth to city walls to even literary writing—a synthesis of cultural expression that may well enliven a student's mind to one day make bold connections across time and space. Meanwhile, when no more school time could be used for the harvest of materials and the crafting of tablets, we can imagine that Abraham delighted in the making of the linguistic signs, arresting his teacher's eye on the duration of each impression made with the stylus. It was all a postponement of the deadening of the clay, the moment when it would become too fixed to change or move. Unlike the egotistical students who were possessive to the point of seeing their reflections in the finished tablets they made (though the tablets turned opaque in dryness) Abraham was as through with a dried clay tablet as it was through with him.

Yet as an inquisitive student, he had an interest in collections, and so the archive of tablets maintained in his teacher's office was of a different order, revealing surprising turns of history and artistic ambition. He felt the same about the god-statues created by his father. Once complete, Abraham felt he might as well have been transporting bricks to the temple. But once *installed* with the other members of the god's family, he could gaze forever, until pulled away by his father. It was the *body* of work rather than the work itself; it was the history or hand behind the work, the intangible spirit that held a collection together. As a probing student, Abraham would have wondered why there was no god for this. Yes, scribes had their own god, but this is not what he had in mind.

Abraham's teacher had stored the tablets of his archive in the manner going back to the last royal family of Sumer. Many of them were indexed at their rims and layered in baskets with clay labels indicating the contents. These were mostly copies that he or others had made; originals were handled differently, bundled with strings and tagged with inscriptions detailing their origin or content. The teacher even had a catalog listing what was on the tags and labels.

The collection represented every area of study and possible duty of a scribe, from religious and music texts common to temple activities, to records of temple transactions and readings of the lights in the sky. There were lists of royalty, plants and medicines, mathematical and surveying calculations, military records and tax collection documents. Even common contracts between landholders, traders, and craftsmen, made at the hand of gate notaries, were in his collection. Abraham was trained in all of these, each having its own predetermined genre that had to be learned in order to proportion the text and select the proper shape for the tablet. All was tied to the activities of the city, but nothing *utilitarian* in nature could explain the existence of the tablets of poetry and stories that were in his teacher's collection, or even the stories of scribal life and school days, which he and the other students would copy out for practice—and as relief from the stress of learning over 500 signs and variations.

And mere utility could not explain a tablet from the basket containing the diary of his teacher. It told a story from his teacher's 30 years as a scribe for the palace, yet not as a record of events but as something that could be read for pleasure or thought. Because it was necessarily unfinished, it had not been put in the fire. Its fragility provoked an anxiety, only settled by his teacher's reassurance that *instructions* had been given for its firing, and for it to be placed in a clay jar next to his own when deceased, beneath the floor bricks in front of the family chapel. Without the fire, the inscriptions could be washed away someday by a flood.

There's an irony in the composition of these texts, designed not to be read by living contemporaries. They are meant for the eyes of gods or history. Unlike his teacher and many of the scribes, most of the population avoided speaking of their own deaths. If necessary, they made indirect references, such as "traveling the road of one's forefathers." But the scribes could always do more with death—no one would be reading those words for some time—and snatched up occasions to refer to it, just as his teacher did.

LISTS

Once, Abraham and other students at his level accompanied his teacher on a field trip to a chapel of the patron goddess of the scribes, Nissaba. This one was a small restoration of what had originally been a temple before the fall of Ur, now only a shadow of a memory of what had existed generations before. It was common knowledge that some of the scribal profession still went to such a chapel to make a votive offering. Such an offering was known to be different than what was possible for the rest of the population, who went to their own chapels or made presentations to the main temple. His teacher presented a finely inscribed tablet. Other tablets were also there, several made of unusual combinations of materials. But Abraham's teacher left a perfectly shaped elongated tablet, upon which the cuneiform signs seemed to float, like boats on the shimmering Euphrates. And as the students each read from that river of boats, the words formed in their mouths and went down artlessly like stones thrown in water:

> *Your land like one who has multiplied . . . shuts tight its mouth. Your house has been laid bare; how has your heart led you on! Your* en *dwells not in the* gipar*; how now can you exist! Oh Nissaba praise . . .*

It was written in Sumerian and Akkadian and some languages not known to the students. Forming the waters for each line were duplicates of each of the signs, beautifully wrought, as if put on display, with antiquated incarnations of each, and seeming to float just below. The signs recreated lines taken from the old lament for Ningal, the wife of Ur's city-god, Nanna. But now it addressed Nissaba, the Sumerian goddess of scribes. The reed in the writing hand had emerged the most enduring; its mistress, Nissaba, the most worthy of an offering. No matter what happened, it was the signs of the reed that endured. Real immortality was only achieved through what was communicated and passed down. Thus, kings pretended to write, even when they could not.

What happened after the visit to the chapel of Nissaba was what always happened at the tablet-house. A return to the scores of exercises that comprised the school day. This time, it might have been unaltered excerpts from the original *Lament for the Destruction of Ur* and their task was to copy. Their teacher wrote out the exercise tablets this time, instead of the "big brother." They sat in a circle as he molded a small round tablet, and began the lines of the lament, speaking them out loud as he impressed: "Having placed the harp of mourning on the ground . . . " He passed the tablet to one of us, and molded some more clay into another round tablet, and continued, "the woman is softly, in the silent house herself intoning the dirge." He paused and said quietly, "This was when our scribes could hear Ningal at her harp, even in desolation." He passed this tablet, too, to one of us, and molded another, writing the dirge that she sang, "The day that came to be for me, was laid upon me heavy with tears, because of which I moan and moan." And he made yet one more round tablet, and wrote "the bitterest of days that came to be for me." This one he might have handed to Abraham. Each of the students studied the excerpt assigned to them, as their teacher repeated the lines once more, and then again. The tablets were then reversed, and each tried to copy from their minds what they had seen and heard.

This is what school life was like in Abraham's day, and we shall see how it built up a discernment about history. When Abraham would have been ten, the class had passed through the grades of copying signs and lists. Their studies had begun with the very first signs, created by the first scribes, more than 1500 years before. They were pictures, art signs. Writing the signs made Abraham and the others feel like artists. Admittedly, there was an abstraction to the pictures of the objects they were rendering, but any tablet of such signs, particularly one that contained a list, could have been followed by anyone with an eye for looking.

Typically in these history lessons of signs, the teacher and big-brother came before them and began a contest of writing between them. They began with the picture signs, finishing each other's sentences on tablets they passed back and forth between them. The demand of their thoughts became more and more complex, and each began to take shortcuts with the signs, so as to not interrupt the pace. The students seemed to understand that the first to drop the pace would be the loser. Soon the signs passed from matching the object in the mind's eye to linking with the different sounds of a word on the lips. Tablets that became too full of signs were discarded at the feet of the students. And as the tablets built up on the ground, the students saw the history of the scribes pass before them, until the topmost tablets revealed the signs that they would all ultimately learn and make a living with.

But it was the tablets of lists that held Abraham's attention, even beyond the literary texts and the scores of imposing mathematical tables, cubing, squaring, and converting numbers for categories of purpose. The Kings List was just the beginning and not even the most impressive, since the kings came with their names. It was all the other lists of things found and that had to be named, which Abraham could copy repeatedly without boredom. Their first lessons based on these lists were introduced by his teacher with a passage from the Sumerian legend of the world's beginnings, the *Enuma Elish:*

When a sky above had not been mentioned
And the name of firm ground below had not been thought of;

When only primeval Apsu, their begetter,
And Mummu and Ti'amat—she who gave birth to them all—
Were mingling their waters in one;
When no bog had formed and no island could be found;
When no god whosoever had appeared,
Or had been named by name, had been determined as to lot . . .

At which point, his teacher had departed from the tablet he had been reading from and said, "Our beginnings began with naming. These lists that you copy—from this day forward, until you die or become old—are a history of those beginnings."

To his teacher, this story of beginnings was more than legend. "One day," he said, as he referred to early gods, "the wise ones would find the first ancestors in the ooze of the plain of Euphrates." He continued, "Their discovery will be open to those with ears closest to the ground, where Enki dwells, himself 'With ears wide open, wise, mighty in strength . . . with no equal among his fellow-gods.'"

In another story of beginnings that would resonate with Abraham as he developed an ear for the cosmic theater, the wise ones were not in the temple but in the groves of date palms. Unlike the other things grown in field and garden, the date palm required little brute strength, but much wisdom. The ears of the wise ones were larger than those of other men. These cultivators did not deduce their strategy of planting as other farmers did; they heard the palm in communication, inviting the time and gesture for reproduction. Abraham's favorite list was the "Cultivation of the Date Palm." Its different parts were named. Its different uses and products were itemized. The details of its planting and handling of fruit were recorded. The only thing absent was what the wise ones heard, which led to more palms, more dates, the promise of a future fecundity.

There were an abundance of lists during Abraham's school days. The palm lists were just the most illustrious. There were lists of medicinal plants, all kinds of stones used for seals and jewelry, including statues, and many long lists of trees, insects, birds, and other animals.

And of course, there were lists of all the geographic names and administrative and legal lexicons. This textbook vocabulary of Sumerian culture was learned by copying. And in his teacher's tablet-house, all texts, even copies, were concluded with a colophon. Students wrote their name, their title, the date, and the city. The date began with the month, followed by the day and year. Years were very descriptive and were named after some distinctive contemporary event. Abraham's title was *school-son,* for he was not yet a *dubsar.*

His first instruction in the colophon came after copying a tablet in his teacher's archive, which carried the name *Enheduanna.* His teacher read aloud the entire colophon, which in this case repeated the title, "Lady of all aspects of life," the first line of the tablet. They all knew, then, it was a literary composition in honor of the turbulent and voluptuous goddess Inanna, whom many of them pictured by her other name, "Lady of the Date Clusters." The students also knew that the scribe of the tablet had to be a woman. It was a female name. They knew, but it did not become real until their teacher said her name out loud. He explained that she had been the daughter of the great king Sargon, who began the rule of the Akkadians centuries before—the first to unite all of the lands north and south. He said that she became the high priestess of the main temple in Ur, the temple of the moon-god, Nanna.

Years later, the students of his grade would sit down to make their own copy of this precious copy. Most of these, inherited by each scribal generation, sifted through and re-catalogued, would eventually become the potsherds filling the ground of the ruined cities and rediscovered in our time. Just as it is up to us to restore the history of Sumerian civilization by interpretation, Abraham was learning to discern the authentic from the copy. This was the education that would lead to Abraham founding an authentic new culture in Canaan, one that would not disbelieve but rather absorb the lessons of history.

CHAPTER 9

Contracts

In c.1750 BCE, Terah and his family prepared for their journey to Canaan. Since they could take little of their statues and materials with them on the long journey to Canaan, the entire business had to be sold. Abraham was in charge of drawing up the contract for the sale of the workshop. His education had required the study of Sumerian legal codes, since these were based upon venerable accounts of actual cases and carried a literary authority parallel to the great poems. Both legal and literary writings were concerned with historical origins (from Gilgamesh's ancient gates to the history of the city in Ur's *Lamentations*) and so too was the Sumerian contract, which carried the sanctity of history.

Private ownership had been established for many centuries already, and so, as with the sale of the house, each contract would include details of the history of both the ownership and the family. After a precise description of the property, the names of those with rights to it would be listed along with those acquiring it followed by the amount of the transaction and the date due. In the case of the workshop, more than one contract would be involved since there would be buyers for the property and the materials. All of this information was stated tersely, as strict as the form of a poem but without the flowery language of some modern legal documents. When all was complete, the seals of the parties would be affixed, and then the names of the witnesses, their seals, and lastly, the seal of the scribe—which in this case was Abraham himself.

These contracts—also known as covenants—were finally confirmed by a ritual, whether an oath and special meal or by a dramatic act, such as the movement of the signatories between the portions of a sacrificed animal. Thus when the covenant between Abraham and God would be cut, it refers to this halving of the sacrificed animal. Indeed for Abraham, the legal contract would be precedent for the covenant with Yahweh in its conciseness. And while one did not ask for witnesses and seals when dealing with God, their equivalent was nevertheless offered poetically in the form of a promise—Yahweh seals his promise with an oath, which was a common ritual recitation of covenantal treaties. When it came to the covenant with Yahweh, only a story of the encounter was to be written down, and history required no seal.

But for Abraham, his literal seal on a contract was his bond—a historical necessity prior to any oath or covenantal promise. We have such seals today in museums. The one Abraham used, given to him by his father, might have depicted a bull standing on its hind legs like a man, with the head of an unnamed Sumerian king in profile. The bull, its back to us, had its front legs resting on a table, on which were to be seen the engraving chisels of a scribe. It was as if the bull-man was writing. To Abraham in his youth, the figure could have represented his father at his business table; but in his mature years, Abraham saw himself in the broad forehead and well-oiled beard of the ancient king.

SARAH

In preparation for the journey, the family gods, packed on donkeys, were also accounted for in another contract made by the mother of the family with the children, describing each god's history and to whom it would be allocated. The retrieval of such contracts in archaeological sites attests to both the household gods and the access to them by women. Sarah would have been in a position to be charged with protection of these personal gods. In the absence of her mother-in-law, who is not mentioned in the narrative, Abraham's personal god would become Sarah's as well.

As for the proceeds of the sale of Terah's property, it would have been used to purchase a new business that could travel—even as far as Canaan, which was Terah's original destination. In Ur, a special breed of donkeys was raised whose pedigree went back to Sumer, and Terah was well placed to purchase a herd for transport to Canaan, where they might also be bred and sold. These highly prized, black donkeys could carry ninety kilos and travel twenty-five miles a day. They were the measure of all domestic animals, so that the domesticated camel, which was still an expensive and rare item in Abraham's time, was called in Akkadian, "donkey of the sea" (since its earliest travels were in sands by the Arabian shores). Some kings would be buried with their donkeys.

Terah, Abraham, and even Sarah were on familiar terms with the donkeys and their masters at the temple. The temple had its own stable of these black donkeys, bred for use in temple ritual journeys. On the river journeys, a god would have his own donkeys transported on ship, and on road travels, the donkeys wore special garments that were made in the temple clothing workshops where Sarah's expertise would be valued.

Sarah had her own business to sell. Abraham's half-sister before becoming his wife, she had already found a place in her father's workshop before the marriage. Sarah designed and supervised the making of the ceremonial wardrobes for the temple statues. It's not hard to envision the depth of the partnership felt between the two, Sarah and Abraham, going back to childhood and holding together through childlessness and uprooting.

Of the many different garments worn by the gods, including tunics, undergarments, sashes and belts, scarves, jackets, and the *kusitu* for goddesses, only the finest, luxury textiles were woven in Sarah's factory room. Ur was not known for the sophisticated dyes used by the early Phoenicians, and in order to achieve a royal effect various colors and textures of material were woven onto each other, achieving a three-dimensional effect. Wool was what Ur was known for, and palm fibers, and the inventive uses for them developed in the royal workshops became a tradition passed down to Sarah. Her own contribution was probably similar to Abraham's. Just as Abraham used and restored many passages from classic Sumerian literature, Sarah would seek to re-create some of the ancient designs that Abraham found described in the library.

While the statues and models in Terah's possession were too heavy to transport to Harran, Sarah was able to take samples of her clothing designs, a personal archive, on the journey to Canaan that Terah mapped out. Once they had stopped in Harran, visiting relatives, the demand for his donkeys as breeding animals might well have caused Terah to stay on for a while, and then eventually decide to settle there.

HARRAN

Today the evidence of Terah's family roots in Ur and Harran has been reinforced. The name Terah has a root that is shared with lunar terms, and we are about to see how that affirms his origin in Ur and later residence in Harran. On the site of ancient Harran, in the 1950s, a trove of cuneiform literary tablets was unearthed belonging to the temple of Nanna, the moon-god. We even have the name of the priest, Qurdi-Nergal. Among the texts are Sumerian classics, adding to the evidence that Harran was a major city. Prior to its discovery as an archeological site, scholars supposed that Harran was a minor outpost frequented by nomads, a notion that propped up the mistaken view of Abraham as a wanderer. But Harran had been a city comparable to Nippur and Babylon, with special status and exemptions from taxes and military service. As partner in commerce and culture with Ur, Harran's history was every bit as ancient in Abraham's day. Meanwhile, the pressure to join the Babylonian cause, felt by Terah and Abraham in Ur, was missing in Harran. At the time of Abraham's arrival there, the city had recently become an independent principality.

Harran was a sister city dedicated to the same god as Ur, Nanna, but the echoes of Sumer were growing faint in Harran. At Babylon's insistence, Nanna was now called by his Semitic name, S'in, and the cosmic drama in which the moon-god figured prominently, though secure, would feel the aggressive influence of the cult of Marduk and his suzerain, Hammurapi. Yet Harran was familiar with competing influences; it was an established crossroad on the East-West Road linking the Tigris and the Mediterranean, and on the North-South Route between the Euphrates and Anatolia. Its ancient name in Sumerian means caravan station.

It was also the center for the raising and trading of donkeys, a business engaged in by distant relatives of Terah. Some of these relatives had also journeyed on to Damascus and Canaan. So with Semitic relatives there, it would be certain that Abraham stopped in Damascus on his own later journey—and surprising if he didn't look up distant relatives already settled in Canaan when he arrived, part of an earlier migration. None of this needed explaining to an audience in Jerusalem however; they knew of both the migration history and what Harran was like. In later centuries, after Israel's exile, Harran was characterized as a cow town, but in Solomonic Jerusalem it would have been known as a center of culture. For those listening to J, it would have made sense then for Terah to prefer Harran over Damascus or Megiddo in Canaan. She does not need to dramatize this; instead she re-directs her audience's attention toward Abraham's growing need to go further than his father—not to a city in Canaan but to the whole land as a crossroads of a future civilization.

The moon-god, who served as guide to journeys, held donkeys—a symbol of trade and freedom of movement—in high regard. The moon-god veneration also contributed to making Ur and Harran a center of writing: Nanna was a conduit of creativity from his father, the creator-god Enlil, and there was a close relationship between Nanna and Nabu, the god of writing. Abraham's role in his father's statue workshop would have included engraving the bodies of the statues with writing. The work draws one close to the Sumerian literary texts, which are combed for excerpts. The writing on the statue was an artistic embellishment, a testament to the figure's authority. Poems like the Gilgamesh epics were choreographed as a reading with actors in the Sumerian king's palace and also set to music—yet even in this dramatic form their effect was less momentous than the cuneiform writing on clay tablets. Writing was on the way to becoming the definitive stage.

READING AND THEATER

The idea that a single person could read "to himself"—that is, to read and hold an entire book-length work in mind—was a Sumerian invention, but it had already become a lost art after the destruction of the last dynasty of Ur, several hundred years before Abraham's birth. Of course, original authors and translators in Akkadian and some scholars continued to imagine entire works, but this kind of reading was now confined to an extremely small circle in Harran. What had been common in Ur was precious in Harran, Abraham discovered.

Nothing had been more common than the scribal dictionary in the temple edubbas. Although their function was to provide the meaning of the Akkadian vocabulary, each page and each line began with the Sumerian word. Only a scribe could imagine what was lost in the literal translation; a dictionary could not do it by itself. It took a creative work of art to identify and dramatize the loss of Sumer. This is what Abraham now learned about the Akkadian rendition of the *Epic of Gilgamesh.* The older Sumerian version of the epic, originally a much larger collection of poems, resembled a Sumerian Bible, the written embodiment of the culture that was now both behind and within him. Abraham's Semitic ancestors from Akkad, who had conquered and assimilated Ur, had preserved the Sumerian originals as sacred works. (In the same manner, the works of ancient Greece were preserved by the later Romans, and although they were translated into Latin they were still venerated and read in their original Greek.) Now reading to himself in the palace library, the loss left Abraham dumbstruck: only these ancient tablets remained, small tombstones to the liveliness of the cosmic theater of Sumer.

In the absence of the living breath of the Sumerian theater, the gist of Abraham's recognition of this can be grasped. It's one thing to put on a play and another to create a theater that one lives with, day by day, as if in eternity. As we have seen, the makers would cease to know the god-statues they made and then watch them as others in the audience could, with a suspension of disbelief. This transition to becoming part of the audience required theatrical rituals of its own, as the sculptors in essence denied their knowledge of being creators of the statues. An imaginary cutting off of the maker's hands was one of these rituals.

And it was not only participation in this theater that was becoming lost to Abraham in Harran, but also the questions about boundaries that the theatrical rituals dramatized: Is the work believable? Will the audience believe that this statue is something a god would want to inhabit? Although these statues have a life of their own, it's not what the gods knew as life. All that humans can do with the social and psychological sciences, the Sumerians accomplished by creating a setting for the imagined forces of the gods, in which to watch and study. Yet one problem remains, and that is the problem of the stage. A stage requires our willing suspension of disbelief, and so immense attention was paid to the verisimilitude of the "life" of the gods. The Sumerians were a culture at play with this experience, able to hold illusion and disillusion in mind at the same time. This also supported the quality of their written works—and the necessity of an expansive imagination in the individual reader.

The great cosmic drama of Sumer revealed that a human being is not perfectly seamless clay like the statue, but has faults in it, holes in it, mortal holes. The holes of ingestion and excrement were obvious, likewise those of tears, sound, breath, and the hole of birth. But the biggest hole was unseen, the hole of death. The statues, which have none of these holes beneath their exquisitely painted surfaces, are not perfection but rather a means to connecting inner feelings with outer reality.

Yet the secret that the statues were not really alive did not require enforcement; everybody knew the secret of the solid core of wood and stone to the statues, in the same way that the priests and priestesses who spooned out the meal to the statues understood that it was theater and that they themselves were an important element of the theater when *they* ate the food that had been set before the gods. So how would this knowledge be transferred to a solitary reader, seated before a text written in clay?

For one thing, the edges of the cuneiform letters could be physically felt, like miniature sculpture. Everything could be inscribed into the clay and held there, just as in the statues. One did not have to know it all, keep it in mind; and since nothing in the writing would be forgotten, the reader could imagine himself an observer of a literary theater. It was always there in the library, as it was in the cosmic theater of the temple. And thus the library was also a Sumerian invention.

But in Abraham's circumstances in Harran, the time was already lost when a civilization's imagination and sympathy were big enough to hold every dream, every thought, and put it all on stage, constantly before themselves, whether each person was a daily witness to it or not (if not, the votive statues would stand in for them). This was the human creation whose loss, felt by Abraham in Harran, may have driven him forward on his journey.

While living for many years in Harran, Abraham worked with his father in the donkey business, drawing up contracts, handling correspondence from as far as Egypt and Canaan. But he could still occasionally find himself at the palace library with permission to make a copy—of the Gilgamesh epic, for instance. For a trained scribe like Abraham, a tradition had long existed that allowed him to copy a classic for his personal library. For him it was now a private matter: to read to himself and remain in touch with the Sumerian civilizing spirit.

ABRAHAM READING TO HIMSELF

Enkidu made for Gilgamesh a House of the Dream God,
He fixed a door in its doorway to keep out the weather.
In the circle he had drawn he made him lie down
And falling flat like a net lay himself in the doorway.

Did a god not pass by? Why is my flesh
    frozen numb?
My friend, I have had the first dream!

I have had this dream, Abraham said to himself, of encountering a god but not seeing it. The dream is like a stage shrunk to its essence, a theater of two, or of three. And I sit here as with two others: myself, copying, and the author who wrote. He has created this place for us, and it is also of what he writes: "Enkidu made for Gilgamesh a house." It is a strange intimacy, what Enkidu has done, as the dream that Gilgamesh has is shared. In the same way, the author has shared with me a presence that neither of us has seen—but I have felt the same feeling of it as he, so long ago. It could only have happened in this place, in this dream house that I am copying, on these tablets.

The one born in the wild knew how to give counsel,
Enkidu spoke to his friend, gave his dream meaning:
My friend, your dream is a good omen,
The dream is precious and bodes us well.

So the dream is named, precious, but only as Enkidu has listened, the wild man who is at home anywhere in the world, and with the wildness of dreams.

My second dream surpasses the first.
In my dream, my friend, a mountain rumbled
And then threw me down, it held me by my feet.
The brightness grew more intense. A man appeared,
The comeliest in the land, his beauty astounding
From beneath the mountain he pulled me out and
He gave me water to drink and my heart grew calm.
On the ground he set my feet.

The mountain is like a god, it buried Gilgamesh, and to me it feels like the mountain of words I am reading. "A man appeared"—and that is me as I read and give life back to the text. But it is Enkidu, too, who interprets the dream of Gilgamesh:

Enkidu spoke to him, saying to Gilgamesh:
My friend, we shall overcome, he is different altogether.

Humbaba is not the mountain.
He is different altogether.
Come, cast aside your fear.

Enkidu tells his friend that Humbaba is not as frightful as a mountain, not to be so feared as a wild mountain. This, Enkidu the wild man, knows. He is here the wise man, King Gilgamesh the fearful child.

In this manner, the author of these tablets has turned me into his interpreter, I am the man alive with a mind still wild—yet he, the author, long since dead, he can live only by the breath of a comrade still alive, a friendly reader.

Locking horns like a bull you will batter him,
And force his head down with your strength.
The old man you saw is your powerful god,
The one who begot you, divine Lugalbanda.

His friend Enkidu reduces the mountain to Gilgamesh's size, someone to lock horns with. And who is this mountain but the one who stands in for the father of Gilgamesh? This is what Enkidu interprets for his friend, who has failed to recognize how the creator god has turned into his personal god in the dream. But a wordless god in this dream—until Enkidu supplants the god with his own words.

And I had thought, from seeing the dramatizations in Ur, that Enkidu was no more than a wild man. As I read the tablets, now, I see that he understands the drama of the gods in his wildness, as King Gilgamesh could not. It is as if the gods are wild too and the natural man in his wild element, Enkidu, is close to them. This makes the gods come closer to my mind, and I think how the fear of them and the love is mixed together, as with a father.

You loved the speckled allallu-bird
But struck him down and broke his wing:
Now he stands in the woods crying "My wing!"

It is easier to see the details now; I had not thought much of these words before. Why did Inanna harm what she loved? It is because she is divided against the bird in the wild, her anger cares not. But what of the poet who writes these words? His love for the allallu-bird is stronger, for he interprets the song of the bird to mean—and to sound like—"My wing!"

In your presence I will pray to An, father of the gods,
May great counselor Enlil hear my prayer in your presence,
May my entreaty find favour with Ea!
I will fashion your statue in gold without limit.

Though he prays to the gods and promises statues of gold if they will spare Enkidu, King Gilgamesh would be ruining his intimacy with his friend by giving it a price. He disfigures the value of the statues of Sumer by reducing them to a matter of gold—he has turned spirit into gold. And it is gold I, too, pursue, the price of creating my own stage in life: I write contracts and not poetry. It makes me sad to read this.

May the high peaks of hills and mountains mourn you,
May the pastures lament like your mother!

May boxwood, cypress and cedar mourn you,
Through whose midst we crept in our fury!
May the bear mourn you, the hyena, the panther, the cheetah, the stag and the jackal,
The lion, the wild bull, the deer, the ibex, all the beasts of the wild!

May the sacred river Ulay mourn you,
Along whose banks we walked in our vigour!
May the pure Euphrates mourn you,
Whose water we poured in libation from skins!

What a grand list, a list like the lives of kings, these plants and animals of the wild, and the grass of pastures and the wild rivers. As if the gods are not necessary, as if the wild things form the great stage—here Gilgamesh invokes them like personal gods, intercessors to the high god. Gilgamesh speaks it. The poet writes it. Sumer enacts it: it creates the same place for these words as for the living things. A place where the loved comrade cannot be forgotten.

O my friend, wild ass on the run, donkey of the uplands, panther of the wild . . .
Now what is this sleep that has seized you?
You've become unconscious, you do not hear me!

But he, he lifted not his head.

He felt his heart, but it beat no longer.
He covered, like a bride, the face of his friend,
Like an eagle he circled around him.
Like a lioness deprived of her cubs,
He paced to and fro, this way and that.

It is no dream, this loss of a comrade—of a love as dear as a personal god. Like a personal god, the memory must be fixed for all time, an immortality, for what was life without it, or what could life be had he not lived? And here it is, before me, an immortality fashioned in clay, in this artful clay a mind may caress in the future.

At the very first glimmer of brightening dawn,
Gilgamesh sent forth a call to the land:

O Sculptor! Lapidary! Coppersmith! Goldsmith! Jeweller!
fashion my friend . . . !

Your eyebrows shall be of lapis lazuli, your chest of gold, your body shall be of . . .

I shall lay you out on a magnificent bed,

I shall lay you out on a bed of honour.
I shall place you on my left, on a seat of repose;
The rulers of the underworld will all kiss your feet.

The people of Uruk I shall have mourn and lament you,
The thriving people I shall fill full of woe for you.
After you are gone my hair will be matted in mourning,
Clad in the skin of a lion I shall wander the wild.

It is as if I am being called, the sculptor, to make the friend's statue, and all the occupations of the temple are on display, the jeweler who fits the turquoise of the eye, the lapis lazuli of the eyebrow. But it cannot have a mouth opening ceremony, Enkidu is not a god, and the king knows this, his hair torn. "In the skin of a lion" he returns to the home of Enkidu, the wild—but it is only a skin, a costume.

And it is as if the poet has lost Sumer, lost the enlivening of the statues, and it is me—I, too, have lost the great drama! But King Gilgamesh tries to impress Enkidu everywhere, on Uruk and even on the underworld, this is the depth of impression that the loss of Enkidu has left.

Further, it is as if he is founding a new culture, a burst of creative arts dedicated to Enkidu, and yet I feel it is futile, it is all lost, Enkidu is dead and Gilgamesh knows it. And the poet? The poet who makes me weep for the loss of Sumer, the loss of the spirit of the poem, the author is as myself. It is lost, but it may be remade in words, in the voices that words evoke, in those who are still to be born, in the promise of a future.

For his friend Enkidu, Gilgamesh
Did bitterly weep as he wandered the wild;
I shall die, and shall I not then be as Enkidu?
Sorrow has entered my heart!

Gilgamesh "wandered the wild" but he has lost it, he cannot even see it, it is a civilized sorrow that allows him to see only his own death. Death shows that everyone will be lost, even Gilgamesh himself. That is why he finds a new attachment to Enkidu in death—"shall I not then be as

Enkidu?" But it is an attachment frozen in time; it does not admit how it is inevitable in every affection that it leads to death and separation. Gilgamesh is a king, and so it was hard for him to believe in his own death. What comes after? He does not know yet, but the poet knows. It is the making of memory. But Gilgamesh does not know this yet, and must repeat himself until he can discover what to do.

My friend, whom I loved so dear,
Who with me went through every danger,

The doom of mortals overtook him
Six days I wept for him and seven nights.
I did not surrender his body for burial
Until a maggot dropped from his nostril.

Then I was afraid that I too would die,
I grew fearful of death, and so wander the wild.
What became of my friend was too much to bear,
So on a far path I wander the wild.

How can I keep silent? How can I stay quiet?
My friend, whom I loved, has turned to clay.
Shall I not be like him, and also lie down,
Never to rise again, through all eternity?

I heard in this now the Lamentation for Ur *and for other cities. The city was destroyed, the road of Sumer had come to an end, and only the words remained. Something more than the words, too. The inspiration. The breathing of the words of Gilgamesh even after his death—this the poet knows. We give in to death, acknowledge that it belongs to the gods—no, to the whole creation, to the wild. At the same time we do not give in, we do not mistake the god for the statue, we hold on to the memory, although "what became of my friend was too much to bear." In the very words, it is borne. If not by Gilgamesh, then by the poet. Each by ourselves bear it alone, reading the clay.*

Said Gilgamesh to her, to the tavern-keeper:
Where is the road to Uta-napishtim?
If it may be done, I will cross the ocean,
If it may not be done, I will wander the wild!

In place of the wild, it is a journey into the unknown that Gilgamesh finds, "I will cross the ocean." To visit Uta-napishtim, the flood survivor—who would think of that? Out of a lost and desperate way, a journey appears.

So we are here, in Harran, and in place of the temple drama I have words and donkeys that travel the greatest distances.

Man is snapped off like a reed in a canebrake!
The comely young man, the pretty young woman—
All too soon in their prime Death abducts them!

No one at all sees Death,
No one at all sees the face of Death,
No one at all hears the voice of Death,
Death so savage, who hacks men down.

What a need is here to make of Death a presence, a statue with a face, a voice, an arm that hacks. The absence of the lost friend is complete disillusion: the comrades were not as one, though they felt it so. It could be true only in spirit, only for a time, and then in death they are separate as they were in life. Without the poet, the terror of death—that it cannot be affected, cannot be stopped—would be too much to bear. The poet has made of Death a presence.

Ur, too, was only for a time, but the poets of the Laments have kept the memory alive. The poet of Gilgamesh has kept all Sumer alive, beyond what powers King Gilgamesh had. As I read I feel the absence of it—of Ur—so keenly that it is present again.

It was only for a time, this is the hard thing, and then it is rendered invisible, even as it still stands. The Ur that is usurped by Hammurapi and Babylon is still visible, but the loss of Sumer becomes an invisible presence. It is only for a time that anything lives. The toy model chariot on its woven palm frond rope, joy of my childhood, made by my father, was only for a time. The rope was never repaired when it frayed; the clay wheels never refinished. And yet never discarded, always on the shelf it remained, even after it was no longer an object of play. Finally left behind when we set out for Canaan, it remains with me as a memory in Harran, an invisible thing.

Not a seed. The invisible might be seen as a seed that falls and replants itself through time. A future from a seed. Here man is a reed only, a mere toy; broken off, there seems no future, but the broken reed is also a writing implement for the poet.

Ever do we build our households,
Ever do we make our nests,
Ever do brothers divide their inheritance
Ever do feuds arise in the land.

Ever the river has risen and brought us the flood,
The mayfly floating on the water.
On the face of the sun its countenance gazes,
Then all of a sudden nothing is there!

The abducted and the dead, how alike is their lot!
But never was drawn the likeness of Death,
Never in the land did the dead greet a man.

Two faces meet, the sun and the mayfly. All other faces are summed up in these faces that we never look into, the sun's and that of the mayfly. The faces around the hearth, the scribes drawing up the inheritance contracts, the sad faces of the burial—all are just as vulnerable to the flood, all the faces.

But here the poet has revealed what is most strange: the disappearance of the face of the mayfly, for there can be no likeness of what we have not known. How to remember what has not a face? The poet knows our dependence on it, on putting a face on everything to make it present. The face of the sun, the face of death—though "never was drawn the likeness of Death." What can we know without facing the absence of a face, what is unknown? The poet gives me the face of the tablet to read.

Gilgamesh found a pool whose water was cool,
Down he went into it, to bathe in the water.
Of the plant's fragrance a snake caught scent,
Came up in silence, and bore the plant off.

As it turned away it sloughed its skin.
Then Gilgamesh sat down and wept,
Down his cheeks the tears were coursing.

Here is a scene almost too hard to see, too close to death. It is the plant that holds the gift of immortality Gilgamesh has found at the end of his journey. It is his for only the shortest of time. In a moment, a natural thing, a water snake bears it away. The man loses the secret of immortality to the snake.

It is as if Gilgamesh does not want it, does not smell it as the snake does. The smell of the plant, the desire for it, the man does not possess. What does he lose? His dearest one, Enkidu, he has already lost. The knowledge he too must die—but is this a loss or a gain of knowledge? Something is left in Gilgamesh's tears; the poet has left a clue. The old skin must be let go, just as the snake sloughed off its skin. In the feel and taste of salt tears on his lips, an old life is leaving.

The king, Gilgamesh, will return to his city and build a new kind of skin of great works and deeds, the doors to Uruk renowned through time, older than Ur. But it is as nothing compared to the living man that the poet has captured.

His name lives on, simply a name, the fifth name of the kings of Uruk, included among the hundred kings on the Sumerian King-Lists until the First Dynasty of Babylon and Hammurapi today. It will be the same for Hammurapi, for all the monuments and copies he will commission, only a name on the list of kings. But it will be the next work that I copy for my private collection, the Sumerian King-Lists, a frame of history that holds the passage of time since before the Great Flood.

Men, as many are given names,
Their funerary statues have been fashioned since days of old,
And stationed in chapels in the temples of the gods:
How their names are pronounced will never be forgotten!

Temples have been destroyed, statues broken, but all can be rebuilt. So the temple in Ur, as here in Harran, can stand and the temple life go on, and it is still capable of being lost, the life in them growing stiller the more they are copied, without the poets and the craftsmen alive to Sumer. Here in these tablets I have the living Gilgamesh to weep with, but in Uruk today, already Hammurapi has destroyed the city.

For the life of a scribe in Ur, even today but perhaps not for long, everything has a name. Everything is listed. This is how we learned the words, how to write—from lists. The great Sumerian lists were inspired. A copy only says "Remember"—the spirit to actually remember disappears without the sharp pinch of knowing that Sumer was long ago. The Sumerian King-lists say: This existed, apart from me, and is gone. What does the new Babylonian copy say? We can copy and keep everything for all time, it says, as if there is no loss.

What is the future of Abraham's copy, my own copy? A pinch of loss when I see the name of Gilgamesh again but the name of the poet is lost. For I have only the name of the scribe who copied it in Ur. He has set his seal, but not remembered the poet.

PART III

THE JOURNEY

CHAPTER 10

The Journey

Abraham crossed into the land, as far as the sanctuary of Shechem, the oak of Moreh; he found the Canaanites in the land, back then. Now Yahweh revealed himself to Abraham: "I will give this land to your seed." He built an altar there: to Yahweh, who appeared to him.

"Abraham crossed into the land"—but from where? It appears that the entire journey from Harran was unspoken, unaccounted for. What happened along the way? It seems there is no apparent interest in a critique of the cultures along the way during Abraham's journey, no interest in his experiences and ideas. Yet, the journey is what the audience must have anticipated, given the way it is used as a motif in all classic literatures. In Exodus, the book that follows Genesis, J describes in detail the journey of the Israelites out of Egypt and the other peoples they meet.

And her well-educated listeners must have been familiar with the classic from Sumer, *Nanna's River Journey to Nippur,* which Abraham and the families of the patriarchs (including those left behind in Harran) would have inherited. (It was also known to J that in both Harran and Ur the moon god Nanna guided the religion.)

To Ur he then went.
In the river he received overflow,
In the field he received abundant grain,

In the swampland, grass and reeds,
In the palm-grove and vineyard, honey and wine,
In the palace he received long life.

Indeed, all sorts of itineraries have been found on cuneiform tablets that describe what is met with along the way. Even today there are popular tours in the Middle East entitled "Follow in the Footsteps of Abraham," and "Follow in the Footsteps of Moses," as if the villages and people they encountered along their way were of paramount interest (and in spite of the ecological changes that have turned what was a wetland in Abraham's day into a desert today).

Given this natural interest in journeys, certainly the older sources for the life of Abraham, the ones available to the J writer, would have told of his journey through Mari and Damascus and Ugarit. Perhaps—even as it is strange and unknown to us—it was too familiar to J's audience to be interested in. By not accounting for the journey from Harran to Canaan, J expresses the boundary that Abraham has crossed—he has now entered into Yahweh's realm. Once in this new domain, Yahweh's uniqueness enlarges beyond a personal god and extends to becoming visible. If we have any doubt about this boundary, it is answered in the next sentence when "Yahweh revealed himself," which is bolstered by "Yahweh, who appeared to him."

Abraham heads first to a "sanctuary," a refuge for strangers, and the apprehension he must have felt is reinforced when "he found the Canaanites in the land, back then." That would have meant walled cities and sophisticated civilization, for the Canaanite libraries, such as the one at Megiddo recently excavated in Israel, contained Sumerian tablets of the *Epic of Gilgamesh.* Canaan was hardly a new world. If J seems unconcerned about this, it is because it was common knowledge among her audience, and it is the unfolding of a personal relationship between God and man on a new *cosmic* stage that is urgent for her.

Whatever surprises Abraham encountered on his journey then (is there such a thing as a journey without surprises?) they clearly remained in the "back then" for J's audience. After the reigns of David and

Solomon, the Temple to Yahweh was well enough established that there had to be irony in J's emphasis. It was a "back then" in which the cultural developments of Hebraic kingship and temple had not yet been made, lending an air of innocence to Abraham, or what some commentators have mistakenly identified as nomadism. But J has cancelled any hint of Abraham's innocence by carefully noting at the very outset his provenance in Ur. And thus the appearance of Yahweh as a personal god is a sophisticated elaboration of Abraham's Sumerian cultural experience.

The best way to avoid the complex texture of history would be to frame the meeting of God and man in idyllic, pastoral terms. There is nothing more ahistorical than the desire to ignore Abraham's past and his roots in Ur. This is what the ahistoric "Abrahamic" tradition does, portraying Abraham as an obedient servant and peacemaker. But J has made of Abraham a more dynamic figure, even more uncanny than the shepherd boy, David, or the royal son, Solomon. These latter men, who became kings, are faced with complex political and religious issues, while Abraham's are exclusively cultural: what will happen to him and his family, and how will he found a new covenant and culture all by himself? Yahweh's problems, on the other hand, are cosmic: how will he enter into mortal time and the life of man permanently? The negotiation of the covenant, therefore, will be turned by J into the most complex of issues, a persistent dance around the central problem of human death and its effect on sexuality and inheritance. It will be a drama about the origin of culture—which was also crucial to the much older Sumerian *Epic of Gilgamesh.*

When the seventh day arrived . . .
The sea grew quiet, the tempest was still, the flood ceased.
I looked at the weather; stillness had set in,
And all of mankind had returned to clay.
The landscape was as level as a flat roof.
I opened a hatch, and light fell upon my face.
Bowing low, I sat and wept,
Tears running down my face.

The raven went forth and, seeing that the waters had diminished,
He eats, circles, caws, and turns not round.
Then I let out all to the four winds and offered a sacrifice . . .

The gods smelled the savor,
The gods smelled the sweet savor,
The gods crowded like flies about the sacrificer . . .

Only at this last stanza of the Gligamesh flood story do we recognize a Sumerian view of the cosmos of gods, yet it startles for its irony: these gods, the object of the holy sacrifice, are described irreverently, "crowded like flies." How could such a deeply loved text and its author refer to the gods as flies? The answer is in the self-confidence of the Sumerian audience, who are predisposed to making light of their oral folk tradition and its magical superstitions about animal sacrifice. This use of irony by the Sumerian author would have impressed J as well, and that may be why she took the flood story almost whole into the Bible (except for the Sumerian folk gods, of course).

The flood itself was embedded in human memory, so the historicity of the long-standing Sumerian text serves to anchor the origin of civilization. For even antediluvian culture is contained in this story of the great flood, written down almost two thousand years before J creatively translated her version as the story of Noah. While primitive religions were built around some accommodation with the gods over the fear of extinction, God himself, in J's version, provides the rainbow as a sign that he will never wipe out humankind again. Yet the fear of personal extinction was strong and justified: the landscape of Abraham's time was dotted with ancient cities in ruins, and the remnants of the last destruction of Ur were still visible.

Personal extinction is vastly different from our personal deaths. When we die we are remembered, whether by family, friends, or even the state in a public graveyard. We die into the culture in which we are born. But if our culture is wiped out altogether—as almost happened to the European Jews in our time—it is like becoming an extinct species: there is no context left in which to be remembered, other than as extinct.

When Abraham arrives in Canaan, the very first words are Yahweh's: "I will give this land to your seed," as if to alleviate any fear of extinction. It says nothing to reassure Abraham about his personal death, but offers something stronger: he will be remembered within a culture for he will be the founder. Having studied the destruction of Sumer, and witnessed the slow suffocation of Sumerian spirit in the rise of Hammurapi's Babylon, extinction would have been uppermost on Abraham's mind.

Yahweh has been concerned with sexual inheritance, how the "seed" is going to develop, but Abraham is focused upon what he must know and convey to his son, Isaac, once he is born—in short, upon education and culture. In that sense, both Yahweh and Abraham are concerned with family first, apart from any religious devotion. This is also what one would expect of a personal god from Ur or Harran.

Abraham was the first Zionist and the first survivor—the first to establish a right to exist for himself within his own culture in a specific landscape, not simply a city—and at a time many centuries before his seed would emerge from Egyptian slavery. Fleeing Egypt four hundred years later, the Israelites arrived at the mountain in the Sinai desert where they symbolically received the Torah narrative containing Abraham's life. It was actually composed by J four hundred years after that in Jerusalem, on the palace hill earlier known as the Stronghold of Zion (that is how Abraham would have known it). And if we look further ahead in history for a moment, to the sixth century BCE, we find Jewish poets writing Hebrew psalms in Babylon, to which they were exiled by the Assyrian civilization. Now we can see how Abraham's descendants would look back to the Hebraic culture he founded in Israel:

Into the canals of Babylon
We cried like babies, loud
Unwilling to move

Beyond the memory
The flowing blood
Of you, Israel . . .

If I forget thee
Sweet Jerusalem
Let my writing hand wither

My tongue freeze to ice
Sealing up my voice
My mind numb as rock . . .

The latter-day Babylonians who exiled these Jews had long ago relegated Abraham's Sumerian culture to a distant memory. But that was not yet the case in the time of J, when those educated at court read the classics of civilization from Sumer.

THE PROBLEM OF ARRIVING

It would nevertheless come as a surprise to J that the Sumerian founder and counterpart to Abraham, King Gilgamesh, was also a historical character. This would have been revealed to her only through her own reading, because in the popular mythology Gilgamesh was godlike, almost indistinguishable from the gods he called upon. Yet Gilgamesh was the first king whose life history survived, a story of facing death, accepting it, and establishing a culture—from the literal gates he designed for his city to the poems he inspired. If we think, however, of the full range of Gilgamesh epics (there were many in the Sumerian language that were later left untranslated by the Akkadians who superceded Sumer) we see that they serve as a kind of Sumerian Bible for J. They describe the founding of civilization as a desire for establishing a written historical record, and they usually emphasize the separation between human culture and the realm of the gods, even when supernatural or mythological figures are involved. The encounters and journeys of Gilgamesh were set down on a written stage of words, in parallel to the Sumerian cosmic theater.

Imagine the amazement J must have felt then when she read the later Akkadian translation of Gilgamesh, on the cuneiform tablets in the Jerusalem palace archives, which described him as *two-thirds* human, one-third god—an astute joke by the original Sumerian author, since the requirement for godly status was *one-half.* But beyond the joke, or the poignant necessity for it to establish the heroic bona fides of a conventional hero, it was quickly forgotten. Gilgamesh acts and feels as a human being, and we must pay attention to this, as J no doubt had absorbed his character when she portrayed Abraham. Long before Abraham was born in a different city, but not far from the Uruk of Gilgamesh, the latter's disbelief that his friend Enkidu will die, or that he himself will, is shown to be but a hope, a supremely human wish that must be brought down to earth by real experience.

Since his mother is still alive in the drama (Gilgamesh's father died when he was too young to remember) the death of Enkidu becomes his first intimacy with dying. Because of this, and because of his closeness to Enkidu, it is not surprising that he decides to go anywhere he can in search of something to bring back his friend. There were plenty of mythical dramas in which one god would go in search of a dead god and bring him back to life (most famously the story of Inanna retrieving Dumuzi from the Underworld—Ishtar and Tammuz in the Akkadian translation). Yet it is also appropriately ironic that the search leads him to a man, not a god, Ziusudra, who was the Sumerian Noah (Utanapishtim in Akkadian). The shock of recognition for J comes in how the *Gilgamesh* author made his drama rest upon the attachment of one man to another, Enkidu, whose part-god ancestry is also rendered irrelevant when he accepts the constraints of human civilization. Here are two mythically heroic, partly divine characters from a great tradition of divine intercession in reversing a death, now rendered as historical men.

The popular mythology among the Hebrews also contained legends of Abraham that made him seem superhuman, a man subject to godly miracles, but it would be the task of the J writer to render Abraham more human than any hero that came before. Abraham is no victim, like other founders of religion. He was neither a slave nor imprisoned nor put to death. The trials that he lives through reveal that he is a survivor, above all, and that this survivor who maintains a link with past and future will stand in for the origin of the Jewish people, replacing a conventional, superhuman hero. From J's vantage point in history, the Jewish condition becomes one of carrying a special compass, tuned to past and future rather than north and south, which seems strange to others.

Abraham, the first Jewish hero, is already an anti-hero. How could there be no resentment of him by his relatives and neighbors? For even there, at the beginning, he is a founder who is taking away what humanity had felt entitled to in abundance: heroes and gods. As for Yahweh, he is other—a high god absorbed with human rather than godly history. He must *worry* about his human characters, as if he too wished to be human—worry, that is, if they will listen and even if Abraham and Sarah will have a child to carry on the covenant.

But first, there is the problem of arriving. What or where is the place?

> *He rose, came to the hills east of Beth El, pitched his tent there—Beth El to the west, Ai to the east. It was there, building an altar to Yahweh, he called on him by name, Yahweh. Yet Abraham kept on, journeyed down toward the Negev.*

What is Abraham looking for? Why does he not seek sanctuary—is he above it? The audience has been listening and waiting for him to arrive somewhere on this journey without momentousness. But he arrives nowhere. Canaan was in the middle of the Bronze Age and a lucrative tin trade as well. There were interesting, thriving cities like Shechem and Megiddo, Gezer and Hazor. Although Abraham has come to two of them, Beth El and Ai, he stays in between the two. Yet there is not necessarily something to cause fear for a man like Abraham who is well endowed with family and herds and retainers, and who speaks the language. In place of fear, we sense an anxiety not fully revealed.

He is not running away and he is not arriving. He and the journey are one, and it is this that pleases the J writer's audience. This is the most anticlimactic journey that ever was, the opposite of all the heroic journeys—even Gilgamesh's bittersweet journey to Uta-napishtim. The audience may already be smiling: they know this life, this very Hebrew and Jewish life. To build an altar to Yahweh in the middle of nowhere!

And then, to simply leave it behind. Moreover, if the altar-making was understood by the Jerusalem audience as a Sumerian custom or just a conventional show of respect by a foreign traveler—in other words, as an ethnographic description of "the way it was"—then it is even more ironic, since author and audience know it is nothing of the sort; rather, it is the beginning of becoming Jewish, something entirely different.

BEING ALONE IN THE WORLD

J's biblical characters seem to have no precedent in literature because we have lost earlier narratives of family history. And yet J's Abraham is more alone in the world—and independent of his God—than any earlier biblical character. J had not so much created new types of characters as learned from, built upon, and transformed the great writers in history who preceded her. If we look at a precursor, we may discern where J's particular inspiration came from and how it diverged just enough to allow for the characters of both Abraham and Yahweh. Anchored in literary history, we can begin to see how Abraham's journey turns into the problem of his arrival—how to preserve a cultural uniqueness into the next generation. For it is not just a man and his family that arrives in Canaan; it is the new Hebraic culture.

Trained as a translator, the J writer was made intimately aware of the great authors who preceded her. The author of the Sumerian Temple poems, Enheduanna, was acknowledged as the first great author, writing more than a millennium before J, and being a woman she no doubt influenced J in her particular affection for the predicaments of women characters. For Enheduanna, the women were goddesses and she herself was a priestess, and yet, although J was probably a princess, her life as a translator at court resembled Enheduanna in its cultural acuity, for the Sumerian poet was also a translator.

In a characteristic passage, Enheduanna translates and transforms an earlier myth, playing upon the stereotypes of gender.

Inanna
Dressing a maiden

Within the women's rooms
Embraces with full heart
The young girl's handsome bearing

The maid a woman evilly spurned
Taunted to her face
Sways beneath the wrath
Thrown on her everywhere
Her only path a wanderer
In dim and lonely streets
Her only rest a narrow spot
In the jostling market place
Where from a nearby window
A mother holds a child
And stares

This dreadful state
The Lady would undo
Take this scourge
From her burdened flesh

Over the maiden's head
She makes a sign of prayer
Hands then folded at her nose
She declares her manly/woman

In sacred rite
She takes the broach
Which pins a woman's robe
Breaks the needle, silver thin
Consecrates the maiden's heart as male
Gives to her a mace
For this one dear to her
She shifts a god's curse
A blight reversed

Out of nothing shapes
What has never been
Her sharp wit
Splits the door
Where cleverness resides
And there reveals
What lives inside

Enheduanna has written about her personal god, Inanna (Ishtar in Akkadian), as if the god were like herself, an *author,* as she changes a cursed woman into a man to lift her status. The status of J, like Enheduanna, was also no doubt "manly woman," and the kinship between the two authors was sensed by J.

Yet unlike Enheduanna, J was not a priestess herself, so the question arises, what was J's relation to the Jerusalem Temple? For the priests and priestesses, her work appeared adjunct, at a remove from duties involving the sacred drama of the Temple. She would have had no official office of the kind the High Priestess Enheduanna was given. Her work was an important link to the palace, however. It was the narrative of the nation she was translating and giving new form. And since Yahweh was the presiding presence, J would have consulted the Temple hierarchy over the words and deeds of Yahweh. But the Jewish scholar-poet J stands at the beginning of a new cosmic integration in which story and words, not the Temple, come first. In this founding narrative, which appears to be the story of Yahweh's people, we find a new story of being alone in the world, of negotiating a new contract with history. The J writer is focused upon relationships that lead to inheritance—in other words, that lead to society and culture—and not to the Temple religion.

These relationships break down into threes for the J writer, as in the following narrative episodes of Sarah-Abraham-Pharoah, Abraham-Lot-Yahweh, and Sarah-Abraham-Yahweh. And it is Abraham, not Yahweh, who orchestrates the situations in these triangles. Yahweh is the creator god, but he is still in the process of coming-to-be for Abraham, in transition from the personal god of Sumer. For now, Yahweh does nothing.

Even when Yahweh and Abraham are alone, Yahweh's promises point to a third—as yet in the future but very much a reality. How to get to this future is the issue, how to ensure it and the triangle that it will entail: a child. Thus a family drama becomes cosmic drama, for what is the covenant between Abraham and Yahweh but the promise of a third, an inheritor?

In the narrative to this point, it is as if Yahweh is still Abraham's creation, a voice and presence resembling a personal god. Up to this moment, he hasn't had a name, which fits the Sumerian usage, where the personal god's name was invoked only for formal verification (as in, for instance, a contract). The naming of Yahweh would only have struck J's audience as odd if, like us until recently, they didn't know this.

And then, "He called on him by name, Yahweh." How Abraham got the name, what it means, and why God cares—of this there is no accounting. No drama around it either. Were he a nomad we might expect him to ask little, but Abraham knows about cities and civilization and gods. Nothing that exists in Abraham's education can satisfy what Abraham needs to know about the meaning of his journey, and Yahweh tells him nothing, "yet Abraham kept on." It is a very serious "keeping on," it is peculiar, going "toward the Negev"—that is, toward the desert.

Abraham had entered no cities. He saw Beth El and Ai but did not enter. These cities would have had their gods, their civilization, and we would expect the open space between them—where Abraham remained—to be a land of nomads. But after the civilization of Ur, Harran and Damascus, Abraham finds an intimacy with Yahweh here in the wild, in the open space. It is dumbfounding and it is the J writer's intention that it be so.

This is how J's audience heard it: familiar story, strange telling. But upon reflection, and in the context of the whole, a new sensibility is emerging—a new theater of realism in place of supernatural expectations. Now, with an altar in the land, Yahweh's transition from a personal god into the high god is established, a creator who prefers the breadth of the land to cities, who prefers the complexity of what lies outside civilization. J maintains the incongruity of Abraham's journey, so that her audience is left wondering how much stranger it can get. It is easy to lose the wonder of it if you forget where Abraham has come from. If Sumer is not in mind, the uncanniness is lost. For Abraham has called on Yahweh by name as if he was merely a personal god, though we already know he is the creator.

The altar, the naming of Yahweh—these are a further making of culture, a mark of something to be passed on. Abraham is a man in need of society and this is what Yahweh provides in the form of his presence, but it is inadequate and Yahweh knows it. It will be expressed in the anxiety about inheritance: for Yahweh, how human life unfolds, and for Abraham, how to establish a secure culture. And so, the obsessive concern with a child will soon take center stage.

WHAT CAN BE INHERITED

Now look: a famine grips the land. Abraham went down further, toward Egypt, to live—starvation ruled the land.

Who would have imagined that, given the power of Yahweh behind this journey, a famine could jeopardize it? But at this point, we are not meant to know what problems exist for Yahweh in founding a relationship with humans. Yahweh is potential, not yet actual—his coming into being is a background drama. He has no control over Abraham's journey. It would be easy to assume that Yahweh intended for this to happen, that here was another test or lesson for Abraham to absorb. But the story is not written that way. We have just been exposed to the promise of the land—yet the land itself is ambivalent, dangerous, other.

Despite this frequent danger, the constant potential of Abraham's death is barely of interest to the J writer. (No doubt the Gilgamesh poet and translators helped J to concentrate on the central drama of the Sumerian epic, the facing of death.) But for her, there is only the issue of what can *survive,* what can be inherited. The crucial difference from Sumerian culture is that now Abraham and other biblical characters are not in service to priest or king—that is how J envisions it, even as she and her audience live in a later time of king and Temple.

There is a new sense of separation from it, of aloneness, that is projected back upon the character of Abraham. Although some religious commentary refuses to face it, Abraham is not in service of Yahweh. He truly is on a journey, both his and Yahweh's, toward a re-negotiation of what it can mean to live as a mortal creature in an infinite cosmos.

In place of the tragedy (victimhood, for instance) and comedy (literal mindedness, for instance) of service comes the tragicomedy of aloneness. Long before, the comic side of service was recorded in various ways by the Sumerians. Here, for example, is a letter from the King of Mari's governor in a city downriver, sent to the king:

> *I had previously written to my Lord as follows:*
>
> *"A lion has been caught in the granary of Bet Akkaka. Let my Lord write me whether that lion should stay in the granary until my Lord comes, or I should have it conducted to my Lord."*
>
> *Let my Lord write back to me! Now, tablets of my Lord have been slow in arriving here and the lion has been sitting in the granary for five days. They threw a dog and a pig to him but he refuses to eat. This is my worry: Heaven forbid that that lion passes out! So I feared and made the lion enter a cage made of wood, and loaded it on a ship to have it conducted to my Lord.*
>
> *—Yaqqim-Addu, your servant*

Thus the comic predicament of a servant left alone, preoccupied with his role as servant. In contrast, there is the tragicomedy of aloneness found in Abraham's relationships where it is never clear or simple who is in service to whom. Is Abraham doing Yahweh's bidding? Or is it actually Yahweh who is serving Abraham's need to survive? The latter, for example, seems to be the case in the story of Abraham and Sarah's meeting with the Pharaoh of Egypt:

> *At the point of entering Egypt, listen: "To look upon," he said to his wife, Sarah, "you are as lovely a woman as I have known. Imagine the Egyptians when they see you—'That one is his wife.' Now I am killed; you, kept alive.*

"Say you are sister to—and for—me, for my good and on your behalf. As my flesh lives, it is because of you and with you."

So it was: Abraham crosses into Egypt; the Egyptians see the woman, how lovely. Pharoah's officers see her, praise her to Pharoah. Now the woman is taken away, into Pharoah's palace.

On her behalf, it was good for Abraham. Look: he had sheep and cattle, donkeys and asses, servants and maids, and camels. But Yahweh struck Pharoah with disease as if with lightning—his whole house stricken—on behalf of Sarah, Abraham's wife.

Now Pharoah called for Abraham: "On whose behalf have you done this to me? Why not tell me this is your wife? Why say, 'This is my sister'—I would of course take her in, for my wife. Yet now, look: a wife that's yours—take her out of here, for life."

Now Abraham rose up from Egypt—wife, household, and Lot with him—up toward the Negev. He was surrounded with livestock, slowed with silver and gold.

Yahweh has acted for the first time on their behalf, but Abraham and Sarah do not know it. He acts in service to Abraham and Sarah while Abraham acts only as a survivor—in service of surviving. Neither is Pharoah the big story, though we might expect him to play a larger role; we see little more than the usual trappings of kingship. And how easy but unnatural it is for Abraham to be in conversation with a king. No, the big story is Abraham's relationship with Sarah. Although she is aware of the drama and misunderstanding inherent in the clash of cultural customs, J is more interested in the best that intimacy has to offer—the unexpected.

The usual betrayals of intimacy do not end J's story. The audience once again sees the story is on a different plane from moral melodrama altogether. Again, it's about survival—do you want to live or not? What is the nature of intimacy and a culture built on these actions?

Clearly we have an uncanny relationship here, one where all aspects can be lived with between two—and with Yahweh included, three. It's his concerned presence that makes things different, that changes things from Gilgamesh. Yahweh will not only need to save Abraham and Sarah from harm and immorality, he still needs to figure out his own natural role (rather than supernatural intervention) in this new relationship with humans.

For Gilgamesh, it had always been but two, he and Enkidu. The gods were present but not as beings to deeply relate to. The time had come for a new story in man's history, the story of three. What does it mean to make room for the third? Different threes are revealed in the Abraham story, including the problematical.

> *At the point of entering Egypt, listen: "To look upon," he said to his wife, Sarah, "you are as lovely a woman as I have known. Imagine the Egyptians when they see you—'That one is his wife.' Now I am killed; you, kept alive."*

Is Abraham fearful? Why isn't Yahweh's promise recalled? The author J lets the future depend upon Abraham's wits, and it is wit indeed that praises Sarah.

> *"Say you are sister to—and for—me, for my good and on your behalf. As my flesh lives, it is because of you and with you."*

Abraham now charges Sarah with his life, and by implication with the future of Yahweh's covenant. All hangs on the free decision of a woman, for it would be more in moral character for her to refuse telling a lie. J's feminine sensibility is at play; she would have known that her original source for this story was relating a cultural custom regarding marital and filial status. It may have been already ancient in J's Jerusalem, but nevertheless a woman's legal status in Harran was sometimes determined by a tradition that allowed her to be both wife and sister. (These marriage and sister contracts also marked Sarah as a woman of the upper class.) J has used this anachronism to allow the story to turn upon Sarah's apocryphal beauty and to depend upon her wit.

> *So it was: Abraham crosses into Egypt; the Egyptians see the woman, how lovely. Pharoah's officers see her, praise her to Pharoah. Now the woman is taken away, into Pharoah's palace.*

The story turns upon a Mesopotamian custom but we are in Egypt so J writes as if all has become strange, as if Sarah has lost her name: "Now the woman is taken away . . . "

> *On her behalf, it was good for Abraham. Look: he had sheep and cattle, donkeys and asses, servants and maids, and camels. But Yahweh struck Pharoah with disease as if with lightning—his whole house stricken—on behalf of Sarah, Abraham's wife.*

What could be worse than prosperity in Egypt, where he could lose everything? "Look: he had sheep and cattle . . ." That is the crux of J's ironic telling. We are reminded of Abraham's donkeys from Harran, and he even has camels, which at the time were an unusual luxury. "It was good for Abraham" could not be more ironic, since it reveals his utter dependence on Sarah's sexuality. And his predicament is further defined by Yahweh's intervention "on behalf of Sarah"—once again Yahweh is serving mankind but it is Sarah and not Abraham.

How does Yahweh intervene? Disease, lightning, famine—all are natural events. He did not interfere to save Abraham's life, yet he does so to save the triangle, Abraham-Sarah-Yahweh. It is not Sarah's honor that's at stake, for conventional honor does not matter to Yahweh, and whether or not she has become sexually compromised is secondary to just getting her out of there and back to Abraham. Striking Pharoah's whole family with disease—presumably venereal disease to fit the situation—is an exclamation point to Yahweh's desperation at having to do something at last.

Yet because the intervention is by way of natural events, it would be apparent to no one that Yahweh has intruded—not to Abraham or to

Pharaoh. Only J's audience is informed, and all subsequent readers, so that we will not forget that Yahweh is a character as much caught up in the unfathomable dangers of history—of becoming vulnerable, of revealing himself—as is his human counterpart, Abraham. In this story, no one and nothing is in perfect control, and the world in which a covenant between human and nonhuman will be needed is a world continually in the grip of change.

This world will need a moral compass, one that is personal and not only governed by public laws like the regime left behind, that of Hammurapi and his Code. Here, it is Abraham himself who becomes the model, where each person makes his or her personal relationship with the nonhuman, unknown world. Here, in J's understanding of the relationship between man and God, the latter is prudish. Abraham has not expressed sexual fears for Sarah's predicament in Pharoah's bed; it is Yahweh who's exercised.

Yahweh acts now as a personal god—not in the open but behind the scene. No divine act is mentioned when the king of Egypt calls for Abraham.

> *Now Pharoah called for Abraham: "On whose behalf have you done this to me? Why not tell me this is your wife? Why say, 'This is my sister'—I would of course take her in, for my wife. Yet now, look: a wife that's yours—take her out of here, for life."*

Abraham is seen as a stranger with peculiar customs. Yet the implication is that Pharaoh speaks out of convenience, not moral principle, and thereby Egyptian culture is critiqued—just as was Mesopotamian culture—for its literal-mindedness. Pharaoh speaks on behalf of honesty: "Why not tell me this is your wife?" Yet we are made to believe by J that he only understands power, since he first asks: "On whose behalf have you done this to me?" But does he want to hear of Yahweh? Apparently not. This is Yahweh working in the great civilization of Egypt as he did in Mesopotamia, in Harran, in a personal capacity. Like Abraham, Sarah will be "taken out" of Egypt.

Pharoah hurried his men to take him out of the country—with his wife and his whole household.

> *Now Abraham rose up from Egypt—wife, household, and Lot with him—up toward the Negev. He was surrounded with livestock, slowed with silver and gold.*

Abraham was looking for survival, not riches, and yet they came to him. (Is he charmed; is it Yahweh's doing?) But the silver and gold have no positive value; on the contrary, they "slow" Abraham's journey, perhaps even imperil him. And in spite of all this, of dangers and riches, and the danger of riches, the way J writes it, the greatest doubt is whether they will be able to have a son. Everything depends upon this fragile future because the past seems totally lost. But this is not really Abraham and Sarah's concern—only the reader's, who has been allowed to share Yahweh's predicament—because they did not come to Canaan to have a child. They were childless in Ur and Harran, and they expected to remain so in Canaan, or else why would Sarah shortly turn to a surrogate mother arrangement with Hagar? No, they came to Canaan for reasons not yet fully revealed to them and without a real plan for the future. Yahweh's promise—or a personal god's advice—remained imprecise.

Steeped in gods, Abraham is a man who isn't going to tremble or be paralyzed by awe in his relationship with Yahweh. Abraham's adventures in themselves are unheroic; neither are Yahweh's parallel feats extraordinary. But in the Book of Genesis so far we have already learned something about the character of Yahweh and his dealings with men and women, so that we see now that he has become a bit anxious: all rides on a single man. But as J tells it, Sarah is the crucial one. Her origin is vital to give Abraham's civilized history substance (as well their eventual son's) for she too is of Ur. Yahweh's history, however, is illusory; he has a story, but the history of the gods has been supplanted by human history. Gods do not as a rule inherit. Yet Yahweh's entrance into human history depends on the cultural necessity of inheritance and on the natural fact of birth and death—and it is on this he must build a covenant.

Though she doesn't know it, Yahweh already has a relationship with Sarah as well. Instead of tending to her personal god, as she had done in Sumerian culture, this god in Canaan is tending to her without her knowledge. It seems as if God is trying to choreograph these two, Abraham and Sarah, into position, as if they were his statues. Being human, however, they have minds of their own, and here is the tension that the J writer is building behind the scene. J, too then, is part of a threesome. For her, it is the audience, herself, and Yahweh that are locked in a relationship about inheritance.

What will the children of Abraham—J and her audience—inherit? They have received an Abraham who had the complexity of character to negotiate Yahweh's initial promise of land and descendents into a covenant. The J writer and her audience are the proof of it: both are descendents of Abraham and interpreters of the covenant. And so, too, is the Yahweh of the covenant. All three—J, audience, Yahweh—are dependent on Abraham's originality.

This is no miraculous gift for Abraham. He is careful with Yahweh, as Yahweh is careful with him, because what he stands to pass on, via the covenant, is redemption from what he has lost in Ur. We are given another chance to live in the cosmic awareness of Sumer, in conversation with what we do and do not know. Recognizing that the most promising aspect of the Sumerian theater was the daily life cycle of the god-statues, the J writer does not strip her audience of this, but makes it the linchpin of the new cosmic drama, in which Abraham's whole life would be the theater, with God in attendance. The personal god—really just a potential presence in Sumer, since confined to the role of intermediary or in service to the existing cosmic drama—becomes revealed as literal God in Yahweh. J makes Yahweh promise a future to Abraham but then shows that future in continual dependence upon Abraham and Sarah's relationship and fertility. These are the same problems of intimacy and sexuality that we, the contemporary audience, inherit.

CHAPTER 11

Promised Land

In c.1720 BCE, after the famine has subsided, Abraham and Sarah return from Egypt. Abraham is already telling himself his own history in the land. He comes back to the place of first recognition that his Sumerian personal god and Yahweh are the same, and where a new intimacy between man and creator was marked by a place. At the first arrival, it had been as if no place at all:

> *He rose, came to the hills east of Beth El, pitched his tent there—Beth El to the west, Ai to the east. It was there, building an altar to Yahweh, he called on him by name, Yahweh. Yet Abraham kept on, journeyed down toward the Negev.*

But now, what this means to him is still not a grandiose promised land but rather the promise of survival—having prospered in Egypt ("surrounded with livestock, slowed with silver and gold") and returned. He sounds almost nostalgic in his return: if there was any naïve dreaming in making Yahweh his own, it is now the place itself in the land that Abraham belongs to.

> *His journey took him from the Negev to Beth El, to arrive at the very place he pitched his tent in the beginning, between Beth El and Ai. Here was the calling: the first altar made, he called the name Yahweh.*

Unlike his nephew Lot, Abraham has a realistic view of loss, of family and culture left behind. His focus on survival leaves little room for being impressed by the land. It appears that Yahweh will try to impress him with a vision of it—"Open your eyes, and may it please you look around you"—and that act of showing would be most impressive to a man from the Sumerian cosmic theater. Yet the reference to the land is usually about inheritance, and thus, survival:

> *"I am Yahweh, who drew you out from Ur, of the Chaldeans," he said to him, "to give you this land as heir."*

The purpose of the land is shifted to a realism about loss and mortality, and away from a materialistic, promised land motif still embraced by Lot. But it is a *cosmic* realism for Abraham; he is already establishing a story for himself, *culture*, which becomes the basis for the Cosmic Theater of Abraham's God. Both man and God want to sink roots in a natural world that is secured by a cosmic covenant.

> *Lot who traveled with Abraham—he too was surrounded by many sheep, cattle, tents. Now look: argument breaks out between Abraham's shepherds and Lot's—this was when the Canaanites were settled on the land, along with the Perrizites, back then. "Please, hold off this quarreling between us, between our shepherds," Abraham said to Lot. "We are men who hold each other as brothers. You may let go of me and face the whole country, open before us. Please yourself, make your own way: left, and I'll go right; south, I'll go northward."*

What is likely to stand out most to our own sensibilities is the generous spirit of Abraham in this passage. Yet neither magnanimity nor the first case of conflict resolution is what is significant here; what we are meant to witness instead is a further clarification of Sumerian origins. Abraham says to his nephew Lot what Abraham may have wished his father, Terah, had said upon taking leave from him in Harran: "You may let go of me and face the whole country, open before us. Please yourself, make your own way." But that is not what a man of Sumerian culture like Terah would be likely to say. A Sumerian would have drawn up a letter of conflict and presented it to a court; next, a decision would be written down; and finally, each side to the conflict would sign the written decision with their seals along with several witnesses. Here, however, Abraham acts as a man who is beginning to absorb the spirit of the new cosmic theater of his God, Yahweh—one in which the unwritten covenant holds more strength than a written contract. But although it is unwritten, it still must be written *about,* dramatized in a fresh language, so that future generations can inherit it. A man like Abraham, who is aware that he is at the beginning of a new culture, senses that his acts and knowledge contribute to a history that will be remembered in writing.

Abraham is not worried about losing out materially to his relative. He offers Lot the first choice because he has let go of the myth of a promised land at the end of the rainbow, just as he had let go of Ur. Abraham has understood that there are no more Gardens of Eden—the innocence before loss. Like Lot, we continue to this day to have fantasies of finding an Eden, yet watch what happens to him: thinking he has found it, he ends up in Sodom! It is Lot's ignorance of his own culture in Ur and Harran that makes him seem like someone going along for the ride—and blind to the dangerous dead ends of history. Like most of us, he has forgotten, or perhaps never absorbed, the several Lamentations of Ur:

> *"Your city has become a strange city; how can you now exist?"*

When Abraham says to Lot, "face the whole country, open before us," Abraham is creating a cultural theater for Lot and himself that mirrors the cosmic theater. Soon, Yahweh will say almost the same thing to Abraham, "Open your eyes, and may it please you look around you," as if he has been transported into a new theater. But here, with Lot, Abraham refers to "the whole country" as a stage upon which it matters not where you are placed or who else is already there. There is no intention to displace anyone and Abraham is content in his tent. Having absorbed his origins and the necessity of loss, Abraham is aware that in this new relationship with his God the land has become the Sumerian equivalent of a stage: there is no contract, no deed, no official dividing of the land, nothing in writing—there is only daily life and the awareness of living in a cosmic drama. That is all that is necessary, until the time comes to educate a successor and written words take on new importance.

Lot, who is like most of us, will choose what his eyes tell him to: the best land for his livestock and for prospering; Abraham will get whatever is left, for it is all the same to him. It is about survival of the inner not the outer life. This is what Abraham has been brought to understand and why he is not impressed with the lovely parts as Lot is. Inner life and outer cosmos need a stage upon which to meet, and for the first time, beyond temples and sanctuaries, the natural land—divested of myth and spirits—has become a home within the universe.

In any drama that involves the vicissitudes of time, you are either going to be a survivor or a victim, and Lot will end up the victim because he has not seen the land as a theater that both embodies and transcends time. Instead, he is caught up in the very essence of the temporal, concerned over the material advantages of this land and the marriage of his daughters to sons of this land. Why is it that Abraham never acts as if he is a displaced person in any sense at all? Because he chooses to be a survivor with a prehistory that is as portable as a personal god. He arrives not only at a new place but also in a new theater. A promised land is always about a culture's prehistory—the origin of its dreams.

For Abraham, there was a precedent in the Sumerian promised land of Dilmun. But Dilmun contained a vision of its future as well as its prehistory, which Sumerian creation poems were always trying to resolve:

Of Dilmun, that place is clean, that place is bright,
He-who-is-all-alone laid himself down in Dilmun . . .
In Dilmun the raven uttered no cries . . .
The lion killed not,
The wolf snatched not the lamb . . .
The sick-headed says not "I am sick-headed,"

Dilmun's old woman says not, "I am an old woman" . . .
Her wells of bitter water, behold they are become wells of good water,
Her fields and farms produced crops and grain . . .
Dilmun, behold it is become the house of the banks and quays of the land."

This ideal land of Dilmun is not an innocent place. It is a real place in time where the Sumerians may survive in their thriving culture—just as Israel was re-envisioned by the Zionist author Theodor Herzl in Vienna, more than a hundred years ago. In Herzl's 1902 novel visualizing that future, Israel becomes a recognizable modern country with all the normal problems, including relations with its Arab population. It may seem naïve to us now that Herzl imagined a friendly partnership emerging between Israeli and Palestinian Arabs, but he described it as a utopian wish—a kind of Dilmun—and like Abraham, he understood that the wish was complicated by the necessity for survival. So complicated was that wish that only time could contain and reveal the drama.

Now Lot lifted his gaze, drank in the whole Jordan valley—how moist the land was everywhere (this was before Yahweh destroyed Sodom and Gomorrah)—like Yahweh's own garden, like Egypt—gazing as far as Zoar.

With the lush land being "like Egypt"—described by J in sensuous materiality—it's easier to imagine Abraham leaving it to Lot. It suggests the exotic and foreign, and that is not what Abraham has come for. Even if it had been compared to the luxuriant wetlands of ancestral Ur, J and her contemporary audience in Jerusalem already knew that Ur was becoming desert, for the sea at that time receded. In J's time, Egypt and the Nile were a closer paradigm. But there is no more Garden of Eden for J and her audience in any case; they have absorbed their lesson and now can be confident of their *earthly* prehistory. Eden is to be found not in the land but on the page, the written embodiment of a place where Yahweh walked and "the lion killed not," as in the Sumerian Dilmun. It is, in short, a theater of the past, lost and finally transformed into a Dilmun-like land, a Sumerian drama expanded into a

Hebraic vision. J and her audience were living in it and it was no paradise; for them, it was a complex situation to be captured whole only in the written word.

Yet lest we forget too quickly the famine that just recently drove Abraham from this "garden" down to Egypt, the memory remains in the writing. Here, nature has been demythologized, and both Abraham and his God move in a world of change. They bring a cosmic dimension to reality, especially as it contrasts with the literal-minded Lot, who chooses Sodom without concern for what it may represent.

> *Lot chose all the Jordan valley for himself; he set out toward the east—and so a man let go of his brother. Abraham settled in Canaan's land; Lot in the cities of the valley, his tents set beside Sodom.*

More than a place-name, Sodom becomes a cosmic word because that is where Yahweh will face human *contempt* for the cosmic and for the future. Sodom's inhabitants show disrespect for the very principle of inheritance that Yahweh is trying to negotiate with Abraham and Sarah. And so the irony of Lot's tents "set beside Sodom" is a nod to J's audience in Jerusalem, for they already know the fate of Sodom, which was a site of ruins in their time.

For now, back with Abraham and Lot as they part, even Yahweh doesn't know he will destroy the city, since he later agrees to Abraham's contingency of sparing it—for the sake of "a few just men." The audience is granted a kind of omniscience here, looking back into history and forward from Sodom to themselves. It is a taste of the nonhuman, as if seeing through Yahweh's eyes, who has been otherwise relegated to the background of the story.

CHAPTER 12

The Witness

In c.1700 BCE, an Akkadian writer at the royal court of Melchizedek in Shalem gave an account of Abraham independent of biblical tradition yet included in Genesis. Because there is nothing else in the whole of the Hebrew Bible which resembles this writing in style and content, the writer was designated "X" by the translator of the Anchor Bible, E. A. Speiser, and more recent scholars. The names and places invoked by X have been authenticated, but the identification of the writer at Shalem, an earlier name for the Canaanite city of Jerusalem many centuries before the conquest by King David, is made here for the first time. As in the case of other biblical authors, I have paid attention to the sensibility of X by restoring a time and place that is left vague in previous citations.

We know that X was not a Hebrew—he writes from another culture—and that his scribal record would have been attached to a court. He is the first independent witness of Jewish character in history. What is especially remarkable about this is that already, within just a few years of the lifetime of the first Jew, we are spectators to a typical mischaracterization of the Hebrew people throughout history: Abraham is seen as far more powerful than he was. Within his household are counted "318" warriors—a seeming overstatement in itself—who go north to Damascus to "defeat" the combined armies of northern Mesopotamia and send them fleeing, having abandoned all their possessions. Nowhere in the Bible does Abraham have this capability, nor does he desire such might. Even though the Hebraic writers of the Bible did not record a pacifist Abraham, the literary hyperbole of X is clear in itself: Abraham's invincible warriors are a tip of the hat to legend, not history. So, why this idea of illogical power in the first Jew?

The X writer wrote in his own tradition, extending back in time to an older form of writing, popular in the 24th century BCE, at the court of the Sumero-Akkadian king, Sargon (who was also the father of Enheduanna, the renowned writer). "The King of Battle" is an epic poem written at Sargon's court in which invasion and capture are major themes. In one part the king rescues his subjects in the manner that Abraham saves Lot, suggesting a likely source for the X writer's point of view. Many poets wrote about Sargon and his royal line's exploits over the following centuries, including descriptions of conflict between rival coalitions of rulers, so it makes sense that X wrote in the same manner about Abraham. Among other aspects of Sargon's story that turn up in the Hebrew Bible, the childhood of Moses is adapted from the legendary history of Sargon (he was found as an infant among the bulrushes of the Euphrates, in a basket sealed with bitumen).

Why write about a realistic Abraham in this exaggerated way of writing about Sargon? It was due to King Melchizedek's friendship with Abraham, and there are many clues for this, as we shall see. The king's real name was Sarrumken in Akkadian, which means "Sargon is just," and when translated many centuries later into Hebrew by J, became "Melchizedek," meaning "the king is just." So both Abraham and Melchizedek shared a Sumero-Akkadian background, or at least were fellow Amorites historically, along with "Mamre the Amorite" and "the allies of Abraham, Eshkol and Aner." Melchizedek's court writer, X, duly emphasizes this fact.

Seven centuries later, writing at the Jerusalem court of Rehoboam, J chooses to translate the tablets by X into Hebrew and embed that narrative like a touchstone within her own. In this way, her precursor in pre-Hebraic Jerusalem, shown writing about Abraham near or within his lifetime, becomes an authentic autograph: of Abraham, but also of J's own presence as a Jerusalem court writer in the process of translation.

Most commentators responding to the X narrative have searched around hastily to account for all the names and places that suddenly bombard the reader of Genesis. Philologists especially are immediately prompted to do so when they begin to recognize the Akkadian-sounding names. What is more important than the etymology of places and names in this passage is what J is trying to achieve by it. She is saying in effect to her audience at the Jerusalem court, "You want notes? Here are the notes." And her great compensation is that she can do it with nothing more than a quotation—as sophisticated as any modern or postmodern text. She makes a point of quoting, and it is this detail that is most important because it, rather than all the verifications of the names, adds fullness and complexity to the historical Abraham.

> *These are the days when the four kings—Amraphel of Sumer, Arioch of Ellasar, Chederlaomer of Elam, and Tidal of Goiim—went to war with the five: King Bera of Sodom, Birsha of Gomorrah, Shinab of Admah, Shemeber of Zeboiim, and the king of Bela,* or Zoar as it now is called. *These last joined together in the Valley of Siddim,* or the Dead Sea. *Twelve years they had served Chederlaomer, but in the thirteenth they turned away. In the next year, Chederlaomer and his allied kings returned and conquered the Rephaim in Ashteroth-karnaim, and then the Zuzim in Ham, the Emim in Shaveh-kiriathaim, and the Horites in the hills of Seir, near El-paran, which borders the wilderness. After that, they turned around to En-mishpat,* now Kadesh, *overpowering the region of the Amalekites, including the Amorites who inhabited Hazazon-tamar. At that point, the kings of Sodom, Gomorrah, Admah, Zeboiim, and Bela,* which has become Zoar, *who had joined together in the Valley of Siddim, were attacked there, five kings taken on by the four, Chederlaomer of Elam, Tidal of Goiim, Amraphel of Sumer, and Arioch of Ellasar.*

Reading more than three thousand years later, we earn a double glimpse into this writing: first at the time of Shalem (1700 BCE), and later at the time of translation in Jerusalem, when J quotes the original since a trace of her actual hand is found inserting the notations about place-names. She adds such phrases as "or Zoar as it now is called" and "now Kadesh" to familiarize the audience with name changes in the intervening centuries since the X episode was written.

There is more historical background that can be gleaned from this passage, however. The Sumerian background of Abraham is palpable from the start, since at least two of the invading kings are connected to King Hammurapi; Amraphel, in particular, is associated with the region of Ur. Yet their appearance in Canaan is not remarked upon as unusual; and thus Abraham's journey from Ur and Harran suddenly does not seem unusually ambitious.

One bitumen pit after another—that was the Valley of Siddim. They dove into them as they ran—the kings of Sodom and Gomorrah hiding there, the others escaping into the hills. The conquerors took all the goods of Sodom and Gomorrah, and all their food, and left. Also captured was Lot, Abraham's nephew, who had been living in Sodom; they took him and all that he owned.

It had been many decades since Abraham's father, Terah, had decided to leave Ur and migrate to Canaan, following the reshaping of Babylon into an empire by Hammurapi. To have left all that behind, especially to have escaped what one feared was destroying the culture of Sumer, and then to hear of the kidnapping of his nephew Lot by a king from his homeland must have come as quite a blow to Abraham.

He is called to action on a completely secular errand, the rescue of Lot, and this calls to mind his Sumerian origin in another way: In order to take care of business, Abraham is able to put aside for a while the cosmic theater, a trait of an educated Sumerian. There is no Yahweh or covenant in this episode, no cosmic background; the motivating idea appears to be that it is just too much to bear that Lot is being carried back to Mesopotamia.

To a reader at the Jerusalem court, it might seem strange that, having reunited with Lot beyond Damascus, Abraham doesn't continue on a bit further to Harran to visit his father (Terah was also Lot's grandfather, of course). What dispels the incongruity is that the reader knows that this is a non-Hebraic source, a writer to whom Abraham's family history is largely unknown. Instead, this writer, X, knows everything about the nearby bitumen fields of the Dead Sea—which J needs to remind her audience was in that day also a verdant wetland, a valley, rather than the desert it had become.

While bitumen may have been a part of Canaanite life, it was at the center of life and the arts in Mesopotamia. On the ark of life built by the precursor of Noah in the Sumerian flood story, bitumen is one of the few insentient things valuable enough to be brought aboard. In daily life, bitumen was an essential part of the waterproofing of the precious things made or held together by clay. But the most interesting connotation of bitumen is purposely reserved for the kings of Sodom and Gomorrah. Emerging blackened from the pits, this image might have suggested nothing special to the X writer, but for J and her audience, these besmirched kings foreshadow what would soon happen to their kingdoms when Yahweh visits, hears their contempt for him, and responds as if justifying an earthquake and their destruction.

While this historical account seems legendary simply by virtue of its improbability, nothing supernatural comes into play. God is not invoked. We are meant to react as did J's audience: the earlier the history, the more fragmentary, and that in itself can be a sign of its authenticity.

An escapee brought the news to Abraham the Hebrew at the terebinths of Mamre the Amorite, who was related to the allies of Abraham, Eshkol and Aner. When Abraham heard that Lot his relative had been captured, he gathered his men—all those serving or born into his household, numbering 318—and pursued the captors as far as Dan. He positioned all his men around the others at night, overcame them, and stayed on their heels as far as Hobah, north of Damascus. All the goods were recovered, along with his relative Lot and all that he owned, including the women and others.

The number 318 lends an air of accurate history, and it may be one of several genuine details recorded by Abraham or Isaac themselves in the household chronicle (though probably a reference to some other accounting of persons than that they were warriors). More importantly, as the news about Lot reaches Abraham, the picture sharpens of the region into which he has moved. His family had relatives and friends here, just as in Damascus, which is what would be expected of those who knew the ways of trade and migration. This kind of extended, geographical relations is not hard to envision since as far back as the third millennium, Sargon had extended his reach from Egypt to India by posting traders along the caravan routes.

To be involved in real-world diplomacy, to have friends and enemies, to defend himself like others more than seven centuries before King David—this lengthens the history considerably of defense-minded Jews. Now we learn that he is not alone; that he is located at the terebinths not because it is a spiritual site (its history as a sacred grove would have been known in Jersualem) but because he has an associate there, a fellow Amorite. And yet Abraham has just been set apart, called "Abraham the Hebrew," the first—and only—Hebrew named as such in the Bible.

If that is how Abraham was already known to the local kings, and to the king of Shalem and his court writer, then the word "Hebrew" has acquired new meaning from its Akkadian sources. In Sumerian and Akkadian, *Hapiru* referred to various peoples who lived outside of cities but were not nomads. Here the word is applied to Abraham as if to signify that this migrant, although he also lived beyond cities, represents a civilization of equal significance to a city-state. In the eyes of King Melchizedek and his court writer, X, Abraham's Sumerian learning would have been deeply impressive, perhaps lending an uncanny power to the first Jew. Even in this early context, "Hebrew" had already acquired a unique cultural resonance.

X shows Abraham winning more back than Lot; he recovers everything looted by the invading kings, including the women, and what is unspoken here: perhaps the gods. It was well known from the genre of Sumerian laments that invading kings would carry off city gods and hold them hostage, further humiliating their conquered kings.

In Mesopotamian tradition, such shifting of fortunes could be attributed to a failure by the king, causing the city god to withdraw affection. However, there is no such attribution here. Instead, X writes straightforwardly of people orchestrating their own lives. When the gods are eventually invoked in the following paragraphs, it will be about a drama of something else entirely:

> *As Abraham came back from defeating Chedorlaomer and his allied kings, the king of Sodom came out to the Valley of Shaveh, known as the King's Valley, to receive him. There too Melchizedek, king of Shalem, came out with bread and wine. As priest of El-Elyon, he blessed him, saying "Honored is Abraham by El-Elyon, creator of heaven and earth. Honored is El-Elyon, who brought your enemies to you." So Abraham allotted to him a tenth of everything.*
>
> *Then the king of Sodom said to him, "Give the people to me and you take the goods." Abraham demurred. "I have promised Yahweh, El Elyon, creator of heaven and earth, that not even one thread or a sandal strap would I take of what belongs to you, saving you from ever saying, 'I made Abraham rich.' For me, nothing but what my men used up, but for the allies who joined me, Aner, Eshkol, and Mamre, a fair portion."*

X could not have known about the covenant between Abraham and Yahweh, yet he recognizes the name ("Yahweh, El Elyon—the Highest God") as does Melchizedek. Perhaps the real witness to the covenant is X's silence: when Abraham names Yahweh, the strength of a personal god comes forward, to join together with "El Elyon," the supreme god of Canaan.

It is striking how the invocation of the gods emerges as personal drama as well as cosmic. Personal, because there is much unsaid and unknown about Abraham's Yahweh. A Sumerian from long ago could have sensed a serious theater here; instead of mindless worship, there is a disguised vulnerability, for both Abraham and Melchizedek appear to know that they are the producers of this theater of the gods ("Honored is Abraham by El-Elyon" *and* "Honored is El-Elyon."). The ironic smile and wide eyes on all the sculpture of the Early Dynasty of Sumer comes clear in retrospect, for here is the empowering recognition of mutual dependence: both god and man need an audience. But now the god-drama bears on relations between people, as the different parties—Abraham, the King of Sodom, and the others—decide how to divide what was recovered. This is crucial, echoing back to the core of the Sumerian cosmic theater, where the spectacle of daily life and family relationships is played out.

The Sumerians would often refer to themselves quite playfully as "the black-headed people." It was a distinction that wasn't real, but which others who superceded them took as literal. References to the black-heads by the Akkadians and others betrays an uneasy suspicion that it designated something about them that was chosen, and some scholars still consider Sumerians as thinking they were somehow chosen by their gods. Actually, they were the first to have achieved the awareness of *something being* chosen, through the dramatic energy of their cosmic theater. This something was about more than themselves; it represented what we would call today humanity. For the Sumerian, it was an awareness of the human species among a vast realm of others, enacted by both visible and invisible gods. Sumer achieved this awareness by fully imagining the daily lives of the god-statues in their different habits and habitats.

Now, in the writing of X, the cosmic theater begins to emerge as a species drama of different peoples who represent a shared origin, and who face each other with the sense of an obligation to something beyond their individual kingdoms. Yahweh is neither a statue nor like anything else, but a link to this emerging consciousness.

In the mutual greeting of "El Elyon"—the supreme god, who is normally not approachable except through the local gods—Abraham and Melchizedek allow a glimmer of the Hebrew future. From an initial high regard, resentment eventually develops of the Hebrew mission to the world: that it is chosen by mere humans. The Hebrew culture and its God will therefore be in need of reinforcement in every generation; it will be a written culture, reenacted in more writing and including all dramas, secular and divine.

As the audience at Jerusalem's biblical court read this passage, they did not imagine that Abraham and Melchizedek were alike, or that cultures are universal. On the contrary, they would note the great differences between them, for in seven centuries the Jebusite culture of Melchizedek had disappeared, unable to withstand the extinction of its capital city. The message embedded in J's quotation of the text by X is that the differences between us are as critical as the divergence between species. All species live and die, eat and excrete, reproduce—that much is universal. But the uniqueness of each one is precious, its extinction a loss worth keeping in memory. The J writer—and the Hebrew Bible throughout—has kept the loss of the Jebusite culture in living memory.

The monotheism that arose from Abraham's journey was not the consequence of blind groping but the product of a very real effort to found a culture. It was to be different in its focus upon survival, a culture that would know how to survive the extinction of Sumer and Akkad that Abraham had absorbed. Sumer was becoming a mistranslated literary culture in Abraham's time, and Abraham's struggle was rooted in its fate. His inner battle—to unite personal god with the creator—was driven by the fear of extinction.

J and her audience at Rehoboam's court in Jerusalem were also facing an unstable future and were trying to secure their culture, many centuries after Abraham. The kingdom of David and Solomon was breaking up. Even today, the issue of extinction, in the form of a questionable future, is still real for us, and we can identify with Abraham's fear of the extinction of his name and family, culture and religion. From a dying Sumer to the dramatized "dying" of his son, Isaac, as we shall see, Abraham braved extinction no less than Noah, whose story had been documented in Sumer.

CHAPTER 13

The Cosmic Theater in Ur and Harran

The culture and religion of Sumer making up Abraham's education was a crucial influence upon the Bible's writers in ways we are just beginning to understand. In the year 2250 BCE, a Sumerian poet in Ur composed the poem for Nanna's journey to Nippur, an enactment of the cosmic theater. Nanna, the city-god of both Ur and of Harran, god of the moon, was the son of Enlil, the supreme god seated at Nippur, spiritual capital of Sumer. Every year Nanna and his attendant statues embarked by boat on a journey upriver to Nippur and back, to visit his father. Nanna's boat is loaded with plants and animals, gifts to his father, and along the way he makes stops at other cities, Larsa, Uruk, and Shuruppak among them, in all of which his statue has dramatic meetings with the god-statues of those cities. At last Nanna arrives at his father's city.

At the lapis lazuli quay, the quay of Enlil,
Nanna drew up his boat . . .
"Open the house, gatekeeper, open the house . . .
That which is at the head of the boat I would give to you,
That which is at the rear, I would give you."
The gatekeeper joyfully opened the door;
With Nanna, Enlil rejoiced.
"In the river give me overflow,

In the field give me much grain,
In the wetland give me grass and reeds,
In the palm-grove and vineyard, honey and wine,
In the palace, long life,
To Ur I shall go."
He gave him, Enlil gave him,
To Ur he went.

A form of documentary poem, describing an actual journey of the god-statue on its way to meet his father, also a god-statue, *Nanna's River Journey to Nippur* is composed to be enacted, not imagined. This is the theater of the mind laid bare, so it can be seen. Somewhere between dream and physics, the land of Sumer was turned into a stage upon which the cosmos could be seen and experienced by all. The poem was written to accompany the journey and to be voice accompaniment to the cosmic drama as it unfolded in each city. There was musical accompaniment as well; also dancing and other art forms, and the statues, bejeweled and painted, and dressed in various costumes.

But in the time of Abraham's youth in Ur, in 1750 BCE, the Sumerian cosmic theater had already become an ancient ritual that was reenacted—a classic rather than a contemporary drama—and the audience was more dependent on the written text for documentation than in the actual days of Sumer and Akkad. Once his family moved to Harran, Abraham had only the written words in the temple library of Nanna. It was like reading an opera libretto, because it had been written strictly as accompaniment in a theater of the gods.

THE SEED OF INTIMACY

In the years since he left Harran to journey to Canaan, Abraham has not lived in cities nor has he been witness to god-statues moving between them. The voice of Yahweh has taken their place, but the only drama is a repetition of the invitation to imagine a poetic future. Unlike Nanna and his father Enlil, with family status at the crux of their relationship, Abraham is not in a filial relation to Yahweh—the dynamics of their intimacy are still to be worked out. At first, Abraham hears Yahweh as an inner voice that represents his Sumerian personal god; then, once in Canaan, it becomes the voice of Yahweh, a Canaanite (West Semitic) creator-god. Although we have been told that Yahweh appeared to Abraham ("He built an altar there: to Yahweh, who appeared to him") we have not yet been asked as readers to envision the encounter: to become aware that we are in a new kind of theater, one in which man and god are equally masked.

The following passage, which came at the end of Abraham's return to Canaan after Egypt—and before the episodes written by X—seemed out of place there because we still had no clue about how to visualize the scene of the Creator speaking to man as if standing beside him.

> *"Open your eyes, and may it please you look around you," said Yahweh to Abraham after Lot had parted, "from the place you are standing to the north, then down to the Negev, to the sea and back, westward. The whole land you see I will give to you: to your seed for all time.*
>
> *"I have planted that seed, made it true as the dust—like each grain of dust no man could ever count. Rise, walk around on this land—open and broad—it is to you I will give it."*
>
> *Abraham folded his tents, moved on; he settled by the oaks of Mamre, beside Hebron, built there an altar to Yahweh.*

The foreshadowing of Sodom, however, in the sentence that precedes this passage ("Now the people of Sodom had gone bad, parading contempt in Yahweh's eyes") reminds us that Yahweh has other things on his mind besides Abraham (who apparently has no idea of the problem in Sodom). The audience in J's Jerusalem, however, is being prepared for what will emerge about Sodom later. Yet something more important than literary prefiguring is going on as well. The aside about Sodom has also interrupted the emerging relationship between Abraham and Yahweh.

Why should Abraham have to know what preoccupies his God? The Sumerians had many stories and mini-dramas to express the preoccupations of their gods, but the obsessions and concerns of the gods are anxiety-provoking and only made tolerable for humans by the slowly unfolding drama over time of the cosmic theater. Yet here Yahweh expects Abraham to be in sympathy with his feelings about Sodom.

And to reach this new kind of sympathy between natural and cosmic worlds, a new theater is emerging that expands the possibility of intimacy even when the participants, man and god, are each of two minds. Yahweh's mind is on two futures at once: Sodom's and Abraham's. Abraham accepts but is not wholly persuaded by the theater Yahweh is inviting him into—he still has one foot in the Sumerian theater. He does not speak in reply to Yahweh. There is a mask over Abraham's interior self. He moves on, builds an altar, and his thoughts are his own. And Yahweh does not ask for them. We've been here before—the first time Abraham arrived at the oaks of Mamre and Yahweh offered a vision of the land ("'I will give this land to your seed'").

Abraham having returned from Egypt, Yahweh is trying again; this time, Yahweh says to Abraham as if a director to his actor, "Open your eyes, and may it please you look around you." Abraham did not feel as if he were part of the land after the first assurance, or he wouldn't have felt compelled by a famine to leave so quickly for Egypt. Now, Yahweh is directing him more explicitly to imagine himself there, to look this way and that way,

> *"I have planted that seed, made it true as the dust—like each grain of dust no man could ever count. Rise, walk around on this land—open and broad—it is to you I will give it."*

Beyond showing him, Yahweh is dramatizing the land and each particle in it. In a vast and entertaining sublimation, Yahweh states that no man could count the grains of dust. That no man could have *created* the land—for Yahweh himself is the creator—would be just too obvious for Yahweh to say. It would also make it more difficult to find some form of commensurate relationship with Abraham. We see Yahweh here trying to cut himself down to Abraham's size, to establish a cosmic theater in which both participate.

Although he is present and speaking to Abraham, we do not yet have a way to envision Yahweh—to see him. Nor was there any real conversation that might have helped us flesh out the scene; when Yahweh was finished, Abraham only "folded his tents, moved on." Neither did Yahweh ask Abraham to see him, merely to "open your eyes. . . look around you." Yahweh remains chiefly a voice here, still not sure of how to approach Abraham. He uses the trope of counting (as in the grains of dust) which is appropriate for Sumerians, for whom a quantity that could not be counted did not exist. (They had even created art forms of their weights, dressed out in precious alloys and shaped into creatures: an ounce weight might be a duck; a pound, a dove.) Yet Yahweh's presence remains vague.

Regardless, Abraham is now in a drama where counting does not count. It is how something is visualized or *seen* that counts. The hint of what will make the new cosmic theater real is already here—a further intimacy, a coupling—whether between Yahweh and Abraham, when Abraham will finally speak back on level ground ("'Lord Yahweh,' said Abraham, 'what good is prospering when I walk toward my death without children'") or that immensely complex intimacy between man and woman that yields the one and only offspring who can inherit the drama and pass it on.

Yahweh had spoken to Abraham before of offspring—of seed—after Abraham and Lot separated. Now he has seeded the land and deeded it to Abraham ("it is to you I will give it") in an oath, an oral contract, sealed not with a cylinder or a stylus on clay, but by Abraham going into the land—for a second time, after the retreat to Egypt. Now, he is to go into it again with changed eyes: as if the first time was a false start, he finds himself going through the land and redoing the altar scene. This must have seemed curious, perhaps even comic to J's audience. Yahweh is saying, in effect, Do it over. This time when you go out into the land, imagine that it has been seeded by me in order to write a new drama for you. Getting used to the words of Yahweh changes the experience of the land for Abraham.

THE THEATER OF ABRAHAM'S GOD

These things had passed when Yahweh's word came to Abraham in a vision passing before him . . .

Yahweh's words have blossomed into a visual theater where Abraham can see Yahweh—a fearful situation that Yahweh quickly calms: "Have no fear Abraham." But what is it that Abraham sees? First, he is presented with a new kind of passing: instead of time passing, as in "these things had passed," it is a vision passing; it is timeless. For Abraham, as for the historically aware audience in Jerusalem, this is the realm of cosmic theater, where time does not count, since gods do not normally age or die. What Abraham will see is an aspect of God, speaking behind a shield—a masked God. What kind of shield is this? It turns the worn-out, wooden cliché of "I am your shield" into an uncanny metaphor by giving it a visible usage: it literally hides Yahweh's face while revealing his presence.

"Have no fear Abraham, I am your shield and reward, a shield that prospers."

Yahweh speaks now in character, a bit awkwardly at first, since "a shield that prospers" is enigmatic visually and makes sense primarily in the poetic way of before, where the shield symbolizes defense—and normally we expect only an offense to prosper. But this mask offers comfort, a protecting shield, and it makes a sort of visual sense: like God, it is a nonhuman object, and one that grows in value.

"Lord Yahweh," said Abraham, "what good is prospering when I walk toward my death without children, my inheritance passed down to a son of Damascus, Eliezer, accountant of my house.

Now Abraham has a form to which he can speak back, and so he has finally entered the drama. We see him more clearly than ever on this new cosmic stage. Abraham speaks baldly as a Sumerian, focused upon inheritance, and his attitude toward death is the Sumerian one of matter-of-fact acceptance. Thanks to the Sumerian obsession with contracts and counting—everything can be arranged, everything can be quantified with ingenuity—Abraham alerts Yahweh to his accountant, the proper inheritor in the event of no proper child. In effect he is saying, a shield that prospers is fine but let's talk reality, let's talk accountants and not poetry.

> *"Look at me," Abraham continued, "you have given me no seed; and look, a son not mine—though under my roof—inherits my household."*

Despite the changes he has undergone, at this point Abraham remains very much a Sumerian. These cosmic promises cause such frustration that he caricatures Yahweh just as a Sumerian would talk back to his personal god, asking him to "look"—as Yahweh had asked him—and pointing to "a son not mine" as technically inheriting the promise, making a bit of a mockery of it, since he is "under my roof." This is not the way we would act before an all-powerful creator-god, but it *is* the kind of conversation we might expect with a Sumerian house god. Here it marks a restored boundary in the relationship between human and nonhuman worlds—a playing with words between Abraham and Yahweh that can cross between those worlds. It persists to this day, in the playful language of evolutionary biology for instance, where one species supercedes—or evolves into—another and "inherits" the extinct one's history.

> *Now hear Yahweh's word that passed before him: "Not this one for your heir—only what passes between your legs may inherit from you." He drew him outside: "Look well, please, at heaven; count the stars—if you can count them. So will be your seed"—and so it was said to him. He trusted Yahweh, and it was accounted to him as strength.*

Again we are reminded that Yahweh's word has become envisioned—that he is now visible as "he drew him outside." But first Yahweh responds with equal irony to Abraham. "Only what passes between your legs"—the seed, that is—may satisfy a Sumerian's literalness.

Once outside, we become aware that the natural world is Yahweh's stage, as he re-states the promise as if in Sumerian literal terms: go ahead, "count the stars—if you can count them." This time Abraham trusts Yahweh because he has been spoken to at his level: Eliezer has been superceded by a cosmic accountant who points to something that *could* be counted, though it cannot or should not, the stars and semen-seed. Thus Eliezer will be superseded by Abraham's own seed as well.

In this world, on this stage, Abraham finds a new cosmic theater that he is beginning to trust. For now, he is not yet thinking that he was told he would be father to a nation but only that his seed will be potent, that he will have "strength." Yet there is also something missing here that neither Abraham nor the audience in Jerusalem can forget. When Abraham blurts out his concern about inheritance we remember that he has left behind his own father's inheritance. Although Terah remained alive in Harran (the J writer has told us as much when she earlier accounted for his age) there is no attempt to go to see him, and neither will Terah even know of his grandchildren to come. So there is an underlying anxiety here, and it is not only Abraham's. Yahweh must be careful not to come too close or become "unshielded," since his presence would kill a human, as we will see in later chapters of the Hebrew Bible, particularly in Exodus, where Yahweh descends to Mount Sinai before a human multitude. Meanwhile, he is having a problem with managing his anger toward the people of Sodom, and Abraham is about to encounter its consequences.

Inheritance is an enormously important concept in Sumer, overshadowing any thought of death itself. What counted was the transference of what belongs to someone alive to what continues to live—death is not even in the picture. When the inevitable happened, death would be expected and accounted for, and for this reason it could be faced without illusion. But take away the coherence of the laws and philosophy of inheritance, and a great insecurity would naturally threaten. Abraham has felt this anxiety ever since he left his mother and father—and along with them, all the old Sumerian legal solutions to the problem of inheritance. In addition, he has lost the consolations of Sumerian poetry and its unflinching confrontation with death and extinction. The separation from his family is not unlike the one that death imposes on the Sumerian sensibility, where the dead are imagined cut off underground. In the Sumerian epic, *Inanna's Journey to*

Hell, a son freshly buried hears his mother's grieving and wishes he could be mere grass or water so that he might respond to her.

THE SON'S REPLY

There can be no answer
To her desolate calling,
It is echoed in the wilderness,
For I cannot answer.
Though the grass will shoot
From the land
I am not grass, I cannot come
To her calling.
The waters rise for her,
I am not water to come
For her wailing,
I am not shoots of grass,
In a dead land.

All that Yahweh can offer however is the promise of a poetic inheritance that Abraham will leave behind. This is a new kind of consolation, and it will take Abraham some time to assimilate it. Meanwhile, we, the audience in Jerusalem, can imagine that Abraham continues to feel cut off from Sumerian culture and uncertain about a covenant with Yahweh that is unwritten. It is something Yahweh will try to alleviate immediately, offering a consoling ritual of cutting a covenant (a "brit," as we are about to see) that will make the promise of inheritance a more concrete, Sumerian-like phenomenon.

Abraham, however, had never seen animals cut unless cooked and presented as cuisine before the god-statues. Even Gilgamesh offers simply flour to the gods. No one today can identify the provenance of the ritual that Yahweh is about to enact. A Hittite custom seems closest, but Hittite power comes later in history. So while the audience in tenth century BCE Jerusalem would have known the custom (and since the Hittite culture would become a strong influence in Canaan, it makes sense that Yahweh would consider it of international sanction) it would have been quite foreign to Abraham eight hundred years earlier, and thus he must be told what to do by Yahweh.

It is this very dissonance between the Canaanite Yahweh and the Sumerian Abraham where the drama of a new intimacy is born, although awkwardly. Abraham and Yahweh are actors from two different schools of theater trying to create something between them, and for posterity. What should he do about it, what can be done about it—this is what Abraham is thinking. Yahweh hears Abraham's bewilderment as a wish and fulfills it as neatly as he can: seed is needed, seed it will be; proof is needed, an elaborate sacrifice must be served up. But nothing is solved in these passages. There is no actual contract for Abraham and no conception or birth for Yahweh—not for a long time.

> *"I am Yahweh, who drew you out from Ur, of the Chaldeans," he said to him, "to give you this land as heir."*

But it was Harran, not Ur, where Abraham heard the voice of a personal god advising him to move on. Either Yahweh is giving little credence to history or he is emphasizing Abraham's cultural origins. But it is definitely not "Ur, of the Chaldeans," for the Chaldeans were a dynasty that arose long after Abraham. They were barely emerging when J wrote in Jerusalem. It was probably J's intention to submerge Harran's importance beneath its identification as a satellite and sister-city of Ur, the more significant cultural capital.

> *"Lord Yahweh," he said, "how may I show it is mine to possess?"*

Once again, the Sumerian in Abraham is hinting broadly about the contract. Yahweh responds with a "cutting" of a covenant.

> *"Bring me a heifer of three," he said to him, "a she-goat and ram, three-year-olds also, a turtledove and fledgling dove." All these he brought, cut down the middle, placed each one's half opposite the other; the birds he left unparted.*

The word "covenant" comes from the Sumero-Akkadian term, "birit," which later becomes the Hebrew "brit," meaning "between"—as in "to cut in half" or "to walk between." In Akkadian custom, a covenant was sealed by the sacrifice of a donkey. "The cutting of an ass between" was the complete term in Akkadian. The covenant between man and God is founded upon this ritual stage where Abraham and Yahweh will both appear, Yahweh in the mask of smoke and fire. In preparation, Abraham must also be masked in a "covering darkness thrown over him."

And the vultures descend on the carcasses, but Abraham scared them off. Now look: as the sun goes down, a deep sleep falls over Abraham—a covering darkness thrown over him: underneath he is plunged in fear.

"Know this within," he said to Abraham, "your seed will be strangers in a land not theirs; slavery will be their state—plunged in it for four hundred years. Yet the nation which enslaves them will also know judgment.

"After, they will come out prosperous, surrounded with it.

"You will come to your forefathers peacefully, when good and old be settled in your grave. They will be a fourth generation before they return: that long will Amorite contempt build, until the glass is full."

Enigmatic though it may be, Abraham has been shown the future in much further detail now; Yahweh has again stressed that it is "his future"—Abraham's—and although he is still not receiving the proof that he requires, a written contract, the audience in Jerusalem for the actual writing down of J's covenantal history is being more deeply convinced, for they know the history of slavery in Egypt that Yahweh foretells here. At this point, it means more to them that it is part of their legacy in the form of history than it does to Abraham that it is to be part of his future. As a Sumerian, Abraham is not particularly impressed by promises and futures, including the promise of prosperity ("they will come out prosperous"). He would also be perplexed by the forecast of his death in terms of "you will come to your forefathers," since he has left his father and forefathers behind.

So it was: the sun gone, darkness reigns. Now look: a smoking kiln and its blazing torch pass between the parted bodies.

The smoke and the fire are Yahweh's mask here—just as they will be later in Exodus, in the Sinai desert, where he leads them: "Ahead of them, it never disappears: a pillar of fire by night, a pillar of cloud by day." And later: "Mount Sinai was wrapped in smoke. Yahweh had come down in fire, the smoke climbing skyward like smoke from a kiln." All of this fire and smoke originates in Sumerian rituals, and Yahweh would have expected Abraham to be familiar with them. Now Yahweh has transformed them into masks for his appearance in the theater of Abraham's God.

It was that day Yahweh cut a covenant with Abraham: "I give this land to your seed, from the river of Egypt to the great river, Euphrates—of the Kenite, the Kenizzite, the Kadmonite; of the Hittite, the Perizzite, the Rephaim; of the Amorite, the Canaanite, the Girgashite, the Jebusite."

These are peoples known in J's Jerusalem but not all of them to Abraham, who lived many centuries before. To make clear to Abraham that he has not forgotten his family back in Harran, Yahweh pushes the border of his promise to the far-off Euphrates. Although he can't provide one witness (and most Sumerian contracts provide for several) Yahweh needs a multitude to be his proof of having entered into time. The host he describes to Abraham as coming out of Egypt will be transformed into an audience, the "uncountable" number of listeners and readers through time—the real proof is in the assembly of those listening in Jerusalem to J's history, and thereby attesting to the covenant. When Yahweh promises Abraham a multitude of descendants, he might have known that the writing of J would be a form of written covenant that would have satisfied in Abraham the Sumerian spirit for both documentation and poetry.

CHAPTER 14

Arranging a Child

Now Sarah, his wife, had no children with Abraham; she had an Egyptian maid, Hagar her name. "See how it is," Sarah is saying to Abraham, "Yahweh has held me back from having children. Please go into my maid now; maybe a child will come out of it." Abraham grasped Sarah's words; his wife Sarah had taken in Hagar the Egyptian, her maid (it was ten years since Abraham had settled in the land of Canaan), and hands her to Abraham to go into as a wife.

Now he came into Hagar so that she conceived; she saw that she was pregnant and looked down at her mistress with contempt in her eyes. "I have been hurt on behalf of you," said Sarah to Abraham. "I gave my maid into your grasp and now, seeing that she's pregnant, she looks down at me—may we know Yahweh's judgment between you and me."

Eight centuries later, in the year c.920 BCE, at the royal court in Jerusalem, J's audience believes it is hearing a typically Sumerian solution to the childless problem when it comes to the subsequent problem with Hagar. It is typically Sumerian because it's a legal solution; by their time it is an anachronism.

However, the situation is still surprising, considering that the story up till now has been built upon an underlying structure concerning the covenant between Abraham and Yahweh. Abraham will have a child, father a multitude . . . but here we discover that this child is to issue from an Egyptian, a concubine. And if Yahweh had foreseen that Abraham would have intercourse outside of his marriage, why not warn him? Yet it is all perfectly logical to Sumerian thinking, which Abraham and Sarah share: a legal solution can be found to every problem.

But where is Yahweh on this stage of cosmic significance, considering that Abraham and Sarah's child will provide the necessary heir? To the audience in Jerusalem, Yahweh is present by his absence. He has previously enacted a ritual drama, in the cutting of the covenant, to satisfy Abraham, yet as soon as he's not there, the human drama seems more startling—stands out in relief—than had the cosmic drama of man and God. The covenant cutting scene must have seemed strange and exotic to the Jerusalem audience (nothing like it was know by that time) but as a consequence, the human drama of enacting it via Hagar's womb will show itself even more foreign. What at first might sound like a sensible, logical solution of surrogate parenting is made to seem quaint in the context of the glorious historical perspective that was Yahweh's poetic envisioning of the covenant ("'Look well, please, at heaven; count the stars—if you can count them. So will be your seed'").

Not only is Hagar a concubine, she is foreign too, an Egyptian in fact! But what else is poor Sarah to think in this tragicomic attempt to fulfill the covenant? She has heard from her husband that Yahweh expects a child, and she has heard the exact words as well: "Only what passes between your legs may inherit from you." Now the drama has turned around—from Yahweh taking Abraham too literally in his desire for proof of the covenant, to Abraham and Sarah taking Yahweh's words literally. Yes, Abraham's seed will pass between his legs, but Yahweh failed to specify that Sarah be the one to receive it. Assuming she was too old to conceive, she was wise enough to figure out the solution. But did the tragedy of Hagar's expulsion and her son Ishmael's irrelevance have to happen?

Using this very immediate and essential problem, J has dramatized how strange the cosmic drama is when it comes down to real time and real history. Of course, our notion of reality involves the literal, an expectation of fact and true event, yet these things are not an integral part of that drama. Thus, through her depiction of this story, J deftly shows how the literal is to be always a mistaking of true intentions.

The scene is simply set: it is perhaps ten years after Yahweh's promise, and no child has appeared. Sarah is a level-headed woman. Not only has she not allowed her head to be spun by her husband's claims of a promised child, she describes it satirically, as if she were highly active sexually: "Yahweh has held me back." Yet she remains practical, even if her plan will be rendered with a bit of exasperated punning, which J's audience would have recognized as Sumero-Akkadian custom by the ritualized description of the process: Abraham "grasped"; Sarah "hands her"; and the repeated "going into" and "coming out."

After the going and coming, the perspective changes to up and down. Pregnant, Hagar "looks down" at Sarah. But this human aspect of the theater isn't yet in focus. It is missing a new version of the Sumerian idea of what constitutes normal reality: that there's an inside and an outside; or rather, that there's an inner reality that must be dramatized on a cultural stage. It is becoming clear that there must be a new culture to accommodate the situation of Abraham and Sarah, and J is making her audience acutely aware of it by showing how anachronistic the Sumerian solution had become.

For Abraham and Sarah, who have already found themselves within a new cosmic theater with Yahweh, their immediate drama is to make room for themselves on the stage that is this land. Their roles are to survive—Yahweh has seen to the prospering. And so J has equated the drama of survival with that of the family drama, which hinges on sexual reproduction. All the difficulties of a new culture based on the covenant are represented by Abraham's and Sarah's problem of sex: How are they to take having a child literally in their circumstances of advanced age and foreign land?

Sarah asks Abraham for "Yahweh's judgment between you and me," asserting her equal part in the drama. But Abraham misunderstands and offers her a Sumerian judgment: although Hagar had become his own (perhaps even as another wife) Abraham, according to law, reverts rule over her to Sarah. It was *Yahweh's* judgment, specifically, for which Sarah had asked, but Abraham has no confidence yet in his recourse to Yahweh.

> *"See how it is: your maid is in your hands," said Abraham to Sarah. "Do as you see best." Now Sarah punished her; she fled beneath her eyes.*

It turns out that Sarah's feminine intuition—as in so many instances in J's narrative—is superior and foreshadows what will actually happen: Yahweh would assert judgment.

> *Yahweh's angel found her by a watering hole: a spring in the desert on the track to Shur. "Hagar, maid of Sarah," he called, "from where have you come, where are you going?"*

Yahweh appears before Hagar in the mask of an angel and pretends not to know what has happened. He is still hesitant about interfering in, or even acknowledging, the temporal sequence of events, in order not to upset the natural world and endanger humans. (In the previous passage, he mystified Abraham by describing events many centuries in the future, including four hundred years of slavery in Egypt.) Even by referring to Hagar as the "maid of Sarah" rather than the wife of Abraham, Yahweh reveals his deference in judgment to Sarah.

> *"I am escaping," she said, "the cold eyes of my lady, Sarah." "Go back to your lady," Yahweh's angel said to her, "hand yourself back to her desire."*

> *Now Yahweh's angel said to her: "Your seed I will sow beyond a man's eyes to count." "Look," said Yahweh's angel again, "you have been made pregnant. You will give birth to a boy: Ishmael, you will name him. Yahweh heard your punishment: you will hear a* male.

Once again, Yahweh is given to poetic visions that might baffle Hagar, including his high esteem for women over men in general: "Your seed"—he tells Hagar, though it be a man's—"I will sow beyond a man's eyes to count." But he gives her something more specific to hold onto as well, a prediction of a boy and even his name. Nevertheless, even here he cannot resist the poetic flourish of deriving the name *Ish*mael from an airy pun, since "ish" means man, and "mael" means from God. Nor can Yahweh resist showing the future, but in Hagar's case as previously with Abraham, it is J's audience in Jerusalem who are the ones to be impressed.

> *"Impudent, he will be stubborn as wild donkeys, his guard up against everyone and theirs raised against him. The tents of his rebellion will rise before the eyes of his brothers."*

> *Yahweh had spoken to her and the name she called him was, "You are the all-seeing God," having exclaimed, "You are the God I lived to see—and lived after seeing." That is why the hole was called "Well of Living Sight"—you can see it right here, between Kadesh and Bered.*

The disguise of an angel has been discarded—"Yahweh had spoken to her"—and Hagar answered him. In fact, she had seen him and without any threat to her life, although this was the common fear of mortals in God's presence as well as Yahweh's fear of coming too close to his creatures. Hagar confirms this and in so doing confirms that Yahweh is both public and personal god: "You are the God I lived to see—and lived after seeing."

Being a woman, and one depicted by J, Hagar has none of Abraham's hesitancy before Yahweh. She understands the angel was merely a disguise, for she "names" Yahweh in the same playful spirit with which he had named her son, Ishmael. For written verification, J gently interrupts the narrative with her own historical proof of the site, almost as another footnote for her reader: "you can see it right here."

A far more blatant interruption occurs in the next passage. It is the hand of P, however, not J (one knows this through textual analysis).

He is the third of the four writers of the Pentateuch, the Priestly author writing almost three centuries after J and her audience were forgotten. P is a stickler for historical accuracy, and in place of proof he offers exact dates and other "facts" to make it seem that J was too literary an author to be a scientific historian like himself. But P's "science" is far closer to fiction than J's impervious gaze: "Abraham was 86 years old"—should we be more impressed by Abraham's potency at such an age or by his fidelity to Sarah (since it was she who commanded the act)?

CHAPTER 15

The Court of the World

Three hundred years after J first wrote down her narrative at Rehoboam's court, another writer at the court of King Josiah, who was also a priest, was commissioned to write a new version of Hebrew history in the world. This would be one that would correct and refocus the documents of both J and the E writer. In particular, what appeared as moral ambiguity, paradox, and too much sympathy for human idiosyncrasy was now to be hardened into black and white by the P writer. He was also to verify and insert dates and ages in an effort to shore up literal authenticity. Moreover, the version commissioned of P was in tandem with the religious reforms of Josiah, which centralized the temple and codified the religion. But the historical authenticity of J and E was unquestioned and not to be revised. The proof of this historicity has been long lost to us, but in Josiah's time it probably included early editions of the combined J and E narratives, written in the archaic script that the newer biblical Hebrew was leaving behind. Yet P did have a freer hand in the editng of the biblical law in Leviticus, which is why traditional scholarship emphasizes his legalism (another gift from the Sumerians).

J's original text, lost for more than a century, had now been found although it had been combined with another history written in the ninth century BCE by the E writer, an author at the court of the northern kingdom of Israel whom we will encounter in the final chapters of this book. (Beginning in J's time, the biblical land had been divided into a southern kingdom, Judah, first presided over by Rehoboam, and a northern kingdom, "Israel." This division lasted until the fall of the northern kingdom in c.720 BCE.) After the fall of the northern kingdom, the two histories, J and E, were combined but within another generation had already become an ancient document revered though rarely consulted—until it was found again in 622 BCE. Those at Josiah's court read the combined JE text with profound reverence yet also a sense of dismay at its literary provenance. It appeared too full of intimate drama and linguistic invention for a history, with too much emphasis on details of a story and too little concern for the message.

The authority of religion had grown considerably since the tenth century of Solomon and Rehoboam, and the bold theater of Abraham's God with its human inspiration seemed no longer sufficient. Now a very clear literalness was wanted, a certainty that not only was this history divinely inspired but that it was meant to last through time. It was not the wonder of the covenant between Yahweh and Abraham that earned the awe of P and his contemporaries but the religious commandments and their interpretations that had been forgotten.

Although the influence of the Sumerian love of documentation had carried through to P's day, he had lost touch with the intimacy of cosmic theater. In place of intimate dialogue, we find authoritarian encounter; in place of the masks that allowed closeness, awesome fear. Thus what had been cosmic theater receded into static scenes when P rewrote parts of the history—ostensibly to make clearer what the reader was to think. The P writer could not have known anyone's exact age, of course, but he *needed* Abraham to be ninety-nine years old, so that he could be one hundred at the time of Isaac's birth. Historical congruence was to override emotional truth.

Because the origin of J's narrative is unknown to the P writer, so too is the cultural context that created it. He assumes the biblical text that has come down to him was written by poet-dramatists and that it therefore needs to be re-focused as a statement of evidence—of testimony in a court. In place of an audience, P speaks as a defense lawyer before a jury of priests; the defendants in the dock represent the seed of Abraham. They must be proven to be that seed—that is, the literal inheritors of the covenant—in front of the priests, who represent the newly institutionalized religion.

In this context, who then is the accuser? It is the world, now—the entire known world of nations who project their power in the name of gods who have no ultimate obligation, no covenant that lifts the human realm into intimate relationship with the cosmos. The result is a world in which human wishes for power can be marked as the will of the gods, and the monumentalizing of power serves the local god. Hammurapi's will to power in Abraham's day has become the norm.

Or so it seems to the P writer and his audience of priests. There were, of course, all sorts of religious sects in the world at the time that renounced the world in favor of cosmic mysteries. There are probably branches of these sects in ancient Israel even, but the P writer is defending his people against a generalized vision of the world's religions and gods. Far from seeing it in terms of cosmic theater, as the J writer had, the P writer views the foreign nations as representing a kind of prosecutor who denies the covenant of Abraham, the chief innovation of the people of Israel. The P writer himself probably did not see the Hebraic culture—the actual "people of Israel"—as an originator; instead, he put Ancient Israel's history in the dock as defendant. They must be proven to be who they are by their knowledge of and obedience to the judge. That judge is the sole God allowed in this court, the one God who has entered into and become intimate with time and human history, the only God who can sit in judgment in the court of the world. It is Yahweh.

WRITTEN IN THE FLESH

In his first words to Abraham about the covenant, the God of the P writer identifies himself not as Yahweh but as "El Shaddai," or "God of the Mountain." P uses this name as a deliberate anachronism, thinking that is what a Sumerian would know him by. But P knows little about Sumer (to begin with, mountains were not a feature there), and the name comes from a different source, possibly Canaanite and much better known than the obscure god Yahweh whom Abraham appropriated. Further, Sumerians are not ones to "throw themselves on their face"; when they speak with a god, it is a personal god, and El Shaddai is clearly not that. This El Shaddai inspires fear and face-saving prostration; he is probably the god who Hagar expected when she was surprised to have survived a face-to-face meeting.

And yet, El Shaddai remains a uniquely personal creator-god, speaking to humans in person rather than through mediating gods, as is usual for creator-gods. He is offering too, as seal of his unwritten covenant, a change of names, from the Sumerian Abram to Abraham. This change is a not very clever pun since Abraham means the father of many—but in Hebrew, and it is not possible that anyone was speaking Hebrew in Abraham's day. It appears that the P writer is nothing like the scholar and historian that J was.

To make up for his lack of interest in language and culture, and in the human confrontation with death that centers on the problematics of inheritance, P has a poignant agenda of his own. He shows in defense of the people of Israel that the unwritten covenant is actually written in the flesh and in time. In his literal-minded yet fecund imagination, the seed itself is a kind of writing, and God tells Abraham he will be "exceedingly fertile," a promise of preternatural seed.

When Abraham was ninety-nine years old, the Lord appeared to Abraham and said to him, "I am El Shaddai. Walk in my ways and be blameless. I will establish my covenant between me and you, and I will make you exceedingly numerous."

Abraham threw himself on his face; and God spoke to him further, "As for me, this my covenant with you: You shall be the father of a multitude of nations. And you shall no longer be called Abram, but your name shall be Abraham, for I make you the father of a multitude of nations. I will make you exceedingly fertile, and make nations of you; and kings shall come forth from you."

Now, in the emerging theater of Abraham's God, having his name changed would have Sumerian echoes for Abraham. He would recall the classic poems about Gilgamesh, in which the name of a man or woman is raised to cosmic dimension when it becomes part of his votive statue in the temple—and then "immortalized" after their death. This was a drama that he had already put behind him but whose influence would remain fundamental.

FROM *THE DEATH OF GILGAMESH* (SUMERIAN)

Men, as many are given names,
Their funerary statues have been fashioned since days of old,
And stationed in chapels in the temples of the gods:
How their names are pronounced will never be forgotten.

These votive statues, the type that Abraham himself might have sculpted, or at least inscribed with the names of their possessors in Terah's workshop, suggest how deeply involved was the Sumerian person in the cosmic theater—to the point of having his name immortalized in the presence of the daily life of the gods.

From Abraham's Sumerian roots to P's retelling of his story, the obsession with male seed also persists. But there is a crucial difference: In the Sumerian creation epic, *Enki and the World Order,* it is the seed of the creator-god of water, Enki, who engenders the living landscape, while in the P writer—two thousand years later—it is, perhaps for the first time, a human phallus that is to become "exceedingly fertile." In terms of poetry, the Sumerian poem is perhaps more sophisticated, for the bull and the river Tigris are not anthropomorphized but aspects of even older, archaic myths—played with by the Sumerian poet tenderly, metaphorically.

After Enki had lifted it over the Euphrates,
He stood up proudly like a rampant bull,
He lifts the penis, ejaculates,
Filled the Tigris with sparkling water.

He lifted the penis, brought the bridal gift,

Brought joy to the Tigris, like a big wild bull proud of causing birth.
The water he brought is sparkling water, its wine tastes sweet.

The P writer is not so much mistrustful of metaphor as he is of "making" metaphor himself. It seems slightly crude to him, for he has transferred creative power to the creator, as it were, and this power is one of speaking literally. Of course, Yahweh's literalness is always grand metaphor in itself, as in the following passage, where "my covenant shall be marked in your flesh as an everlasting pact." Yahweh is made to speak in the guise of a judge by P, who is anxious to make literal every phrase of his judgment. "Making literal" becomes a making as well, a creative act, and in this act Yahweh is focused upon the male penis as the document upon which the covenant must be written—literally inscribed in its circumcision. It is Yahweh's way of acquiring a phallus—of partaking in the creative diversity of time—without having to resort to animal metaphors as in the bull of Enki.

"I will maintain my covenant between me and you, and your offspring to come, as an everlasting covenant throughout the ages, to be God to you and to your offspring to come. I assign the land you sojourn in to you and your offspring to come, all the land of Canaan, as an everlasting holding. I will be their God." God further said to Abraham, "As for you, you and your offspring to come throughout the ages shall keep my covenant. Such shall be the covenant between me and you and your offspring to follow, which you shall keep: every male among you shall be circumcised. You shall circumcise the flesh of your foreskin, and that shall be the sign of the covenant between me and you. And throughout the generations, every male among you shall be circumcised at the age of eight days. As for the homeborn slave and the one bought from an outsider who is not of your offspring, they must be circumcised, homeborn, and purchased alike. Thus shall my covenant be marked in your flesh as an everlasting pact. And if any male who is uncircumcised fails to circumcise the flesh of his foreskin, that person shall be cut off from his kin; he has broken my covenant."

The judgment of the uncircumcised is harsh but nonetheless poetic and metaphorical: he "shall be cut off from his kin." The pun on cutting echoes not only the literal cutting of a covenant but also the threat of cultural castration. Ultimately, it is a re-sacralizing of seed, reiterating in its way the sacred seed of Enki. But no real change comes to Hebrew seed, and there is nothing special to it—it is the same as all human seed except that it has become a powerful metaphor for Yahweh's entrance into time and the bodily history of all flesh. This grand Hebraic metaphor of P extends to imbuing the seed with a power over life and death—it survives the decay of the body—and that is why it is such a delicate but decisive matter to offer a written covenant at last to the people of Israel.

It would not entirely satisfy a Sumerian, but the P writer has already lost that awareness of Abraham's origin. It is a loss that resembles the Babylonian loss of Sumer as well—a cultural forgetting, rendering Abraham's deeply civilized background as "lost in translation." This will remain the central problem of the P writer: he puts the Hebraic culture, the people of Israel, in the witness stand, but does not allow it to speak.

Abraham is not allowed to speak either; instead, Yahweh speaks for him in the form of a Canaanite covenant, in which a superior party grants rights to an inferior. Although there are examples of this covenant-granting of rights to humans by the gods, especially to kings, that go back to Abraham's time and before, they are not found in civilized Sumer. P's version is quite different from what the J writer envisioned when Abraham participated with Yahweh in hammering out a covenant-contract, in which each party has rights. Abraham, for his part, had been arguing on behalf of all humanity, of course, while Yahweh had been aware of the complexity involved in entering time.

Under P's hand, Yahweh has turned from the complexity of intimacy to the complexity of the law. It is an undeniably civilizing trend, but it would be a huge loss if it replaced the cosmic theater of Abraham's God entirely. That does not happen however. The P writer is only inserted into the narrative in a way that adds a dimension of complex interruption.

> And God said to Abraham, "As for your wife Sarai, you shall not call her Sarai, but her name shall be Sarah. I will bless her; indeed, I will give you a son by her. I will bless her so that she shall give rise to nations; rulers of peoples shall issue from her. Abraham threw himself on his face and laughed, as he said to himself, "Can a child be born to a man a hundred years old, or can Sarah bear a child at ninety?" And Abraham said to God, "O that Ishmael might live by your favor!" God said, "Nevertheless, Sarah your wife shall bear you a son, and you shall name him Isaac; and I will maintain my covenant with him as an everlasting covenant for his offspring to come. As for Ishmael, I have heeded you. I hereby bless him. I will make him fertile and exceedingly numerous. He shall be the father of twelve chieftains, and I will make of him a great nation. But my covenant I will maintain with Isaac, whom Sarah shall bear to you at this season next year." And when he was done speaking with him, God was gone from Abraham.

The Sumerian "Sarai" becomes Sarah, but without any insight into what is lost by cutting off the echo, retained in her name, of her civilized origins in Ur. Presumably, Sarah will be satisfied to be a vessel for "rulers of people," and this will come about by God allowing a son—though God himself had refrained from any supernatural sexual interference. Where the J writer creates a dramatic scene (in the chapter to come) in which Yahweh confronts Abraham and Sarah by the oaks of Mamre, the P writer merely recapitulates it stiffly here. "Can a child be born to a man a hundred years old?" asks Abraham. But P seems to have forgotten that Abraham has already fathered Ishmael at age ninety-something, so any dramatic steam from this question has been lost. Here is conclusive evidence that P felt compelled to retell J's history as if Abraham, the defendant, was in disbelief of the Judge's explanation of the verdict.

Earlier Abraham was falling in prostration out of fear of God; now he "threw himself on his face and laughed." These separate acts just don't go together, but they seem to suggest that Abraham is having a problem trusting God. God, too, is mistrustful and that is why he devises requirements, like circumcision, for Abraham to prove his trust.

Previously in J's narrative, it was Abraham asking for proof. God supplied it as one would in reply to a child's question of, "How shall I know it is really, really true?" ("Now look: a smoking kiln and its blazing torch pass between the parted bodies.") Now however, God is the one asking for proof, and here a poignancy is lost in the telling of Jewish origins. The thing abrogated is the childhood of Jewish culture, as represented by Abraham and Sarah, in the transition from Ur to the possession of their future. God asks for proof as parents might ask for proof of their children's love before formalizing their inheritance. But holding inheritance over their heads is always about the parent refusing what it is to be a parent. If J had been writing this excerpt, the circumcision would make more sense in the context of the story of Abraham thus far, assuming Yahweh had offered it in answer, once again, to Abraham asking for proof. In P's context, however, it is God's demand, not his answer to a request for proof.

Now Abraham interrupts God, asking for favor of his son, Ishmael—again mistrusting that any other son will be born to him. As God continues his verdict in the guise of a judge, allowing for Ishmael also to become "a great nation," the P writer appears to have forgotten that Abraham was not impressed with promises of the distant future. Abraham wanted at least some written proof of the covenant that he could show, and once again God has offered only the verdict of a Judge: "I assign the land you sojourn in to you and your offspring to come, all the land of Canaan, as an everlasting holding."

The theater of the gods has been turned upside down; formerly, the people envisioned the gods as seeding the earth, and now Yahweh is transferring this power to Abraham, in order that he, Yahweh, may enter mortal time. Where the J writer recognizes this as a new cosmic theater, involving the intimacy of the family drama, the P writer is limited in his conception to the courtroom drama of judge and defendant. It will be left to the poetry of the prophets to make of this judge an intimate father, and for the Hebraic writers of literary books, like the Book of Job, to dramatize the existential condition of the Hebrew man defending himself against a charge of disbelief.

> *Then Abraham took his son Ishmael, and all his homeborn slaves and all those he had bought, every male in Abraham's household, and he circumcised the flesh of their foreskins on that very day, as God had spoken to him. Abraham was ninety-nine years old when he circumcised the flesh of his foreskin, and his son Ishmael was thirteen years old when he was circumcised in the flesh of his foreskin. Thus Abraham and his son Ishmael were circumcised on that very day; and all his household, his homeborn slaves and those that had been bought from outsiders, were circumcised with him.*

The vision of this tremendous cutting and pain is a sign of Abraham's belief in Yahweh's entitlement of land—and disbelief in his own entitlement to the seed of life. But can we as the audience of readers believe in the drama enacted here? As courtroom drama, it lacks suspense; as cosmic drama, it lacks J's genius. As a writer, P does not know how to enact belief in a human drama, and his Abraham is not a real or historical person. Nevertheless, the theater of a courtroom that P has suggested, of judgment and disputation, will be developed further in Jewish tradition and commentary. This will all take on cosmic dimension within a few years after P's time.

Judah, the portion of the Hebrew kingdom that has survived, will be invaded in the seventh century BCE by the power-hungry descendents of Hammurapi and taken into exile to Babylon. There, subjected once again to the sophisticated codification of laws that was Hammurapi's legacy, the beginnings of the Talmud will be written, a form of cosmic disputation that will elevate the drama of Israel into a portable yet unforgettable land.

Why law and disputation rather than lamentation—such as the great lamentations of Sumerian cities? There would be profound poems of lamentation written by Hebrew poets and prophets. But the P writer has provided a basis for a uniquely Hebraic expression of loss.

CHAPTER 16

Acting Out the Drama

In c.1750 BCE, when Abraham was still a youth in Ur, he heard about the prayers for the dead beneath the house. This tradition of burial and prayer originated in Sumer more than a millennium before. Whether he heard the prayers voiced in his own house is doubtful, due to a progressive trend toward public temple participation. Yet Abraham's ancestors in Ur, buried beneath the older house that had become the workshop, may have spoken at one time these words:

> *I want to invoke your names. Let me pour cold water down through your water pipe.*

In this home ritual, water was literally offered to the dead family members buried beneath the floor, poured down a tube laid into the earth. The tube, in fact, was a hollow reed, so that the verisimilitude of a natural process would be enforced: a growing thing, a reed, implanted in the earth beneath the house.

Now, even Abraham's ancestors knew that the dead were corpses and bones (there was no significant afterlife imagined in Sumer), but by feeding water to the dead of the family a cosmic drama is created. The living can pretend their immediate ancestors are alive while knowing they are not, and in the same way Abraham is about to confront Yahweh—who is pretending to be a man when he is not. Abraham knows it is Yahweh who appears as a stranger before his encampment at Mamre, but will nevertheless act out the drama—just as Yahweh does.

> *Now Yahweh was seen by Abraham among the oaks of Mamre; he was napping by his tent opening in the midday heat.*
>
> *He opened his eyes: three men were standing out there, plain as day.*

Abraham says,

> *"My Lord," he said, "if your heart be warmed, please don't pass your servant, in front of his eyes. Take some water, please, for washing your feet; rest a moment under the tree."*

Returning here to the narrative of the J writer, there is an opening up of the theater of Abraham's God: a dramatic focus is suddenly placed on the importance of individual lives. Yahweh appears at ease now in the disguise of a man. Abraham respects the mask, as does Sarah, both of them discovering that it is Yahweh accompanied by two angels, the latter also in the disguise of men. Yahweh, for his part, also respects Abraham and Sarah in their character as human creatures.

How different things now seem after the episode with Hagar and Ishmael. That whole affair had been based upon a confused understanding of the inheritance of the covenant. In the end, Yahweh found a way to rescue Hagar, to bless Ishmael, and to return to his original plan. After that, and after the earlier awkward attempts to help establish the stage for the God of Abraham's theater, including the covenant-making scenes, all will now come smoothly together to reveal a drama of God and man in conversational intimacy.

As a God who has unified the personas of personal god and cosmic creator, and one who has just re-named Abraham and Sarah—according to the P writer's addition—Yahweh is now developing a more subtle understanding of disguises. The Sumerians, pretending the gods were alive in the statues and knowing the statues were disguises, developed a dramatic subtlety of naming and inhabiting their cosmic theater. In one ritual enactment, the orchard area behind the Sumerian temple was imagined to be a vast steppe or grassland traversed by the statues and their human makers, in which memory of the human origin of the statue is lost. As they walk through this "steppe," the sculptors and artists, who would have included Terah and Abraham on occasion, chant the names of the different materials and woods with which they made the statues. They even chant the names of the tools and the names of the artists themselves, as they escort the statues from workshop to riverbank, where the mouth-opening ceremony of the statues would begin.

In transforming her archaic source, J is clearly up to the task of matching the rich attention to disguise in the Sumerian cosmic theater. Even with little more to work with than a naming of the occasion of renewed intimacy between Yahweh and Abraham at Mamre, J interprets and expands this source into a complex drama of inhabiting the covenanted roles of man and God. The setting at the oaks of Mamre is a camping spot in thc vicinity of a sacred grove, but we have also learned earlier from the X writer that Abraham's relatives in the area had extended hospitality to him ("An escapee brought the news to Abraham the Hebrew at the terebinths of Mamre the Amorite, who was related to the allies of Abraham, Eshkol and Aner").

Abraham is almost dreaming—"he was napping by his tent opening in the midday heat"—but now Yahweh appears to him upon *waking.* The theater of Abraham's God has matured into full bloom, where daydreams and "a shield" and other devices can be laid aside for the intimacy of natural encounter. Abraham is changed now, "at home" in the drama. It is an opportune meeting for Abraham, since Yahweh was not specifically on his way to see him but was instead passing by on his mission of judgment to Sodom and Gomorrah.

> *He opened his eyes: three men were standing out there, plain as day. From the opening in the tent he rushed toward them, bent prostrate to the ground.*

Abraham's response to the sudden appearance of these strangers is a gesture of hospitality so extravagant and generous that it is as if he were still in a dream. It is not the heat of the sun that renders it dreamlike, however; instead, it is the first time Abraham is not passive, at least initially, in a meeting with Yahweh. Abraham, we find out, can actually initiate a new intimacy by changing Yahweh's course (since he was on his way to Sodom). There is also something deeply humorous in the scene about to unfold: a mutual willingness on the part of Abraham and Yahweh to observe the "rituals" of daily life—eating and washing—as if it is a new theater of intimacy between them.

> *"My Lord," he said, "if your heart be warmed, please don't pass your servant, in front of his eyes. Take some water, please, for washing your feet; rest a moment under the tree. I will bring a piece of bread to give your hearts strength. Let your journey wait; let your passing warm your servant—to serve you."*

Abraham asks the cosmic strangers if they will wash their feet, and what is even more astonishing, if they will eat. Although he is perhaps not certain who the strangers are, Abraham is willing to pretend they are strangers like himself, from somewhere far away, such as Ur. What enables the scene to arrive at new depths is Abraham's knowing and not knowing. It is Yahweh or not, but both possibilities are present, because Abraham is half-expecting him. And that is what Yahweh has accepted about these humans: they know and do not know at the same time, for they have inherited the sensibility of Sumer.

The audience in J's Jerusalem already knows it is Yahweh, just as we do today, for the passage subtly tells us so. But we are no different from Abraham when we accept the necessity for Yahweh's disguise, since we also know and do not know what to expect of the unknown. What renders J's narrative authentic for her audience is the uncanniness of the drama.

> *"You may," they said, "make what you've said true."*

This response of the strangers is a bit theatrical too, matching Abraham's. They will pretend to eat because Yahweh has accepted the cosmic theater that Abraham has established. It would not have happened had Abraham not been immersed in the Sumerian cosmic theater, where the audience pretended the god-statues were alive, and where there was some degree of not knowing, some suspension of disbelief as the theater unfolded each day with its morning meal rituals. The Sumerian background of Abraham comes to fruition in the theater of Abraham's God, where the intimacy of not knowing what may happen is central. Intimacy requires that anything is possible—within an agreed-upon range, or within covenanted limits.

Abraham rushed toward the tent, to Sarah. "Hurry, three measures of our richest flour, to roll into our finest rolls."

From there to the cattle he runs, chooses a tender calf—the best—gives it to the servant boy, who hurries to make it ready.

Now Abraham gathers curds, milk, and the tender meat he had prepared, sets it down for them under the tree, stands near, overseeing: they ate.

Yahweh and his messengers will pretend to eat and Abraham is their witness, "overseeing"—not seeing through their disguises but acknowledging the disguised seriousness of the drama. The mission of the "men," like Abraham's, requires that they not upset the natural order of things, for the created world is sacred (Yahweh's blessing would mean little otherwise). They will "eat" and Abraham will serve them, each remaining in character.

SEXUAL ANXIETY

"Your wife—where is Sarah?" they asked of him. "Look, she is here," he said, "in the tent."

Suddenly they know Sarah's name. And then one is speaking as Yahweh does. More specifically, he is referring to the blessing.

"I will appear again to you—in the time a life ripens and appears. Count on it and see: a son for Sarah, your wife." Sarah was listening by the tent opening—it was right behind them.

There is no mistaking Yahweh now, repeating the covenant he made with Abraham. Since Yahweh was on his way to Sodom, and not to remind Abraham of what he's already told him, it appears to be a spontaneous repetition. The naturalness of the occasion is disarming, as if Yahweh wasn't going to mention the child but now does, so that Sarah can hear. And there is the further spontaneity of Abraham's forgetting; it is as if he had forgotten the promise—or repressed it for being so outrageous—and needed to be reminded.

> *But Sarah and Abraham were old, many days were behind them; for Sarah the periods of women ceased to exist. So within her Sarah's sides split: "Now that I'm used to groaning, I'm to groan with pleasure? My lord is also shriveled."*

Sarah too has forgotten that she was supposed to have a child and is taken by surprise. She responds as if the visitor resembles a Sumerian personal god, of whom it was common to be skeptical (with a hint of the skepticism attached to the personal god's existence within the theater of belief itself). The skepticism might even turn to sarcasm, as in this *Letter to a Personal God*:

> *Thus says Apil-Adad your servant: Why have you been so neglectful of me? Who might there be to give you a substitute for me? Write to Marduk who loves you, bid him wipe away my debt. Show yourself capable of doing something, so I may have a reason to be grateful to you.*

But Sarah's biting irony even shocks Yahweh. It reminds us again of his anxiety over sexual and inheritance issues:

> *"Why is Sarah laughing," asked Yahweh of Abraham, "when she says, 'Now I can count on giving birth, when I'm elderly?' Is a thing too surprising for Yahweh? In the time a life ripens and appears I will appear to you—and to Sarah, a son."*

Sarah hid her feeling: "No, I wasn't laughing"—she had been scared. "No," he said now, "your sides split, count on it."

Is Yahweh promising miracles then? No, he refers specifically to a pregnancy in the natural order of things—"the time a life ripens and appears." It is implicit here that Abraham and Sarah will resume sexual relations, as if they needed coaxing. Thus Yahweh promises something rare and unusual but not unknown. And he is vulnerable to Sarah's irony, her laughter, thus Yahweh responds with his own: the grammatical root of the word for laughter will become the name of the child, Isaac.

On his way to Sodom in the next passage, we're given a preview of Yahweh's intense concern with sexual relations. For to enter into mortal history and the flow of time, Yahweh knows that inheritance is the means to transcend death; for him it means a descent, a coming down to earth ("it weighs on me to go down")—and a coming to terms with sexuality.

EVIL

But once before there had been a flood as well. Once before, Yahweh had faced evil in his creation, and this brought on the Flood. The first time, all life was nearly wiped out; now the evil was centered in two cities. In c.1675 BCE, within Abraham's lifetime, a tablet was incised in Nippur with the Sumerian Flood Story. Within little more than a century it was buried in the fall of Nippur. In the 1930s, the great Assyriologist C. Leonard Woolley recovered the tablet and translated it in his *Excavations at Ur.* In fact, the Flood Story had first been written down in the fourth millennium BCE, at the origin of cuneiform writing, and the Nippur tablet, with the Sumerian Ziusudra as the original Noah, is just one of many re-tellings that pre-date the *Epic of Gilgamesh.* It was *Gilgamesh*, however, where another Noah, the Akkadian Uta-Nipishtim (in translation from the Sumerian), provides the source for the J writer's history.

. . . a flood will sweep over the cities
to destroy the seed of mankind . . .

by the word of the assembly of gods . . .

After, for seven days and seven nights,
The flood had swept over the land,
And the huge boat had been tossed about by the windstorms on the great waters,
Ziusudra came forth, whose goodness reflects on heaven and earth,
Ziusudra opened a window on the huge boat . . .

Expanding the history of the Flood Story in the Bible, the J writer brings a new focus on evil. In the older versions, the creator finds the world flawed and remakes it, echoing a theme of previous trials and errors at creating the world. Now, in tenth century BCE Jerusalem, J will reveal what lies behind the Sumerian motivation to destroy those who deny the creator's existence. In J's narrative, these deniers are men and women who cannot tolerate the existence of an inner life—their inner desire could only turn into "acts" of harming and manipulating others.

Yahweh looked upon the human, saw him growing monstrous in the land—desire created only evil thoughts, spreading into all his acts. Now Yahweh's pain was hard, having watched the man spread in the land; it saddened his heart. "I will erase the earthlings I created from the face of earth," said Yahweh, "from human creature to wild beast, crawling creature to bird in the air—it chills me to have made them." But innocent Noah warmed Yahweh's heart.

In Sodom, it was the same evil, which slowly becomes known as "contempt" for life. In both stories—both Sodom and Flood—it is not a matter of individuals but always a mass fixation on a common desire in which no different thought or feeling is tolerable. And more than that: there is no room for origins, for a creator. When Yahweh says the

Sodomites have contempt for him—and that he must "see what contempt this disturbance signifies"—he means they have contempt for the cosmos as well, for consciousness of the unknown. As we shall see, the realm of the unknown extends to the innocence of children, who must trust the unknown motives of their guardians.

In the J writer's Jerusalem, no less than in our own time, there were many who believed that evil was relative, and it may seem as if J made Abraham speak for that point of view in her narrative. Abraham's question to Yahweh at first seems to be a philosophical one from Sumer: Why must the innocent be punished along with the guilty? "Can you not hold back for the fifty innocent within it?" asks Abraham, assuming that evil can be accepted in Sodom short of its destruction. And if accepted, then perhaps there are relative evils—or no evil at all.

But it is Abraham who ironically shows Yahweh the direction to Sodom, and he will "draw close" to ask his questions.

> *The figures rose, starting down toward Sodom; from there they could see its upturned face. Abraham walks with them, showing the way.*

This is the Abraham who has left Ur and Harran, who hasn't gone into any other city, and whose drama has centered on the personal: inheritance and seed. Now the Sumerian Abraham, conversant with a great civilization, comes forward. In a tent encampment by a grove of sacred trees, Abraham is revealed to have fashioned a counterpart to the Sumerian cosmic theater: the theater of Abraham's God. Instead of sculpting a Sumerian god-statue inscribed with verses about the god's powers—as had been made in his father's workshop in Ur—Abraham will orchestrate a conversation. It is a dialogue with Yahweh, who appears to Abraham as a man. And instead of writing, Abraham shapes the conversation with Yahweh by asking questions that speak directly to God's power.

> *Abraham drew close: "Will you wipe away the innocent beside those with contempt? What if there are fifty sincere men inside the city, will*

you also wipe the place away? Can you not hold back for the fifty innocent within it?"

Both sides, man and God, will now be seen as observing and negotiating the boundary between them. While Yahweh stays within the bounds of human conversation, Abraham probes God's motivation. His unknown purpose, inferred by Abraham, will translate into human terms as moral purpose. We see Yahweh is now dealing with more than just Sodom and Gomorrah for it is part of the same necessity that brings him to deal with human sexuality and inheritance. Thus the issue of absolute evil will open up for Abraham all the other questions he has harbored, including the problem of having a child with Sarah. It is, in fact, Yahweh's coming to terms with sexuality that now requires him to deal with the evil of the Sodomites, for whom the innocence of conception and childbirth is worthless. In contrast, for Abraham and Yahweh innocence is precisely what allows for the drama of inheritance and survival that will lead to the new civilization of Israel.

Once again, there is an issue of survival: On behalf of his creation, Yahweh must survive both the denial of his existence, the marginalizing that other gods impose on the creator, and the mortality of humans. The latter fact requires that Yahweh support the human creation of a culture and religion that can contain knowledge of him. Since a culture has to be inherited from one generation to the next, its sexual origins must form a basis for a story, for a re-telling of history in poetry and narrative. This is the background for Genesis, in which Abraham plays both the part of progenitor and narrator.

The encounter with Yahweh on the way to Sodom was fashioned by Abraham in the sense that he retold the conversation so that it could be recorded. Perhaps the details of it were even written down by Abraham himself or his son Isaac, but it is J who renders the scene for us. It would be natural to presume that Abraham had first created this cosmic theater, since he was familiar with the "opening of the mouth" ceremony that turned statues into gods in Ur (a cosmic drama so deeply imaginative that the orchards beside Ur's riverbanks could be conceived as a vast grassland steppe). And the J writer has preserved Abraham's encounter in this sense: it is seemingly inherited by her audience in Jerusalem as spoken history.

TRUTH AND JUSTICE

The theater of Abraham's God is now so well established that one could suspend disbelief knowing that the gods were present neither in statues nor in supernatural acts. Abraham is about to firmly establish instead that Yahweh's presence is in acts of "truth and justice . . . "

In reality, the supernatural is never at issue; on the contrary, it is the allowance for natural processes that preoccupies Yahweh. For humans, life and death are everything, while for Yahweh the fragility of time is only something he has promised to keep in mind. This is implicit in the question that Abraham will raise, knowing the truth about evil from Yahweh's mission to Sodom: Can there be justice and truth at the same time? The human Abraham among the disguised figures of Yahweh and angels would seem to be in a delicate position, but J shows how stable this new theater of Abraham's God has become: Abraham stays solidly in character, "showing the way."

> *"Do I hide from Abraham," said Yahweh within, "what I will do? Abraham will emerge a great nation, populous, until all nations of the earth see themselves blessed in him. I have known him within; he will fill his children, his household, with desire to follow Yahweh's way. Tolerance and justice will emerge—to allow what Yahweh says to be fulfilled."*

Yet Yahweh has a greater problem emerging from the dual issues of human sexuality represented by Abraham and Sarah on one hand, Sodom and Gomorrah on the other. How could Yahweh insure a child to Abraham and Sarah—so that "he will fill his children, his household, with desire to follow Yahweh's way"—and at the same time overlook rape, the intolerance of the body's dignity? That is his problem with natural processes, and it will be revealed as the issue in Sodom: a contempt that makes everything from friendship and hospitality to sex and intimacy indistinguishable from rape.

Natural processes are behind everything that happens (with the possible exception of absolute evil). So, eventually Sarah's pregnancy will seem a marvel to her and her circle but not inconceivable or unnatural. In the same way, the earthquake swallowing Sodom and Gomorrah will be understood by J and her audience in Jerusalem as a natural act, although it interprets Yahweh's concern for "truth and justice." Miracles and the miraculous are not to be confused.

One could see even the evidence of these events in person: the remains of Sodom and Gomorrah are near the Dead Sea; the descendants of Sarah's child, Isaac, are alive, making up J's Hebrew audience. As they hear or read her words, their whole history appears the result of natural processes—though deepened by taking place on a cosmic stage where time and the timeless coexist.

Desire is the focus, not only in the desire for intimacy but in "desire to follow Yahweh's way" and fight for the dignity of the body, of the individual. The Sumerians had desire in their cosmic theater, but it was placed with the god-statues for safekeeping. In the new theater of Abraham's God, there is no more playing it safe. Yahweh will stop to talk to Abraham and will allow himself to be an object of desire within a human drama. It becomes possible because the evil contempt in Sodom has forced Yahweh to "go down" among the humans and wipe out contempt of the body—the human body now standing in for Yahweh's natural creation.

> *"The noise from Sodom and Gomorrah grows; as their contempt grows heavy, it rises.*
>
> *"It weighs on me to go down, to see what contempt this disturbance signifies. If brought down to find offense, I will pull them down. If not, I will be pleased to know."*

Although Yahweh comes down to see if the Sodomites are making a travesty of his will for "truth and justice," the dramatic context is framed in an archaic form of cosmic theater ("the noise . . . rises. It weighs on me to go down"). There is an echo here of the Sumerian epics where the gods are disturbed by human noise resulting from a sexual problem: the people are living too long and having sex without restraint. There is the sexual problem of lack of restraint at work in Sodom too, but this time the creator's focus is on the contempt for tolerance shown by the Sodomites.

Meanwhile, the godlike playing with up and down reminds us exactly who it is in this narrative that is the creator of space and time. Throughout this narrative, as the personal god speaks with Abraham, we are forced to be aware also of the public god on high. But now the creator's thinking about Abraham has been interrupted. He has caught wind of the contempt in Sodom. We're confronted with the nature of divine thinking in a metaphorical paradox: the heavier the contempt, the more it should sink—but it rises. Yahweh exclaims "pull down," as if the Sodomites had made towers of themselves—but towers unlike the Sumerian ziggurats, with no theater inside.

When the evil of Sodom is indicated to him by Yahweh, the question for Abraham will remain how bad can it be when balanced against those who are innocent in the city (his own nephew Lot is there!) and who must die along with the guilty in Yahweh's pre-emptive strike. This was a question in one of the oldest Sumerian Gilgamesh epics, *Gilgamesh and Agga,* when the townspeople of Erech (Uruk) reject their king's decree to attack Kish in a pre-emptive strike in order to avoid destruction.

"Let us submit to the house of Kish, let us not smite it with weapons," cry the townspeople. Better to let the Kishites take over, argue the townspeople, than to kill and be killed in war. Ultimately, King Gilgamesh saves Erech by persuading them to arm and be ready to fight, but first he walks fearlessly into the camp of the Kishites and up to its king, Agga, and launches his own pre-emptive strike.

"Agga, you have brought the fugitive to your lap," says Gilgamesh, flattering the rival king's power to the extent that he and his people are disarmed of their plan to conquer Erech. Gilgamesh has told him, in other words, that Agga is so powerful that he, Gilgamesh, was drawn like a fugitive back to his master—while they, the enemy, are in fact taken aback and even frightened by the courage of Gilgamesh. The result is that war is averted, but King Gilgamesh has made his point to his people that a pre-emptive strike was necessary, and that it was not possible to survive as a civilization while making deals with those who wish their destruction.

Gilgamesh and Agga is listed in the oldest literary catalog known, from c.2000 BCE on tablets found in the ruins of Nippur, the ancient Sumerian religious capital. The poem itself, however, is much older, perhaps a thousand years older. J, writing the early Bible in Jerusalem as many as two millenniums later, is narrating Abraham posing his related question to Yahweh: Why must the innocent suffer in Yahweh's pre-emptive strike on Sodom and Gomorrah?

> So the figures, leaving there, descend toward Sodom. Now Abraham stands aside, facing Yahweh.
>
> Abraham drew close: "Will you wipe away the innocent beside those with contempt? What if there are fifty sincere men inside the city, will you also wipe the place away? Can you not hold back for the fifty innocent within it?"

Abraham does not question the necessity of attacking Sodom, but his concern for justice is what survives. In his questions are the echoes of his reading of the *Epic of Gilgamesh* back in Harran, where it is the individual life that achieves primacy over the drama of the gods.

> *"Six days and six nights*
> *Blows the flood wind, as the south-storm sweeps the land.*
> *When the seventh day arrived . . .*
> *The sea grew quiet, the tempest was still, the flood ceased.*
> *I looked at the weather; stillness had set in,*
> *And all of mankind had returned to clay.*
> *The landscape was as level as a flat roof.*
> *I opened a hatch, and light fell upon my face.*
> *Bowing low, I sat and wept,*
> *Tears running down my face."*

These ancient Sumerian tears of survival resound in Abraham's words ("Consider ten are found there"), who fears that Yahweh may value truth and justice at the expense of innocence and life itself ("I will not pull down on behalf of those ten"). Ziusudra, the Sumerian Noah, has just survived the destruction of the Flood, and Abraham argues against another "wiping away."

> *"Heaven forbid you bring this thing to light, to erase the innocent with the contemptuous—as if sincerity and contempt were the same thing. Can it be—heaven forbid—you, judge of all the earth, will not bring justice?"*
>
> *"If I find fifty innocent inside the city," said Yahweh, "I will hold back from the whole place on their behalf."*

Yahweh so values Abraham that their exchange about justice at first seems to have more to do with their intimacy than anything else. Accepting all of Abraham's arguments about saving the innocent and allowing evil to persist for another day, Yahweh enters into the complexity of his "truth and justice." What is beginning to take place is not a dialogue about whether Sodom is evil or not—this is accepted by both—but about how tolerance works for the father of a new culture in the world. Thus it is a problem not about what constitutes evil, but one brought about by the new theater with Abraham. This is where the investment lies now, in the future.

In the previous scene, the visitors are eating the meal Abraham put before them, when suddenly they ask, "Where is your wife Sarah?" Seemingly out of nowhere, this delicately intrusive question betrays everything, revealing an unforgotten desire by Yahweh to see Sarah with child. It is posed even as Yahweh is on a mission that precedes and supercedes Abraham, Sarah, and his promise. That any child should be desired by Yahweh, and also be preceded by a natural history apart from supernatural wishes, and further, be superceded by a competing concern (Yahweh's desire for "truth and justice" in the world)—that is the paradox at the core of being human, a condition imposed by time and mortality. As we shall see, it is both time and mortality that are held in contempt in Sodom. For Yahweh, the risk of tolerating that evil cancels out his stand not only for justice but for life. The danger of allowing evil to persist carries a tremendous cost: it imperils all of mortal creation and threatens the loss of it.

"Listen please," said Abraham, pressing further, "I have imagined I may speak to Yahweh—I, mere dust and ashes. What if we have less than fifty sincere, five less—for these five will you wipe away an entire city?"

"I will not pull down," said Yahweh, "if I find forty-five there."

Yet he found more to say. "Consider," he pressed on, "you find forty there." And he said, "On behalf of these forty I will not act."

"Please, do not lose patience my lord," he continued, "if I speak further. Consider thirty are found there." And he said, "I will not act if I find thirty there."

"Listen please," said Abraham, pressing further. "I have imagined I may speak to Yahweh—I, made of mere dust and ashes. Consider twenty are found there." "I will not pull down," he said, "on behalf of these twenty."

"Please, do not lose patience my lord," he continued, "if I speak further—for the last time. Consider ten are found there." And he said, "I will not pull down on behalf of those ten."

Now Yahweh, having finished speaking to Abraham, went on. Abraham turned back, toward his place.

By tracing Abraham's drama of these tentative iterations of a final agreement—to spare the cities if even ten innocent people can be found there—J confirms the great risk-taking involved—this danger of allowing evil to persist. Ten innocent individuals existing in Sodom certainly will not erase that evil. But Abraham is articulating what has never before been accessible in any cosmic theater: the decision about evil is no longer a singular drama in the mind of a god. Now, it is one that has been joined in by humankind; that is what makes it more complex and costly.

Abraham is not merely balancing moral weights on Sumerian scales here, but actively engaging with Yahweh in the creation of a realistic theater. Similarly, the vulnerability assumed by Yahweh in turn is staggering, for while ten innocents cannot erase or undo the evil, evil can erase or undo creation. The articulation of truth and justice in this new theater is now outside the mind of gods and will never be marked by decisions that seem clean and consistent. For it is now up to mortal men and women to negotiate and explore the way of God within a cosmic theater, and not to simply struggle with the dictates of a god.

A LEGACY OF ABRAHAM

When last we saw him, Lot parted from Abraham and journeyed toward Sodom. He had chosen to live in the Jordan valley ("Abraham settled in Canaan's land; Lot in the cities of the valley, his tents set beside Sodom"). Now, perhaps a year or two later, we are about to learn how he settled there, and how his daughters took men of Sodom for husbands. It appears Lot was both blind to and unaffected by Sodomite ways. Up until this point, Sodom had remained for him the prosperous city it first seemed to be; he was disinclined to look behind that facade of prosperity and to ask what it was founded upon. Whereas we readers have already understood it is corrupt from Abraham's conversation with Yahweh, and we also know that Abraham has reminded Yahweh of Lot's presence there. With Yahweh represented among his disguised messengers, they will look for Lot in order to warn him of the impending destruction.

But we are still absorbing Abraham's prior interrogation of Yahweh and the meaning behind the mission in Sodom. The issues it raises underlie the scenes to come. Abraham's questioning of the relationship between innocence and evil continues to underscore that scene in our own age, concerned as we are with the values being tested in a confrontation with evil. The issue of what constitutes evil comes often into question, and the easiest answer is that nothing does. There are contending values and points of view involved in any answer, some of which are privileged over others. During the last world war, for example, there were some who called for negotiations with Hitler and Hirohito, not wanting to destroy either Germany or Japan—including innocent children—in a "total victory." Most of us did not have to weigh the risk of leaving Hitler in power versus the firebombing of Dresden or additional Allied casualties. Yet the result may have been a Germany that would not know democracy, as well as a democratic Europe living with an anti-Europe in its midst. Our future may well have been catastrophic, since, as modern physics tells us, matter and anti-matter do not coexist when they meet. This is what lies behind Yahweh's mission to destroy Sodom: the anti-life it represents. Yahweh's concept of evil, as dramatized by J, is as modern as our physics. Who but Yahweh, the creator of life, could know better the threat of anti-life?

When we don't want to consider the cost, we see only Abraham's argument and not his absorption of Yahweh's view. Of course, it's a burden to have to bear two policies, not to let evil stand but searching for innocence, or peace, at the same time. It requires one to have to die by and for killing, instead of the more noble questions about the purpose of human society. In certain periods of their recent history, Israelis make the decision every day, and their right to make it is the legacy of Abraham. On the other hand, the Sodomites, as we shall see, cannot tolerate such complexity of thought in the other; the simplifying mind will prefer to sacrifice the innocent without a thought.

IN SODOM: CONTEMPT

In the evening two angels arrived in Sodom.

Lot was sitting in the courtyard of Sodom's gate. As he saw—then recognized—them, Lot rose, then bent prostrate, face to the ground. "Please hear me, my lords," he said, "and stop at the house of this humble servant. Stay the night, wash your feet, rise refreshed, then go on—the road will wait."

"No," they said, "we will lie by the broad road."

Then he begs them, until they stop, to go with him to his house. Now he makes them a feast, complete with fresh-baked matzah and drink: they ate.

Abraham's encounter with the angels in disguise is repeated by his half-brother and nephew Lot in Sodom. Lot "recognizes" them as strangers—and perhaps as something more, as did Abraham—and makes a sincere show of hospitality. This welcome also stands for something else, a representation of Yahweh's justice, even though both Abraham and Lot were unconscious of the full nature of the encounter. Here too the angels "ate"—although there is no reason to expect a god to eat except in the Sumerian sense. In the Temples of Ur and Harran the cosmic theater of the gods required that they be fed in ritual meals daily, and here the angels are returning the favor by pretending to accept the just hospitality of this family from Ur and Harran. It is another instance of intimate hospitality between host and guest that the Sodomites will violate.

The two representatives of Yahweh, disguised as strangers, are nevertheless on his personal mission. Whatever other divine presences may be presented, they are all disguised aspects of Yahweh, who in each dramatic instance is shown to be more and more the one God being served—and, having come from Ur with Abraham, the last personal god of Sumer.

Yet before they had fallen asleep, the townsfolk—Sodomites—press round the house, from boys to graybeards, the whole population from as far as the outskirts. "Where are the people who visited you tonight?" they call to Lot. "Bring them out for us," they ask. "We want to know their intimate ways."

Here begins the dramatic representation of Sodom's transgression: its people's contempt for justice and tolerance. They have neither respect for the rules of hospitality nor the rights of the individual. The former has been dramatized each time Yahweh enters into history, representing the integrity to all living things in the form of a visitor, a stranger—evil becomes personified by Sodom's disrespect for strangers. More than that, however, contempt for intimacy, a rejection of it, is implicit in Sodom's tolerance of rape. That is, their contempt extends beyond the individual's rights in society to a violation of the rights of the individual at their most intimate core, the private parts of their bodies. A travesty of intimacy is what J most wishes to record; that it takes the form of men handling men is only to portray a greater degree of this human tragedy. Indeed, the concern for seed that Yahweh has already expressed is thrown back at him in the instance of male rape dramatized in Sodom.

There has been a long history of misunderstanding this passage. The word "sodomy" has been misused such that it has come to represent homosexual as well as heterosexual acts. But it is a mistake to suppose that homosexuality was at issue here. It is the invasion of the inner life that is dramatized, the evil that results from rape and its obvious contempt for life and for its origins, for creation. It is an intolerance that is acted out without a cosmic theater in Sodom, without a stage for the inner life and a chance to think or be consumed with something other than oneself. J is careful to depict contempt for tolerance in the form of abuse of the individual. It is rape and not its gender that she confronts here.

Of course, the desire on the part of the Sodomites to rape the angels is the height of irony since we know they are angels, beyond sex, only pretending to be human. But the fate of the Sodomites as well as Lot and his family is not to be construed as supernatural because the Sodomites admit no knowledge of anything beyond themselves. Apparently, they have dismissed any god of their own, which is the antithesis of civilization for a city. It is precisely because the Sodomites see the angels as merely men that their evil is revealed, their contempt for seed and life. No conversation with evil is possible; Yahweh's justice requires that it be cut off.

Now Lot came to the door, closing it behind him. "Brothers, please don't act by showing contempt. Listen, I have two daughters who have not known a man intimately. Let me bring these out for you: handle them as you please. Only leave the visitors untouched, bring no hand to them: I have brought them under my roof's wing."

"Get out of my way," one said. "He comes here to share our shelter and already he hands down the law. Now you will know more than them, a touch of our contempt." They pressed against the man, against Lot, were ready to break down the door.

Again, the drama takes a shocking turn. Lot offers his daughters to be raped—what father would do that? But the honor that Lot seeks to uphold is not only his own, it is the whole justification for society, which is built upon tolerance of the stranger. Now, the complexity of Abraham's questioning of Yahweh is examined in all its grotesque implications. Lot is construed by the Sodomites as conspiring to manipulate them. The Sodomites, however, cannot be manipulated or seduced. For them, there is no complexity to seduction and intimacy, but simply rape.

One would not expect the people of Sodom to respect origins as did the Sumerians, for whom the source of every natural and designed object was commemorated in their cosmic theater. Even the bricks were appreciated: the idea of them, and the making of them, and even their origin in clay, though once removed. Rejecting Yahweh, the Sodomites also do not see the need for disguise; they don't recognize the possibility of disguise around them, as the angels most startlingly represent. In fact, they give every indication of hating the very notion of disguise, for they disparage Lot, threaten him personally, over his disguised attempt to protect the strangers by offering his daughters instead.

THE INNER LIFE

The necessity of disguise is represented for Abraham and for J's audience in Jerusalem by the inner life; in philosophy and religion, it has come to be known as the soul. Our inner lives must always remain in disguise, for otherwise they would be in mortal danger by the disguised motives of others. Language disguises our motives further, allowing us to both reveal and conceal the truth of our thoughts at the same time. The inner life is what Yahweh is on a mission to preserve at Sodom. Evil would wipe out the inner life, and that is why the way Abraham framed his critical question to Yahweh reveals his understanding of the only antidote to evil: "Will you wipe away the innocent beside those with contempt?"

But from within a hand stretched out, brought Lot toward those visitors in the house. Now they shut him in. They blinded them with light: the people at the door, boys as well as graybeards. They would grope for the door handle vainly.

The visitors with Lot said: "Are there others of yours—a son-in-law, sons, daughters—anywhere in the city, to be gathered from this place? The offense has risen to Yahweh's ear. Yahweh sends us—to bring down this loud violence."

Lot hurries to speak to his sons-in-law—those his daughters prepared to marry. "Pack up now, leave this place," Lot said. "Yahweh is prepared to overturn the city." Now watch: the sons-in-law see only—in him—a joke on them.

The angels of Yahweh "blind" the Sodomites, perhaps not intentionally but simply by revealing whom they are. As the Sodomites grope for a door handle instead of a sexual organ, it is clear that the "hand of Yahweh," a figure of speech, brought Lot to safety within and protects him. Blinded by the truth, the numinous light the Sodomites see reveals their moral dimness. It is the same inner confusion that the author J portrayed in the story of the Tower of Babel.

The drama of Sodom's corruption comes clear when the author J shows justice turned into a joke by those with no commitment to Yahweh's truth and tolerance. The men of Sodom who might have been spared by marrying Lot's daughters see their potential father-in-law as someone who's trying to trick them. Sodom has turned truth upside down and the justice of Yahweh's "overturning" is given perfect symmetry by J.

Now the sun began to rise; the angels pressed Lot on. "Get up," they said, "gather your wife, your two daughters that are left—or be gathered into the crush of citizens—in this city's sin." He wavered; the figures grasped his arm, his wife's, the hands of his two daughters—it was Yahweh reaching out to them. They brought him out, stopping only outside the city.

As Lot and his family are brought out, grasped firmly by the angels, it once again becomes Yahweh's literal hand that saves them. The author J has no more tolerance for clichés than Yahweh has for "loud violence." For instance, "the crush" of citizens—in the sense of a crowd—is a cliché here, but it is turned into an ironic foretelling of Sodom's demise, when it will be crushed; and "this city's sin" is another cliché that is destroyed by its sound, echoing the one word, citizen. Language acts as a medium between human and divine in J's narrative, overturning clichés, contempt, false analogies, and twisted justice equally.

So it was: while being brought out, one said to them, "Pity your lot—run, don't look back, don't stop until the end of the valley. Escape to the mountain—or be crushed."

"My lord," Lot said to them, "please not so. Listen to me: if this servant has warmed your heart, evoked your tender pity—you have kept me alive—then see: I cannot survive in the mountains, where the hand of contempt brands me. Look instead at this town within my chosen lot, small enough to overlook. Let me fly there, please, it is small, insignificant—and so will I be there."

"Hear," he answered, "I pity your lot again, will not overturn this city you speak for. Hurry, run—I will do nothing until you're there." And this is how one came to call this city Smallah.

The sun rose above the earth as Lot came to Smallah.

Now Yahweh spilled on Sodom and Gomorrah a volcanic rain: fire from Yahweh, from the sky. These cities he overturned, with the whole valley, all the citizens in the cities and plants in the earth.

Behind him, Lot's wife stopped to look back—and crystallized into a statue of salt.

Abraham arose that morning, hurried to the place he had last faced Yahweh, had stood there with him. Looking out over the upturned faces of Sodom and Gomorrah, over the whole face of the valley, he saw—so it was—a black incense over the earth climbing like smoke from a kiln.

If we apply the same lens to the contempt for life of suicide bombers today, we may find that they do indeed share a cosmic theater of belief in an afterlife. It is a distorted belief, however, with no room for knowing and not knowing—for knowing that the god-statues were not gods or that Yahweh did not eat. Instead, the suicide killing phenomenon is a fixation upon one way of seeing the world, in which no other can be tolerated. If there is no other way of seeing, no hidden motives to the actions of others and no motives hidden from oneself, then one is truly locked in a hell of contempt. Their cosmic theater, when it exists, is bereft of acting, of masks and disguises, of the unknown without and within. There is no chance for something new to be created. Desire becomes a dead end—and worse, the dead ends accumulate until there is nothing but a pile of ash or waste.

And for those who might think there is time to look back at evil, as Lot's wife does, desire deadens. Here the idea of "too late" takes hold in the new theater of Abraham's God. As the episode ends, we encounter Abraham again, a witness to all that has taken place. Lot, who did not look, remains the unenlightened survivor.

CHAPTER 17

The Survivors

Lot and his daughters have been spared. For P writing two hundred years after J, it is important to emphasize that Lot was Abraham's closest relative and that he survived because of Yahweh's "watchfulness" of Abraham—but not because he was one of "ten sincere men." P is not particularly interested in the deeper reasons. So, writing in the seventh century BCE at the court of King Josiah in Jerusalem, P adds the following sentence to J's biblical narrative:

> *And so it was that, when God destroyed the cities of the Plain and overthrew the cities in the middle of which Lot lived, God was watchful of Abraham by removing Lot from the midst of the upheaval.*

By allowing Lot and his children to survive, P tell us, Yahweh indicates to Abraham that those who came with him to Canaan, and who were of Sumerian origin, were as dear to him as they were to Abraham. It is somewhat ironic that P himself has no curiosity about Abraham's human history, nor in Sumerian culture or language. Instead, he was primarily intent upon showing a fondness toward Abraham by Yahweh; he added his own commentary to J's in order to make of Yahweh a more sentimental God.

For P, it wasn't on account of a new cosmic theater that Yahweh involved himself with Lot's fate, but for Abraham's sake alone—a subtle but essential point. Perhaps this is the beginning of a phase in Jewish tradition that no longer knows its historical origins: not knowing the Sumerian origin of attachment between Abraham and Lot, and not knowing of the Sumerian background to the covenant.

Reading the J narrative just two hundred years after it was written, even as he understood that Abraham and Lot came from Ur and Harran, P knew little of the history and culture those cities represented. By the seventh century BCE, those cities had declined and the Chaldean empire, which appeared long after Abraham had died (and in which J located the city of Ur—"Ur of the Chaldees"—to mark the place for her contemporaries), was now becoming ancient history itself. For P, the Hebraic culture was ancient also; ancient enough that it was forgotten how it had emerged from an older one. Already, there is no "older one," and a crucial change has taken place: P replaces the cosmic theater that became the theater of Abraham's God with a tradition of the text that has come down to him. Tradition is often a confusion of legend and history, natural and supernatural; here it displaces the cosmic theater of the historical text with a new drama, a fabrication of "oral history." Indeed, the biblical narrative that came down to P in the 720s BCE was not even J's alone—it had already been combined with that of another author, E, writing in the preceding century.

So, because he is at a loss to know how the Jews came to be caught up in the Hebraic cosmic drama, P can only interpret Yahweh's involvement as an *affection* for Abraham. (Perhaps the audience of priests for whom P wrote thought of themselves as having religious insights into Yahweh's affections and sentiments.) At the same time, P is also absolving Yahweh of direct involvement in the story that is about to be described to us in J's original narrative: the family incest of Lot and his daughters. Since God is not saving Lot for any particular purpose other than his affection for Abraham, P is freed of the necessity to rationalize such regressive behavior.

If we go back to the time of J's narrative, we find that the educated audience at Solomon's and Rehoboam's courts appreciated a greater psychological complexity to this episode and were aware of the echoes of Sumerian lament that J combined with local legend:

> *Behind him, Lot's wife stopped to look back—and crystallized into a statue of salt.*

Later commentators have pointed out the resemblance to human statues that the salt formations beside the Dead Sea often acquire. The Dead Sea, a short trip from Jerusalem, was no doubt a part of the real experience of J's audience. They knew the attribution of legend to the salt shapes was fanciful, but even more compelling was the echo of classic Sumerian laments:

> *O Dignified, turn around and look at your city!*
> *O Master of the Fulfilled Speech, turn around and look at your city!*
> *Enlil, Father of the Nation, turn around and look at your city!*
> *Shepherd of the Black-headed, turn around and look at your city!*
> *O One Who Feigns Sleep, turn around and look at your city!*
> *Lord of Heaven and Earth, turn around and look at your city!*

Many of the fond names for the High God Enlil are invoked here, praying that he pay heed to the destruction of a great Sumerian city (in this case, Nippur). This refrain—"turn around and look at your city!"—would have been known to J and her audience, so that the entreaty to Lot's wife *not* to turn around and look back at her city of Sodom would have held tremendous tragic irony.

FEAR OF EXTINCTION

In the recent video testimonies of Holocaust survivors, each survivor tells his or her story simply as what happens, unadorned, as if engraved in memory by an otherworldly art. By refraining from telling us how they *felt* about what was happening, these contemporary survivors express much more than if they had tried to describe their emotions. They help us to understand that it was *unspeakable.* And thus, the unspeakable resonates within us. In much the same way, J does not tell us what Abraham felt about the destruction he had just witnessed. A lesser writer might have attempted this, but not J. Her intelligence is apparent as the drama and scenes she sets before us require our own responses. Here too the unspeakable resonates within us when we watch Abraham return "to the place he had last faced Yahweh" and had spoken with him.

> *Abraham arose that morning, hurried to the place he had last faced Yahweh, had stood there with him. Looking out over the upturned faces of Sodom and Gomorrah, over the whole face of the valley, he saw—so it was—a black incense over the earth climbing like smoke from a kiln.*

But what of Lot and his family? We have only this minute glimpsed them fleeing Sodom, guided by the angels in human disguise, and now J elaborates this survival into a story of horrible trauma, for the city in which they lived has been utterly demolished. More than Abraham, how might *they* feel? A Sumerian lament for a city destroyed records it this way:

> *A wailing, oh, a wailing, oh, could he only hold back the lament!*
> *Over the shack, this young man is shedding tears,*
> *A dirge over the storehouse, this girl is mourning,*
> *This young man is shaking in tears,*
> *This girl is shaking in tears.*

But that is *not* how we see Lot's family, however true this Sumerian lament would have been to their trauma. The destruction of Sodom and Gomorrah was a lesson in the firm response to evil. In psychological terms, we might describe this evil as a psychotic break that can only be disarmed with the shock of confrontation. As with Abraham, we are not told how they feel, however we do watch the psychological effect of Sodom's destruction on Lot and his daughters, the terrible twisting of their powers of human reason.

> *But Lot went out from Smallah, toward the mountains, his two daughters with him—he grew afraid to stay in Smallah, settled in a cave alone with his daughters.*

From the big city of Sodom to this tiny town, so *small* and inconspicuous that no force of heaven or nature would bother with it—so Lot had reasoned—yet even there he is afraid. Back to a cave then, he decides, regressing in his fears to the prehistoric origins of civilization.

Lot's daughters are equally traumatized; their thinking is attenuated, so that they imagine what they have just witnessed was the end of civilization. The daughters have lost their husbands in Sodom after all and witnessed even their mother being destroyed, so it is understandable that their fear is manifested as a fear of extinction.

> *"Father is getting old," the firstborn said to the youngest. "There are no men left on earth to enter us—to follow the way of the earth."*

They fear extinction not only of their family line but of the entire human species: "there are no men left on earth. . . to follow the way of the earth." Like Sarah, these are clearly J's brand of down-to-earth women; they are not impressed by angels or supernatural events. It is the loss of the *natural* world and its processes that terrifies them. Intercourse with their father, they reason, is the only recourse for human survival, and therefore no blame attaches to them. Unlike the people of Sodom, they do not rape their father—for they are not interested in pleasure but in procreation.

This is not simply a useful distinction: J demonstrates here what nuances of morality and logic Yahweh is ready to accommodate, and how much Yahweh's insight engages human reason and the inner life. We also recall how difficult the precise understanding of sexuality is to Yahweh, how nervous he can be over the issue of seed. Thus we can appreciate the ambivalence with which the J writer confronts us, as we feel the characters' dread—and also the absurd predicament—in the same moment.

"We'll pour drink for our father; with wine we will lie with him—life will follow from our father's seed."

On that night their wine poured out for their father. The eldest now comes, lies with her father; he recalls no sense of her lying there, nor when she rises.

Now listen: "I lay last night with my father," said the eldest to the youngest. "Follow me. We will have him drunk with wine tonight again, so you may have from him. At his side, we will give life to our father's seed."

The wine flows on this night also, for their father. The youngest rises, to lie with him; he senses nothing of having her, nor her rising.

Employing subterfuge, the women in effect disguise themselves as their father's wet dream. Psychologically, they act upon the childhood illusion that the children complete the parent, and at the same time they use the rationality of an adult about the need to save the species—a reasoning that, in evolutionary terms, tells us that no one is complete in himself/herself. This dual understanding also approximates the Sumerian cosmic theater, in which the individual is aware of a suspension of disbelief in living with the god-statues. Lot's daughters are, after all, the children of Ur and of a Sumerian education.

So Lot's two daughters became pregnant by their father. The eldest gave birth to a son named Moab—"from father"—the father of the Moabites we see today. A son was born as well to the youngest, whom she called Ben Ami—"son of my kin"—the father down through today's sons of Ammon.

Like Sarah, these women have been impregnated by an "old man," and like Sarah who names Isaac, they also name their sons—except that these younger Sumerian women lie outside the covenant and the cosmic theater of Abraham's God. So the names Lot's daughters apply are blind to their own incest: Moab literally means "from father," though not in the sexual sense. By providing her audience with the sexual meaning of their neighboring kingdom's name, J is defining the borders of the theater of Abraham's God while hinting at what blindness may lie outside it. Yet the blindness to Israel's history in these neighboring regions is not an impious one but rather acceptable—they are after all one's distant relatives.

In contrast, Abraham is a different kind of survivor than Lot, who is marked by this Canaanite blindness. Lot wants to run away from the catastrophe, but Abraham is shown to be a survivor in the form of historical witness: he was the necessary witness to Yahweh's reaction to evil. The "smoke from a kiln" that Abraham sees reminds us of the smoke at the earlier covenant-making scene between Abraham and Yahweh ("a smoking kiln and its blazing torch pass between the parted bodies"). It also prefigures the later covenant-making scene at Mt. Sinai before the assembly of Israelite slaves recently freed from Egypt: "Yahweh had come down in fire, the smoke climbing skyward like smoke from a kiln."

REPRESSING RAPE

Returning to Abraham and his travels in the next paragraph, we plunge into another scene of blindness and the threat of evil: "Abimelech king of Gerar had Sarah brought to him." Sarah is about to be raped—in the name of a gift to a local king—and it will be as blindly excused as was Lot's incest with his daughters. This time, the rape is risked in the guise of saving Abraham's life rather than the angels in Sodom (and since they were standing in for Yahweh, the ironic dread was posed of the rape of deity itself).

> *Abraham journeyed from there to the region of the Negev and settled between Kadesh and Shur. While he was sojourning in Gerar, Abraham said of Sarah his wife, "She is my sister." So Abimelech king of Gerar had Sarah brought to him.*

We have already heard a different version of this story earlier in Genesis, when Abraham and Sarah were in Egypt and it was the Pharoah who took Sarah for his own. Sarah saved her husband Abraham then by also claiming to be his sister. The implication, once again, is that Abraham would be murdered by this local king if he knew that Sarah was his wife. Yet something quite different and unfamiliar happens now. God seems to intervene and control the scene, as he had not done with Lot and his daughters, and as he had also not done with Abraham and Sarah and the Egyptian Pharoah.

"She is my sister," he said
of Sarah his wife.
When Abimelech, king of Gerar, heard

he took her. And God came too
that night in a dream
saying "Death is the price
for taking a man's wife."

Abimelech had not touched her
when he asked, "My Lord, will you kill
a man who is innocent?
I heard "She is my sister"
from him. And from her, "He
is my brother.

"My heart was innocent
my hands clean
when this happened."

And God answered in the dream
"Because I knew it was innocently done
I held you back from touching her
from committing contempt.

"Now return the wife to the man
and live

for he is a man who speaks up:
he can plead your cause.

"Or else die, if you hold on to her.
You and all who are attached to you."

It would seem that Yahweh will entertain an urgent conversation with an ordinary Canaanite king. And it is every bit as intimate as those between Abraham and Yahweh, breaking the spell of Abraham's uniqueness. Although a stranger, Abimelech questions Yahweh in words similar to those of Abraham's plea on the way to Sodom yet now rendering it hollow: "Oh Lord, will you slay people even though innocent?" If a Canaanite king can question Yahweh's morality, what was the significance of Abraham's interrogation? Our bearings would be really lost were it not for one simple addition that changes everything: "God came to Abimelech in a dream by night." Yahweh had not come to Abraham in dreams but in a verisimilitude of reality. Man and God had appeared together on the cosmic stage of the real landscape.

Now if we are not prepared for this sudden transformation, how would J's audience in ancient Jerusalem have reacted? Were they conversant with dreams in a way that would have rendered this scene probable, even nonchalant? And what do they make of Yahweh threatening this Abimelech with direct intervention and supernatural retribution? It is a form of personal intervention totally out of character for the one who made the covenant with Abraham .

"You are to die. . . . I kept you from sinning against me. That was why I did not let you touch her. . . . If you fail to restore her, know that you shall die, you and all that are yours."

Yahweh had been so careful *not* to intervene supernaturally with Abraham and Sarah that they did not even believe he could have an influence on their childbearing. Yet here he is explaining how he supernaturally orchestrates reality—keeping people from sinning, keeping people from touching one another—in short, writing the whole drama of human history as if by himself.

We are made to listen to Yahweh threatening to kill a man and his entire family, a man and king who is not evil in any way that Yahweh has put forward, and who is not at all challenging Yahweh's way of truth and justice. In fact, Yahweh's name has not been mentioned but rather a pseudonym for God that was common in polytheistic Canaan, "Elohim," and another for Lord, "Adonai." Furthermore, we are barely in the presence of Abraham himself, for Abraham the survivor has taken on a diminished meaning here: his survival is taken out of his own hands by a God who seems to take over the stage. This Elohim almost inhabits the place of a mythic hero, for *he* is the one to rescue Abraham—not Sarah, as in J's earlier history. God now names Abraham his "prophet," and although it was a common calling in polytheistic Canaan we have not heard the term *prophet* before nor has it been associated with a very human and civilized Abraham, a man from Ur and not a religious seer or diviner.

Possibly it is not J at all, but a different biblical author of another time and place who has written this episode. For if J were translating an alternative story of wife and sister, based on an alternative Hebraic source in historical Canaan, then it would be up to her to re-tell and rephrase the source in a way that embodies the Hebraic sensibility of her audience. Her readers and listeners would have wanted to relive the past through their own new sensibility; they had little faith in the supernatural passing down of words. So how could it be that J would suddenly ignore the Hebraic cosmic stage of words, in which the covenant allowed human access to God, and present Yahweh as accessible to *anyone* in dreams? And especially, in dreams where he reveals himself as the stage-manager of reality? Surely the Jerusalem audience would have balked—exactly as we would today, if supernatural tales were inserted into our historical record, as represented, say, by the *New York Times.*

In the theater of Abraham's God, as it was in the cosmic theater of Sumer, neither the gods nor the stage changed character. Instead, what happened was that the stage developed and advanced over time. Later audiences require new translations and interpretations in the idiom of their day. And so we should not be surprised that the uncharacteristic scene we have just confronted, in which Yahweh takes over the stage of human life ("that is why *I did not let you* touch her"), comes from another time—a later time, and written for another audience by a different author.

Now this new author (who is identified more fully as E, the Elohist, in the chapters ahead) would have found J's theater too difficult to accept, especially if his audience was not as educated as those at the Jerusalem court had been. J's Yahweh, along with angels in human disguise, would have startled an audience who did not grasp the cosmic theater of it—the theater of Abraham's God. Less sophisticated, the new audience needed a simpler representation of reality, so the idea that God spoke in dreams would have seemed more accessible to them.

It would also have seemed more real that God's omnipotence take center stage and that Abraham's supernatural relationship with him acquire a supernatural imprimatur as prophet. After all, prophets and visionary dreams and gods with humanlike sentiments—favoring an Abraham like a son—were far more common and historical in Canaan than the negotiation of a covenant between Abraham and Yahweh.

In addition, it would have been hard for this new audience to accept the face-to-face relationship between Yahweh and Abraham. It was already an old Canaanite concept that ordinary humans could not survive a face-to-face confrontation with God. And so it would seem far more realistic to imagine that Abraham was a prophet—and that God was in full control. But imagine the loss if a different telling like this one had replaced J's narrative altogether. Abraham's survival would no longer seem integrated with his own initiative and his own historical circumstances. We might have lost the historical Abraham had not J's narrative been retained as the foundation of a tradition that includes other writers at different times.

Thus we must face the fact that we are now in the presence of a different author and audience, and in another time and place than Solomonic Jerusalem (it is also the case that the ancient literary style has changed). "Abraham then prayed to God, and God healed Abimelech and his wife and his slave girls." For the first time, after all, Abraham is said to have "prayed to God," and God, for the first time, is shown to have responded to a direct prayer—as if in a dream.

Abimelech summoned his servants next morning
retelling the conversation in the night
until the men were overcome with fear.

Abraham was called and heard this plea:
"Why did you do this to us?
How did I move you
to settle upon me
and my kingdom
this charge of contempt?
How have I handled you
that you would touch me with contempt?

"What did you foresee
happening
to cause this thing?"

"I said to myself," Abraham began,
"'There is no fear of God here;
they'll kill me
to have my wife.'

"But she is also my sister
my father's daughter
yet not my mother's
and she became my wife.

"When heaven ordained I wander
far from my father's house
I said, 'Be my loyal wife
in whatever strange place we settle;
tell them this about me:
"He is my brother."'"

Abimelech took sheep and oxen
male and female servants
gave them to Abraham
and restored Sarah to him.

"Here, my land is yours to settle on"
Abimelech said to Abraham
"anyplace your eye prefers."

To Sarah he said
"Here, a thousand pieces of silver
for your brother
enough to cover the eyes
of everyone attached to you
to what has happened,
proof of innocence."

Abraham pleaded his cause to God
and Abimelech was restored
along with his wife
and his female servants:
children could now be born.

For God had closed the womb of everyone
attached to Abimelech
as in a protective dream—
for Sarah, wife of Abraham.

This new author, E, comes from, and writes for, a different sensibility than J. Yet both authors remain Hebraic in their understanding of why the wife's disguise is necessary in this new version of the story. The necessity of passing as a sister underlines the knowledge that Abraham and Sarah are in a precarious situation: they are Canaanite immigrants or Sumerian exiles and in that sense remain strangers.

How do you live among people that might abduct or kill strangers? For the laws of hospitality might have protected Abraham and Sarah if they reciprocated and adopted their host's customs, but if you want to remain *apart,* then a lie becomes possible and perhaps necessary. This passage assumes that Abraham understood the lie—or disguise—can be necessary when it opposes *unreal* things, fantasies—such as Abimelech's fantasy of having Abraham's wife. There is no answer to such fantasies of power except survival: the lie is not a lie, in this case, but a disguise that disarms Abimelech's fantasy. (The same holds true in modern terms: it would take a similar act of survival to disarm the Nazi fantasy of hate behind the monstrous fiction of anti-Semitism. For Abraham and Sarah to survive in our own era of Auschwitz, they might have to disguise themselves as Christians.)

Further, we find out that this counter-fiction of Sarah as sister in fact comes from Ur: "And besides, she is in truth my sister, my father's daughter though not my mother's; and she became my wife." In other words, we have a Sarah who passes as a Sumerian by citing the authority of an older law. The new author and his audience may not have understood the ancient Mesopotamian customs in Ur and Harran, but they were there in J's older Hebrew text. So our new author must insure that the counter-fiction of Sarah's disguise comes from the old world in which Abraham and Sarah originated, and he does this by referring to the wife-sister complication of contract-making in historical Harran.

We have seen, then, the survival of Sumerian customs as well as the survival of actual Sumerians, Lot and his daughters. And yet knowledge of this crucial origin in the world's oldest civilization has already grown hazy by the time of E. (It would be as if Columbus had been forgotten and history referred back to "wanderers" of the sea as the founders of America. In fact, long after E, a Hebrew author depicted Abraham erroneously as "a wandering Aramean.") But since the Bible preserved *both* J and E, it is up to us as readers to discern the process of history at work on the Hebraic culture of Israel.

CHAPTER 18

The Influence of the Writing Prophets

The passages in Abraham's life we are about to encounter were written by E, the biblical author best known for substituting the name Elohim for Yahweh—and we shall soon see why. When we reach the last of these short passages, we will need to comprehend how E came to write the climax of Abraham's life story, the sacrifice of Isaac (the Akedah, as it is known in Hebrew). This episode is starkly different from J: there is little dialogue, no questions, no Sarah, and no complexity of Yahweh. Instead, a silent cinema unfolds, with exaggerated stiffness and sparse sayings that read like written inter-titles. The style of narrative is different too, and it reflects the requirements of a distinct audience. But before we come face to face with this new audience, we need to understand the effects of a new religious current that was taking the words of J and casting them into ethical terms. This newly written literature was directed to a wide audience, considerably beyond the educated court. In cities throughout Israel, new prophets were being read as well as listened to.

Barely a century after the death of J in Jerusalem (now the capital of Judah), the great Hebrew Prophets began writing in the eighth century BCE. One of these was Amos, who came to the court of the northern Kingdom of Israel and told the king that everything must change. This is not what the king and his court, including the religious priests, wanted to hear. They were having a hard enough time just surviving in their

Middle Eastern neighborhood, jockeying among the superpowers of the day, Egypt and Assyria, not to mention political conflicts with Judah. Since the death of King Rehoboam in Judah, the northern Kingdom, now known as Israel, was the strongest of the two Jewish kingdoms but also the most exposed, and in need of wily defensive strategies.

Amos told the royal court in Samaria, Israel's newly constructed capital city, that a new reality was to be acted upon—a reality apart from the status quo of international treaties and politics. No human defense could be permanent, said Amos, and the threat of extinction was always to be lived with. Only the covenant between Abraham and Yahweh was a guiding light, and yet it was being forgotten by Israel's leaders, relegated to the province of official religion, to the priesthood. Only the covenant could bring to mind the cosmic struggle for Yahweh's truth and justice, how it was established between Abraham and Yahweh, and how—as surely as the *Lamentations of Ur* recalled the city of Ur's destruction—Israel must live up to it.

By stressing how the covenant applied to daily life, Amos and the other Hebrew prophets brought to the cosmic stage an awareness of how to live with a more complicated understanding of civilization; of how to keep both history and the present situation in mind at the same time, even when they are in conflict. Unintimidated by the royal court, Amos pointed out their obvious preference for wish fulfillment, for fantasy over this complicated reality. They expected to blend in with the ways of those who surrounded them and they wished to be accepted, but all the while they were forgetting they were surrounded by resentment. When asked—almost accused—if he was a prophet by the court, Amos said, "No, I am a cattle breeder and a tender of sycamore figs." In other words, his role in the cosmic theater was rooted in the land, as Abraham had shown. The theater of Abraham's God would keep them grounded, Amos reminded the court—just as the land supported his own firm vision.

So the poetry of Amos in the Bible drips with irony, as it shows northern Israel's leaders out of touch with the land, the cosmic stage, and how they lay mindlessly "on ivory couches" imported from the Phoenicians.

Ah, you who are at ease in Zion
And confident on the hill of Samaria,
You notables of the leading nation
On whom the House of Israel pin their hopes:
Cross over to Calneh and see,
Go from there to Great Hamath,
And go down to Gath of the Philistines:
Are you better than those kingdoms,
Or is their territory larger than yours?
Yet you ward off the thought of a day of woe
And convene a session of lawlessness.
They lie on ivory beds,
Lolling on their couches,
Feasting on lambs from the flock
And on calves from the stalls.
They hum snatches of song
To the tune of the lute—
They account themselves musicians like David.

If your neighbors become upset when you fail to pay homage to their common gods, you'll have to *deal* with that, said Amos. It is what first faced Abraham: How to inherit and pass down the covenant while living among strangers. Ritual and sacrifice is not a sufficient answer, says Yahweh through Amos:

I will pay no heed
To your gifts of fatlings.
Spare me the sound of your hymns
And let me not hear the music of your lutes.
But let justice well up like water.

Tethered to Abraham's Sumerian inheritance of civilization, Amos stands forth as if a speaking statue in the theater of Abraham's God. The justice he invokes is Yahweh's, on the cosmic stage of the land—where it can "well up like water." The couches of ivory failed to serve this history.

Being at home in the land is a problem continually posed in Israel and Judah. The covenant is no guarantee but instead a promise of living into the future as a natural being with origins that must be continually exposed and renewed. Without a restoration of original knowledge about Abraham's history and that of his descendants—as the Hebrew prophets were restoring and interpreting it—the covenant loses its dramatic meaning and the land loses its place as a sacred stage.

This is what happens when Hebraic history as J had written it becomes lost in legend, Amos insists. The court in Samaria to whom Amos is speaking had forgotten Abraham and Isaac as historical figures and had relegated them to religious lore; at the same time, they had been acting as if their fear of being different was responsible for their neighbors' resentment of them. The centrality of the negotiated covenant in Abraham's cosmic theater required constant re-negotiation, in order for Israel to be reminded of their strangeness and their need to survive in a hostile world.

SURVIVAL AND INHERITANCE

Another prophet writing in the eighth century BCE was the first of three authors writing in the name of Isaiah. While Amos was written in Samaria, the first Isaiah was in Jerusalem, in Judah, perhaps a decade or two later, and both of them are aware of the dire geopolitical situation. Yet Israel and Judah had now been in existence for two centuries, and it was harder for most of the people to imagine their own extinction.

Isaiah dramatized his existential fear by putting the writer, namely himself, at center stage. He became an actor embodying the principal anxiety of the covenant: survival and inheritance. His words to the royal court of his day were intended to educate it about the covenant, as if he was a latter-day Abraham. Isaiah imagines the word of Yahweh just as the J writer had, but now it is a critique of the international transactions in which Judah and Israel found themselves.

Abraham and Isaac and their struggles against cultural extinction among other cultures in the land—all of this history had grown hazy to the Jews in this period. Isaiah satirizes this forgetting of history, speaking as himself but in the process creating vivid, shocking allegory. It is as if Yahweh was himself reading in a history book in order to justify Isaiah's right to speak in Yahweh's name. It is the very "history book" that Israel let "drop from sight." Isaiah was now taking the theater of Abraham's God to new heights.

Roll this testimony up
in a scroll   this revelation
hidden in the inner library

of hearts still open
to the word
mind open to the ear

I am turning in   to wait for him
to look up from his reading
in the book

his face is hidden in
as if his people had become
a history book

a book ignorantly dropped
from sight
by Israel

like a mirror   absently swept away
a shattering insult
but the pages the pieces I will keep

before him
and I will look for him there
when he turns again to face us. . .

Listen to me because I
like my children
are signs of his reality

children of Israel
as it was and will be
in touch with his presence   in Zion

knowing where we come from
where we're going
where we are

on the map   the signs
our lines pass through
in the vehicle of his word. . .

[from *A Poet's Bible*]

ISAAC'S NEW REALITY

The original knowledge "of where we are / on the map" is there in the life of Abraham. The history of Hebraic culture, beginning with Abraham, held out the vision of a future based on truth and justice, but also on the education of Isaac. It was Isaac's inheritance that founded Hebraic culture and the expansion of the Sumerian temple stage into a written theater.

The vision first becomes real history with the birth of Isaac. The problems of how to inherit and how to educate—how to build a culture—are there in J's narrative. Yahweh acts not in a dream but in a theatrical play on words, such as "conceive." The play is joyous, touching upon both mental and physical conception, as it makes fun of Abraham in his "ripe old age" by echoing the earlier words of Sarah: "My lord is also shriveled."

Now Yahweh conceived for Sarah what he had said.

Sarah became pregnant and, the time ripe, gave birth: a son appearing from Sarah, for Abraham in his ripe old age.

"Now who would conceive of Abraham having children at Sarah's breast? But I gave birth to a son—not to wisdom—for his old age."

Sarah can both express amusement at the covenant and signify its momentousness: "a son" (is better than wisdom). The survival of Isaac will be the next step, and it will be echoed back by Isaiah a century later in this question: How will the Jewish tradition survive if it is vulnerable to extinction? How can the covenant be trusted? The answer for Isaac's generation, and later for Isaiah's, lay in education and its examination of history.

For Abraham the urgency would be stark, for he cannot provide Isaac with the same complex education he received in Ur. Isaac is living as a stranger among the Philistines. The theater of Abraham's God becomes the text of how Abraham and his family must live by finding their own way to settle into the land. Thus Isaac must be educated in disguise, as it were. And in order that the Philistines assume that he is Canaanite, Isaac must receive a private education in several cultures. He will have to move among Philistines, Canaanites, and Mesopotamian immigrants while at the same time receiving his father's history: how the daily Sumerian cosmic theater of personal and public gods had become transformed into the new theater of Abraham's God. Dreams will play their part as well in Isaac's unique schooling in his parental home.

This is the new reality that is inferred. Indeed, it cannot be avoided, given J's convincing depiction of Abraham and Sarah in the land of Canaan. But the exhilaration of the journey and the covenant are past. We are no longer in J's explosive theater, with Abraham and Yahweh interacting, but rather in the more intractable, down-to-earth reality of daily life. How to survive in the land and to put the covenant into action is the immediate problem. No prescription is provided; it is entirely up to Abraham and Sarah and their background of Sumerian wisdom. It will all have to be focused upon Isaac's instruction.

But later readers wanted more details. At a vantage much later in time, P added to J's telling his own didactic theater of supernatural verisimilitude, punctuating the birth of Isaac with the *exact* date, time, and ritual. The audience of priests at King Josiah's court in 620 BCE Jerusalem wanted a cosmic theater translated into law—and with the text codified from the supernatural point of view, namely God's viewpoint. History had shown the human commitment to the covenant could waver (and P had seen the desperate criticism of the prophets come to fruition in the destruction of the northern Kingdom of Israel). So P was dedicated to making everything clear and definitive, even if it meant creatively deducing the historical facts. He did this in editorial additions to the combined narrative of J and E that had come down to him.

And when his son Isaac was eight days old, Abraham circumcised him, as God had commanded him. Now Abraham was a hundred years old when his son Isaac was born to him.

THE STORY OF E

The details of how Isaac will inherit the covenant are lost to us, perhaps because J's narrative was replaced in part by E (or by a later redactor, the one who combined the narratives of J and E into a single text). So, the ensuing stories of Abraham's life are written by E and instead of J's play on words ("I gave birth to a son—not to wisdom") we will find a straight-faced description of literal laughter:

Sarah said, "God has brought me laughter; everyone who hears will laugh with me."

While putting down roots was crucial for Abraham, the E writer lived in a time when the threat of uprooting was closer. In 725 BCE, at the royal court of King Jeroboam II in Samaria, capital of Israel, E picked up his narrative with Abraham and Sarah in the vicinity of Beersheba. They have survived their encounter with the Philistine king of Gerar, Abimelech, and the history still to be told describes their acceptance into the local landscape.

"After, Abraham resided in the land of the Philistines a long time."

E does not imagine ancient Canaan in the same way as J; he sees it as the land of the Philistines, a people contemporaneous with the Israelite kingdom at its beginnings, with Kings Saul, David, and Solomon. The Philistines had arrived in Canaan a century or two before the Israelites began to form their kingdom, yet the Philistines brought with them the civilization of Mycenaean Greece. How would Abraham have felt among these people, coming himself from a classical Sumerian education? E may never have imagined this clash because, in his own time, it was the Phoenicians who were dominant on the coast, successors to the Philistines, and they were in alliance with Israel. Not many years had passed since the Phoenician princess Jezebel married the Israelite king in Samaria and exercised a strong influence as queen in northern Israel.

But the fact that would have shaped Isaac's life (and upon which J and E would have agreed, as we shall see in the next chapter) was the need for disguise (as a non-assimilating immigrant) in order to insure survival. In addition to Isaac's private education—within his family rather than with Canaanites—there was the inner need for a *place of telling*. His father's life could not be recorded against the background of Ur, which Abraham had left, or the background of Canaan, whose culture he resisted. Instead, it was the land itself—the landscape—that was intimately tied to the telling and the scenes of covenantal history. The passing on of this history was the result of each later generation's nurturing of the text. That's clearly all there was. There were no statues or sacred places to embellish. There was no new ritual (male circumcision was already an ancient custom). Until the life of Moses, five centuries after Abraham, there are no commandments.

Meanwhile, E has God speak to Abraham without even setting the scene: Is God present? Is he in disguise? Is he speaking in a dream? E does not bother to tell us because he is absorbed in reducing J's theater of Abraham's God to what can only be described as a daydream. What matters is that Abraham lives in the land and dreams. He hardly does anything at all. The highlight of his activity is in a passage about Isaac and Ishmael that doesn't concern itself with explaining Abraham's motives, though it shows us his suffering ("this was wrenching"); instead of Abraham's thought, it is God who tells him what to think:

The child grew
was weaned
And on that day a great feast
was made by Abraham
but Sarah saw the son of Hagar the Egyptian
the one carried by her for Abraham
laughing with her own son, Isaac
and she turned in protest to her husband

"Send away that servant and her son.
No son of hers can divide with Isaac
his inheritance." In Abraham's eyes
this was wrenching:
It was his son too.

Then God in the night said this:
"Do not be torn between boy and servant;
listen to Sarah's voice;
it is Isaac that continues your name.
But the servant's son too
will father a great nation
being your child."

There is an effort to write dramatically by E and to live up to J's literary authority. Unfortunately, the wordplay is lame: Hagar "walked away, far as an arrow flies"—and shortly, Ishmael will grow up to be "skilled with arrow and bow." The device of an angel calling to Hagar is also awkward, as no context is given for a distinction between God's voice and the angel's. Instead of experiencing either's presence, we are given only rhetorical expressions: God "*opened* her eyes" or God "*was with* the boy." Yet E has a talent for the telling detail. When Hagar wanders in the desert "until the skin [of water] was dry," the pathos in the previous sentence—of Abraham "fixing a skin of water/ to her back"—is heightened.

Next morning, Abraham
got together bread and water
for Hagar, fixing a skin of water
to her back, sending her and the child away.
She wandered in the desert near Beer-sheva
Until the skin was dry, then sheltered
The child beneath a bush.

She walked away, far as an arrow flies
and sat opposite, weeping, saying to herself
"Let me not hear the child die"
and closed her eyes

When God heard Ishmael's wail
his angel called to Hagar from heaven:
"What pains you, Hagar?
There is nothing to fear. God has heard
the child's cry, clear as day.
Arise, take the boy in your arms
soothe him, he will become
a great nation."
Then God opened her eyes:

A well of water was visible
before her. She walked over
filled the skin with water
let the boy drink.

God was with the boy
as he grew up
making the desert his home.
It was in Paran and he grew
skilled with arrow and bow.
It was his mother who got a wife
for him, from the land
of Egypt.

TREE AND WATER

As if E is aware of his own shortcomings as a literary genius compared with J, his characters of God, Abraham—and in the following scene, a Philistine named Phicol—are unfinished and tend to appear stiff. And E's accounts of Abraham's dealing as a stranger with the cultures of Canaan conform to the pattern already set by J, in which contractual negotiations are the basis for Abraham's interactions. While these negotiations remain connected to the drama of the covenant in E's narrative, they now appear severed from a particular historical awareness.

At that time Abimelech and Phicol, chief of his troops, said to Abraham, "God is with you in everything that you do. Therefore swear to me here by God that you will not deal falsely with me or with my kith and kin, but will deal with me and with the land in which you have sojourned as loyally as I have dealt with you." And Abraham said, "I swear it."

Then Abraham reproached Abimelech for the well of water, which the servants of Abimelech had seized. But Abimelech said, "I do not know who did this; you did not tell me, nor have I heard of it until today." Abraham took sheep and oxen and gave them to Abimelech, and the two of them made a pact.

Abraham then set seven ewes of the flock by themselves, and Abimelech said to Abraham, "What mean these seven ewes which you have set apart?" He replied, "You are to accept these seven ewes from me as proof that I dug this well." Hence that place was called Beersheba, for there the two of them swore an oath.

A further detachment in the text raises the question—when Abimelech and Phicol say to Abraham, "God is with you in everything that you do"—to which *God* are they referring? The generic term God might apply to the high Canaanite god El—or to another, referred to as *Baal,* Lord. Abraham "swears" to this god, as if it does not matter which god it is. So the "pact" made here has no hint of the Sumerian background to the covenant—until, that is, Abraham puzzles his colleagues with the ewes.

"What mean these seven ewes?" they ask, and for a moment we enter a mystery, a drama. It is quickly dispelled: they stand merely for the number seven, as in "seven wells," which is the meaning behind the name Beersheba. We must face the fact that the audience at Samaria, like E himself, had no ear for poetry and the legitimacy it once granted to names, places, and events. Yet they had their own wish for historical authenticity, indulging it in little rituals like the offering of the ewes.

What E demonstrates in these acts is that Abraham is taking hold of the cosmic theater and integrating it with daily life—just as the prophets of the day are trying to plead with their kingdoms to do. Abimelech and Phicol accept Abraham's promise—his word, his poetic covenant—just as Abraham had to accept it from Yahweh in the cutting of the covenant, when Yahweh promised land and seed (and more importantly, promised that it was "his" to give Abraham, thereby establishing a negotiation).

In another ritual, Abraham will plant a tamarisk, a type of sacred oak that was found at Mamre (where Abraham first settled, according to J). This is a Canaanite ritual that J would have had nothing to do with; instead, when Abraham had called upon Yahweh by name, J showed Abraham making a Sumerian-type altar that marked an arrival. Furthermore, the God invoked by E, Elohim, is thoroughly Canaanite with no suggestion that he is the same God who spoke to Abraham in Harran (in the guise of a personal god).

> *When they had concluded that pact at Beersheba, Abimelech and Phicol, chief of his troops, departed and returned to the land of the Philistines. Abraham planted a tamarisk at Beersheba, and invoked there the name of the Lord, the Everlasting God. And Abraham resided in the land of the Philistines a long time.*

As if the author's distance from the story is so great, E intimates that little needs to be told or explained of Abraham's relations with the Philistines. "Abraham resided in the land of the Philistines a long time." After this, there is little left in Abraham's life that E wishes to dramatize, and that is extremely fortunate, for he is now forced to draw upon the dramatic device he has mastered, the dream. God will no longer need an angel to speak to Abraham on his behalf; instead, he will draw Abraham into a deep dream in which, like a somnambulist, he is speechless, sleepwalking through to the end. In that episode to come, the Akedah, Abraham's "only one," Isaac, will already be a young man.

For J, the land had been a stage upon which Yahweh and Abraham could come into contact, converse, and negotiate a covenant, but here, in E's passages, all we are meant to know is that Abraham is safely ensconced. However, far from disappearing, the cosmic stage has shifted. The drama now enters within Abraham's mind: the dreams and visions in which God speaks to him. To E's audience, it was an element made familiar by the writing prophets, and once we become accustomed to this ambiguous atmosphere, we will be led toward the greatest nightmare in ancient history. The preparation for the sacrifice of Isaac will take place as if within Abraham's mind, as if in a dream.

THE INTERPRETATION OF DREAMS

Since we will be given few new clues to Abraham's mind, we must rely on what we already know from J's narrative. Isaac has been born and the promise of Yahweh has been borne out. Abraham and Sarah conceived a son past the age that would normally have been expected. Now what? Does Isaac really belong to them? After all, Sarah was supposed to have been too old. Yes, he is a natural-born child, but how much is he Abraham and Sarah's—and how much is he Yahweh's child? What expectations might Yahweh have about his upbringing? The anxiety behind these questions will lead to the nightmare of Abraham's life to come, when he will have to face losing Isaac.

The covenant only goes so far, when it comes to educating Isaac; it is not yet a culture. Abraham must still integrate Sumerian and Canaanite into one sensibility, and in order to represent this, E would have to absorb J's familiarity with Sumerian poets. And he seems to have done so, by finding a commonality in the interpretation of dreams by Hebrew poet-prophets. Certainly there was nothing in Abraham's classical Sumerian background or in E's Hebraic background that would have prepared either one for the plausibility of child sacrifice—except in a dream. The gods with whom Abraham had grown up would never think to ask for such things. They were pleased simply to be treated as if alive.

For instance, on the eighth day of the New Year festival in Ur, the statue of the chief servant god is taken down into the courtyard of the temple and placed in front of Enlil, the highest god. This happens early in the morning, prior to breakfast, for there are many more god-statues to be brought into the courtryard and placed in proper position. Enlil and his wife are offered a bowl of water for their morning toilette. And then meat is served, on golden platters, first to Enlil and his wife and then to the other statues standing in the courtyard.

In the Sumerian cosmic theater the convolutions of animal sacrifice were hardly known. What *did* exist was a Sumerian literary use of the dream that tied personal death to cultural extinction. This would account for a partly Sumerian origin to Abraham's nightmare of the sacrifice of Isaac (and its implied extinction of the covenant: How could Abraham's descendants come to exist without Isaac?).

A SUMERIAN DREAM

Dumuzi has a dream that he is close to death, and he composes a lament that tells of the dream and its nightmarish aspect:

His heart was filled with tears,
He went forth to the plain
His flute fastened about his neck
To accompany him in his lament:
Among the crabs of the river, set up a lament
Among the frogs of the river, set up a lament
Let my mother utter the words of the lament
Because on the day that I die she will have none to care for her.
Among the buds and flowers he lay down
And dreamt a dream, trembling.
He arose, rubbed his eyes with his hands, he was dazed.
In the wooded grove, tall trees rise fearsomely about me
My shepherd's crook has vanished,
A falcon holds a lamb in its claws,
The young goats drag their lapis beards in the dust,
The sheep paw the ground with their bent limbs,
The churn lies shattered, no milk is poured,
The cup lies shattered—Dumuzi lives no more!
The sheepfold is given over to the wind.

Abraham must have known this poem, since a temple was built in Ur by a deputy of King Hammurapi, Rim-Sin, for the god Dumuzi and his lover, Inanna, and this poem was part of its liturgy. But there was no significant *awakening* from this dream in Sumer.

In Canaan, however, the Hebrew prophets had developed the precedent of a prophetic awakening, which E would have absorbed, and this is what we will find at the end of Abraham's nightmare of extinction. It was E, then, who drew upon Hebraic source material for this story that had been based upon the Sumerian nightmare of extinction (possibly J's earlier version). And it was E who would wed that source to the Hebraic prophecy of awakening. In this way, he recapitulated the problem facing Abraham himself when he arrived in Canaan: how to integrate his Sumerian heritage with the new Canaanite reality.

To carry the knowledge of a personal death that is also *extinction,* as we have just encountered in the Sumerian poem ("the churn lies shattered, no milk is poured") a dream was required—a nightmare dream of extinction. There was no recompense for it in Sumer. Dumuzi was to learn that his dream was a foretelling of reality. But in the prophetic dreams of Israel, an awakening from the dream becomes possible. This is the knowledge that informs the nightmare of the sacrifice of Isaac, which we are about to face. In the end,

For this thing you have done
your descendants will walk freely
through the gates of their enemy
and all the nations of the earth
will feel themselves blessed
one day, knowing
that your descendants thrive
living among them—
[for it was you who listened
and heard my voice.]

CHAPTER 19

Inheritance and the Threat of Extinction

Why has the Jewish culture that began with Abraham survived all myths of its demise? The continued, inextinguishable existence of Jewish culture (which has never even ceased to invent new languages, from ancient Hebrew to Judeo-Aramaic, and from Judeo-Greek to Yiddish and back to modern Hebrew again) confirms the particularity of Abraham's covenant, holding out against the wish for universality by later religions and ideologies. While the covenant with Abraham was a universal drama of negotiation with the unknowable, the only universal certainty was the negotiation itself. Thus Abraham's identity was not to be a prophet but instead to honor the Hebraic boundary between man and his God by continual study and interpretation of the boundary—and taking the form of a life's journey. And then there was the parallel journey of Yahweh from an obscure spot in the Canaanite pantheon, and from representing Abraham's Sumerian personal god, to becoming the essence of the monotheistic God. This journey also depended upon Abraham's knowledge that God too struggles for identity.

In our own day, the Holocaust exposed once again that Yahweh will not intervene directly in the human realm. What he can do is what was done for Abraham: God will guarantee a future that can be negotiated and survived. When we come to the climax of Abraham's life journey—

the biblical nightmare known as the sacrifice of Isaac—we face the terror of cultural extinction. It will not threaten a universal extinction of humanity but rather the particular destruction of Jewish identity. And it will be overcome by what the immediate future reveals to Abraham, namely, an unassuming animal. A wild ram, whose horns have become entangled in a thicket. It is an accident of nature, yet it reassures us that such fortunate accidents (representing the bounty of nature) will continue to mark the future and provide for Jewish survival. Although the unassuming ram appears when all seems lost, it is not really a surprise. It is like waking from a dream of murder to find one is still alive among natural things; all the civilizing history we have inherited is still real. Since Isaac has become the *human* embodiment of the covenant—the inheritor of Abraham's God—his precarious trial will mirror a more complicated reality in the future: the precariousness of being a nation among strangers.

The paradox of the covenant between natural man and supernatural God is that it requires a belief in inheriting the future as if it were the past. That is, the future is more of the same, except that there is the promise of clarity, of a finer awareness through study of where the border lies between known and unknowable worlds. To erase the border altogether would be to erase the covenant. And yet, the wish to throw off the burden of that knowledge arises in every person and every generation. Wishing for help from above—canceling the boundaries—might seem preferable to further study and further journeys. Who would wish to live in tension, in a theater of our own making, where we act as if there is certainty, yet at the same time we understand that clarity (Yahweh's "truth and justice") is all we are destined to know. Thus, Abraham's covenant is a reminder that all dreams of peace are repressive. A dream can quickly turn into a nightmare that smothers clarity and confuses boundaries. And that is what Abraham is about to experience: it will not be divine intervention but rather a natural awaking to his physical surroundings that will stop the nightmare of Isaac's sacrifice.

The dread of being present at the Akedah is the covenant's primal scene, a struggle against evil and its wish to confuse all boundaries. In the scene we're about to face, we may believe that God can do anything he wishes, but the covenant with Abraham insures that if the eternal one crosses the border into the natural world he too will lose his identity. For it is an identity forged in civilization and history. It is sealed by a covenant but it remains a particular, Hebraic identity.

Now we may ask: If Abraham is at the origin of the covenant that leads to Hebraic culture and to the Bible's writers, then when did the this Jewish identity enter *world* history—that is, beyond their own recording of it? As a cultural and political entity, the destruction of the northern kingdom of Israel, in c.725 BCE, is also recorded by the Assyrian conquerors. We even have an Assyrian picture of the king from Samaria, Israel's capital, bowing in submission. Although there is earlier mention in the records of other countries concerning the House of David and the Hebrews *(Habiru),* the polity and complexity of Hebraic civilization is first noted in the world record in the eighth century BCE. The Israelite writer we call E, writing earlier in Samaria, was sure enough of Israel's place among the nations that he could append this promise to his narrative of the Akedah:

all the nations of the earth
will feel themselves blessed
one day, knowing
that your descendants thrive
living among them—

It turns out that E was wrong—for the time being—about the blessing. Nevertheless, his record of Israel's place in the world will be verified by its neighbors ("your descendants . . . living among them") from that time forward.

"MORE MODERN"

Israel's history had already become valid in itself when J's authority was accepted. It happened several times: first, in Jerusalem, then in Samaria (ratified by E), and it would be repeated conclusively in the creation of JE, a biblical document that stands for the combined narrative of those two great authors. This document was shaped in Jerusalem, the capital of Judah, after the fall of the northern Kingdom. Abraham's tie to Sumer, which had been established by J and accepted by E, was again reaffirmed. And thus J's history remained the genuine bedrock of the Bible over nine centuries of further Jewish additions to it. Even when the authorized Christian translation was made into Latin, J's words were preserved—authenticated long before by E's reliance upon them.

Yet E probably considered J's narrative style to be "primitive." A century later, the Solomonic court was viewed as partial to women and not sufficiently in ideological conflict with other religions, signs of being old-fashioned in the "more modern" court of Samaria. The Sumerian influences and the theatrical disguises Yahweh wears in J's writing confirmed its "backwardness" to the readers of E's day.

E himself had little knowledge of Sumerian history, and he probably could not read cuneiform. His Abraham was a religious man of faith who followed Elohim's commands as if in a dream. His audience required that the power of the dream and the authenticity of prophecy be dramatized, and that is why E extends the theater of Abraham's God into the future of prophecy. For all the prophets who will come afterward, including Isaiah and Jeremiah, will share a similar dream of the covenant—namely, that it encompasses the world. The promise of descendents to Abraham, in other words, will be a blessing to the world, as it too can listen.

Now this larger world was after all a polytheistic one. Polytheism in some ways resembles our secular culture today, in that all religions can be tolerated. Temples to various gods were found in the same city, just as synagogues, temples, churches, and mosques are found side by side today. But it would be a mistake to imagine the culture for which E wrote as if it were our own. The Hebrew prophet's complaint *against* polytheism was front-page news on the streets of Samaria. Not only were the other high gods excluded from the covenant but also their supernatural power was blocked, thanks to Yahweh. So it's easy for us to suppose that they thought the Hebrew God had meant to test whether Abraham would turn to one of the *other* high gods in Canaan (particularly one referred to in their time as *Baal* or "Lord"). But the test that underlies the passage to come, the Akedah, is more significantly about the covenant rather than other gods—and as such, it was *Abraham's* test of the substance of the covenant even more than it was Yahweh's.

As we prepare to follow Abraham's journey with Isaac we will see it is in some sense a recapitulation of Abraham's original journey to Canaan, when Yahweh beckons him,

> *"to a land I will bring you to see."*

Now, Yahweh calls him out

> *"to a mountain of which I will tell you*
> *when you approach."*

This is E's new vision of Abraham, and to comprehend it fully we must return to c.825 BCE when he was writing—more than a generation after Rehoboam's kingdom was split in two. Jerusalem was then the capital of a shrunken land, Judah, and the northern kingdom of Israel began to build a new capital for itself at Samaria (no relation to Sumer, which was called "Shinar" in Hebrew).

SAMARIA

To follow Abraham's journey toward its shattering climax, another crucial history must be filled in. And that is the period in which E was alive, writing the biography of Abraham for a new generation. We will learn what E's audience demands, and we will see why it wanted more of Abraham's life than J had recorded. E wrote in Samaria, a small town on a hill commanding a province also known as Samaria, after it was chosen by King Omri of Israel for the new capital. He was emulating King David, who had built up Jerusalem, and huge construction projects were begun. Independently of Judah, Omri negotiated a treaty with the world-sailing Phoenicians to the north, and the fruits of Israel's agriculture were traded for exotic luxury products. While the Phoenician culture contributed a cosmopolitanism to Samaria, the Phoenician alphabet was appropriated for the writing of Hebrew.

King Ahab, Omri's son, married a Phoenician, Jezebel, and together they enlarged Samaria. Jezebel brought the Phoenician religion, in which Baal rivaled El for the place of Canaanite High God. It's important to understand how cosmopolitan these leaders were; they wanted to impress their neighbors, not rival them. In the center of Samaria, on the high ground of the hill, they built an acropolis, surrounded by inner and outer walls encircling public buildings and pools. There were the king's palace and the storehouses, and there was also a district of houses for upper-class merchants, craftsman, and artists. Ahab beautified the palace for Jezebel, importing large shipments of ivory for artistic embellishment.

A decline in Israel's prestige followed the death of Ahab. Then, in c.800 BCE, King Yehoash fought with the king of Judah, Amaziah, penetrated Jerusalem, and returned to Samaria with a portion of the contents of the Jerusalem palace library, including the J writer's narrative. The son of Yehoash, Jeroboam II, went on to achieve the last military and political victories for the northern kingdom. In a time of economic prosperity he curtailed the Phoenician influence and commissioned one major project in particular that changed the face of Jewish tradition.

In the year c.762 BCE, Jeroboam II, King of Israel in Samaria, ordered a new history of the Jewish people to be written that would incorporate but embellish J. It would reflect the advanced sensibility of the royal court in the northern Kingdom. The audience, of course, was very different from the one at J's Solomonic court a century and a half earlier. There was no long tradition of Hebrew and cuneiform archives in Samaria, no study of classic Sumerian literature, no serious historical scholarship and translation. Instead, there were the Phoenician imports of early Greek and Egyptian literature to temper the reliance on Canaanite literary history. Against this background, the Jewish religion was able to stand out—that is, the tradition as written in Jerusalem. Thus the royal court and the priesthood wanted a new, more official-sounding narrative that would move J into the historical background, just as they wanted to make Samaria into a new Jerusalem.

Far from the court at Jerusalem, the royal court at Samaria specifically read and translated the literature of the classic Canaanite kingdoms, including Ugarit to the north, the Phoenician kingdoms of Tyre, Sidon, and Byblos, and the Mycenaean Greek tradition imported with the Philistines. In Ugarit five hundred years earlier, careful historical records on clay tablets along with extensive literary works were written not only in Ugaritic but in eight additional languages, including Abraham's Akkadian. Ugaritic poetry would have been among the classics known in Samaria, and we can feel its influence in the Hebrew Bible especially upon the E writer in Samaria. It is there in J as well, as in a scene of feeding the gods that recalls the visit of Yahweh to Abraham and Sarah at Mamre:

And then Daniel loudly to his wife does call:
'Listen, Lady Danatiya,
Prepare a lamb from the flock . . .
Give food, give drink to the godhead;
Serve, honor him . . .
Lady Danatiya obeys,
She prepares a lamb from the flock . . .
She gives food, gives drink to the godhead.

When J wrote the scene of Sarah's preparing of food for Yahweh and his angels (as they stopped at Mamre on the way to Sodom) it was many centuries after the Ugaritic poem, which may date from the time when Abraham was still alive in Canaan. J transforms the scene in significant ways ("From there to the cattle he runs, chooses a tender calf . . . "), particularly in the human disguise that Yahweh assumes with Abraham and Sarah. The human disguise reminds us of the influence of the Sumerian cosmic theater in which the god-statues (which are the gods already in disguise) must have their daily meals.

E, with less understanding of the Sumerian cosmic theater, depicts a Yahweh (always called Elohim) who is never in disguise. Instead, E's God speaks to humans mostly in dreams, as if determined to keep himself offstage in the theater of Abraham's God. In the process, God comes to assume the role of stage manager: everything that happens seems to follow Elohim's will—and this is the way of dreams, when we are not in control of events.

HIS VOICE

Because God speaks in dreams, there is no need to characterize him; it is only his voice that we hear, and the audience is not even told what it sounds like. For E's audience at the royal court in Samaria, this was the way they wanted it. The priests and prophets of Yahweh and El were far more integrated into the Samarian kingdom than they had been in J's Jerusalem, and they were less interested in character and cultural history. While J's Jerusalem sought to establish a historical basis for the new nation, the royal court in E's Samaria was skeptical of the tolerant culture of King Solomon and his son, Rehoboam. Still the court of King Jeroboam II needed a cultural basis for the religious alternative they posed to the Temple of Yahweh in Jerusalem.

The obvious way to provide this alternative was to present it as more Canaanite; that is, as more integrated into the history and culture of Canaan. If the high Canaanite god, Baal, spoke in dreams, so would Elohim. Thus God could speak to prophets now in the new kingdom—and not just in the days of the God of Abraham. Samaria grounded the Jewish religion in the history of the land but ignored the origin of Abraham in the history of civilization, and in particular, in Sumer. Here was the beginning of the loss of Abraham's Sumerian origins that continues to today.

In the Ugaritic Canaanite poems "Aqhat" and "Kirta," El speaks in dreams many centuries before either Jerusalem *or* Samaria become Hebraic capitals:

FROM AQHAT

In a dream, O Kindly El Benign,
In a vision, Creator of Creatures,
The heavens fat did rain,

The wadies flow with honey.
So I knew that Baal was alive!
The Prince and Lord of all the earth existed!
In a dream, Kindly El Benign . . .
The Kindly El Benign is glad,
His feet on the footstool he sets,
And parts his lips and laughs!

But there was no covenant with El (as Abraham later creates with Yahweh). Thus Kirta must witness all his descendents wiped out and his children murdered. Nevertheless, El comes to console him in a dream:

FROM KIRTA

He sees his progeny, Kirta,
He sees his progeny ruined,
His dynasty utterly sundered.
All his descendents have perished.
His tears are poured forth
Like shekels on the ground,
Like five-weights on the couch.
As he cries, he falls asleep;
As he weeps, there's slumber.
Sleep overwhelms him, he lies down;
Slumber, and he crumples.
Now in his dream, El comes down;
The Father of Man, in his vision.
Now El approaches, asking Kirta:
What ails Kirta, that he cries?

Although E will adopt the convention of "dream-talk" in Canaanite literature, he overlays it upon J's earlier narrative standards. And so it was that the dreams and angels of Canaanite convention were absorbed into the theater of Abraham's God. When we reach the climax of the life of Abraham, Elohim not only speaks in a dream but the dream has become all-enveloping. God will appear capable of saying and asking *anything* ("Please take your son / whom you love . . . "), and Abraham will say *nothing.* It is the God of a nightmare, who can say anything, abolishing the boundaries of the covenant. This dream we are about to enter is not the theater of Abraham's God but instead the drama of its *absence.*

And some time later
after these things had happened
God tested Abraham
speaking to him
"Abraham"
"I am listening," he answered.

And God said
please take your son
whom you love
dear as an only son
that is, Isaac
and go out to the land of Moriah

There you will make of him a burnt offering
on a mountain of which I will tell you
when you approach

"These things" that have already happened are exactly what E has already written: the further threat of Sarah being raped in Gerar, the birth of Isaac, the claims of Isaac and Ishmael, of Sarah and Hagar, and the negotiation of the well rights with Abimelech and Phicol. Now, E announces to his audience that a new "test" of the covenant has arrived, something beyond J's text. It is purposely written in such an unusual dreamlike way that E's audience would have known it was a dream from the start. Moreover, child-sacrifice was an anachronism in this day.

E's audience, however, also included the priesthood of El, the same creator god who would have been known in Abraham's time as El Elyon (El, Most High). As we noted previously, "El" was a generic term for God, but the same held true for the name Baal, which was a term for Lord. There was more than one god characterized as Baal—and before Abraham arrived in Canaan, Yahweh might have been a name for either El or Baal. E uses the term Elohim for the deity, which means "gods" but in a singular concept, as in "thus spoke the gods." Yet Elohim acquires a new meaning here: "all gods in one." This exalted state is what forbids God from speaking directly with humans as he did with Abraham and Sarah. We are in a dream, and Abraham responds to God as if in a trance: "I am listening."

THE DREAM AND THE NIGHTMARE

When we wake from dreams we remember fragments, and we tend to recreate the dream by imposing narrative logic. We add commentary and interpretation, and then the mixture of the two—dream and commentary—becomes compelling in a new way. So it was with E. The situations, the settings are exotic, resonant of myth, and E's biblical narrative fits into the Canaanite polytheistic context of its day. What happens next in the narrative reinforces the depth of this dream, as Abraham "awakes" for the trip to Moriah the next morning. When we know that an onerous task awaits us, our dreams on the preceding night may be fraught with anxiety.

And Abraham rose early in the morning
saddled his donkey
took two of his young workers
to go with him and his son, Isaac
having already split the wood
for the burnt offering
and he started out for the place
of which God had spoken
to him

There is no protest from Abraham. It is an utter embrace of a journey, though Abraham could have argued as he did at Gerar and outside of Sodom. He could have hesitated, or pleaded with God on the basis of their attachment. He could have threatened suicide. Abraham did none of these things, did not even think about it. He simply *goes.* By placing Abraham in dreamtime, E has created a simulation of deep history, of an unknowable, prehistoric-seeming past, and placed it squarely within Abraham's real history in Canaan. He records details of place and time, which frame the historical vision of J and at the same time provide a "modern" Samarian test of the covenant.

It was on the third day
Abraham looked out in the distance
and there, afar, was the place
and Abraham turned to his young men
you will wait here by yourselves
with the donkey
while the youth and I go on ahead
to worship and then
we will return here to you

Abraham took the wood for the burnt offering
laying it upon Isaac, his son
and in his own hands he took the flint
and the knife
then the two walked on together

While we are in the dream, our attention to detail may seem the whole point of it. Awake, it is these details that we go in search of, ahead of what the dream may have meant. Here, E gives us the details, perfectly recorded. There is no care in E about what it means—yet. If there is one thing certain in the midst of a nightmarish uncertainty about Isaac, it is that there is absolute clarity to Abraham's actions. Isaac carries the wood. Abraham carries the flint and knife. There is no obfuscation or confusion. The dream will unfold, just as our lives will—and we do not know why or how. It is here, with wood, knife, and flint in hand, that we see what underlies the Akedah. It was written with a fear of extinction in mind and as an affirmation of continued existence. E is confident that Abraham's God, representing all that is humanly unknowable, could be held *accountable* for Israel's culture. For in the physical details, it is the covenant that is being recalled, the cutting of it, the burning. And the stark physicality of Isaac.

At last Isaac spoke to his father, Abraham
"Father"
"I am listening, my son"
We have the flint and the wood
to make the fire, but where is the lamb
for a burnt offering?

Abraham answered
God will reveal his lamb, my son
for the burnt offering
and the two walked on together

The flint and the wood are now the tools of *Abraham's test* of God. When Abraham says, "God will reveal his lamb, my son / for the burnt offering," he has stated his test in the word "reveal," for that is what God has still not accomplished. Abraham and Isaac walk on, toward the site where all will be tested. E's audience in Samaria was not looking for *supernatural* revelations; that was for other gods. This was a test of the covenant, of a boundary. If God were to interfere in the natural world, he could never be trusted again. Abraham doesn't argue but he tests. Even when the words said "God tested Abraham," the so-called test took place in a cosmic dream theater created by E and his audience. They knew that a blind faith in the supernatural—confusing the boundary between man and God—would render the covenant useless. They knew that Abraham is sleepwalking—and yet he is helpless to stop the dream, to step outside the theater. For as in all aspects of human knowledge, boundaries must be tested.

The audience in Samaria needed a climax to Abraham's life that would renew and validate the covenant. It is only God the creator who does *not* have to test boundaries. The test of the creator is in whether he can *observe* them—whether he can be bound to a theater and to a covenant. We can feel, dream, and create a theater in narrative or any other form and thus render God, but the test of Abraham's God is that he remains unknowable. And that is precisely why he is partner to a boundary called the covenant. It is by the boundary that we know him, and by trusting the boundary. And that boundary, which resembles the one between life and death, is lost again in every single day. In other words, each day that we awake, we face again the fears of death and extinction—and we are free to explore those fears in a cosmic dream of the covenant, as were the Sumerians upon their temple stage of waking and sleeping.

And they approached the place
of which God had spoken
there Abraham prepared an altar
set the wood upon it
then bound his son, Isaac
and laid him there, on the altar
lying upon the wood

Abraham reached out
with his hand, taking
the knife, to slaughter
his son

WHAT IS REVEALED? (A WILD RAM)

Nightmares are always about a violent or passionate wish. Here the wish is Abraham's: that the thing promised, Isaac, truly seal the covenant, immortalize it. As much as the dreaming Abraham might wish for supernatural certainty, we, the audience, witnesses to this drama, are wishing it turn out as we know it must: provisionally. For even after this, Isaac's life, as any other mortal, will remain in the balance. We are the civilized audience, aware of uncertainty, who are descended from the covenant—just as Abraham will once again be the civilized man from Ur when he awakes from his nightmare. We wish for *civilization* to survive rather than see the boundaries between life and death erased by a supernatural intervention. For we have learned this with Gilgamesh at the origin of civilization in Sumer: we face our own mortality, and we must put aside dreams of immortality (though later eras will reinstate them).

Abraham in this deep dream is having tested within his own psyche the meaning of the covenant. Rather than a guarantee of immortality it provides only for the continuation of a culture: Isaac will get on with his life while the boundary of Abraham's life will end in the purchase of burial sites and finally burial. Abraham will thus face death as a Sumerian, fully aware of an irrevocable mortality. And he will have told this dream to Isaac, his son, so that Isaac and his descendants will also understand how critical the covenant remains for human understanding. (We can be fairly certain that Abraham would have resembled *his* father as a devoted teacher of his son.) It would be up to Isaac to inscribe and pass on the memory of his father's journey—as it will be for others in each generation to interpret it.

There is no record of Israel's founding families telling oral stories because they were able to keep written records. And this helps explain why so little of Isaac's own life is preserved, compared with his father's: Isaac would have been trained to write down the history. Eventually J was confronted with historical sources that developed from Abraham's time. And even from far older sources in Sumer, there was a natural wildness in the threat of extinction that underlies the Akedah. A snake could interrupt paradise, a fruit spoil innocence, a flood end and begin things. Now, something equally wild will wake Abraham from his nightmare.

But a voice was calling to him
an angel of the Lord, calling
from out of heaven

Abraham, Abraham
I am listening, he answered

Do not lay your hand upon the youth
you will not do anything to him
for now I know yours is an integrity
dedicated to God
not holding back your son
your dear one, from me

The scene unfolds with hypnotic intensity to a climactic moment: Abraham's dagger is poised above the chest of Isaac when suddenly a voice breaks the spell. It's an unexpected voice, one not heard before. It's the voice of an angel delivering God's request to end this scene, and it permits a new perspective on the scene. Elohim's messenger jolts us into the awareness that there is another world, unknowable. Still, it is merely a voice, and the scene continues to open out in a natural way. (The angel does not stay the hand or exercise force against the raised knife.) Nothing supernatural has actually been seen; it would have been a betrayal of the covenant for anything supernatural to intervene.

Thus E has honored J's devotion to the natural world. Abraham (and Sarah), so free of supernatural thoughts that even Yahweh's foretelling the birth of Isaac was laughed at, remains in character. In J, Abraham and Sarah struggle with Yahweh's desires, and they test them as well. His divinity is never enough for Abraham. And thus it remains in E's additions to the biography of Abraham.

Yahweh has withdrawn and sent a messenger in his place. The angel's voice Abraham now hears corresponds to an inner one; it is like a man conversing with his personal god in Ur. It is the voice of conscience in the world at last, translated from the Sumerian idea of the soul as inner voice, the mediator between the individual and a personal god.

We need a monotheistic God not because we die but because, as Abraham knew, whole cultures can die, become extinct. A singular "God our Father" holds on to the sexual meaning of fatherhood and our origin in nature. At the same time, it expands the meaning of our unknowable origin in the cosmos. Abraham has also fathered the name of Yahweh (by founding the culture in which it lives) and thereby confronted the issue of extinction. Yahweh's "truth and justice," which are dynamic concepts, complex and changing, are in need of creative interpretation and a culture to support that interpretation. Now E will complete the covenant's rescue of Abraham from his nightmare of extinction with the most natural of acts: "Abraham looked around." It is a waking from this wild, unknowable place, which is where Abraham and Isaac are—in the dream and in real life. It is also a waking into the culture of that day, where a ram may be sacrificed in the ongoing drama of covenant-making.

Then Abraham looked around and there
behind him
its horns tangled up in a thicket
a ram had appeared

And Abraham went over to it
carrying the ram to the wood
for a burnt offering
instead of his son

The name of that place
was given by Abraham, meaning
"The Lord reveals"
and today we still say
"The mountain of the Lord
is revelation"

What is revealed? A wild ram. And to what is the revelation compared? A mountain. Both ram and mountain are part of the natural world and supersede the dream's supernatural voices of angel and God. But now Abraham has named the site, marking it in the landscape as well as the cosmic stage of the covenant. Specifically, the place is named for the benefit of Isaac, who will pass on the covenant. And that is the reason it can pass from landscape to Hebraic culture: "today we still say . . ." reminds us that "we" who read this retain an intimate connection over the centuries with Abraham. As the father of a culture, he has educated his descendents.

The emphasis on inheritance falls here on Isaac's survival; he is the first who can call the God of Abraham "the God of my Father." Later in time, the term becomes "the God of my Fathers"—which was also the Sumerian expression for a family's household god and personal god. (It was his Sumerian personal god who spoke to Abraham's father in Ur and to him in Harran.) When it comes time for Abraham to be buried, however, it will not be beneath a Sumerian house. He will seek out a field and a cave, so that the entire landscape of Israel will be domesticated for Yahweh. Thus "the God of our Fathers" continues to be linked to that land.

Meanwhile, the mountain of the aborted sacrifice is also, figuratively, a reminder in Abraham's memory of the ziggurat in Ur, which represented a mountain. It is Abraham of Ur who has endured the nightmare (whether or not Isaac recorded the kernel of it). E has absorbed J's history, so that the influence upon Abraham of the Sumerian cosmic theater is still there. And even with his limited knowledge of Sumerian, it is apparent that E's construction of Abraham's dream closely resembles the testing of God by another writer-translator: the Hebraic author who adapted the Book of Job from Sumerian literature. (As much as it seems Job suffers the limits of human endurance, he ceaselessly tests God's motives.) From a distance, it can appear that the Sumerian influences go unacknowledged. At the time of writing, however, the more ancient Sumerian sources would have been known to the educated Hebraic audience and thus needed no attribution.

And the ram on the mountain—the ram that appears in the thicket—is a further Sumerian influence upon E. A ram or goat was in some way part of the cosmic drama, and we have dug up in our own time a remarkable Sumerian sculpture of it: the animal is crafted in gold and its hooves are entangled in a thicket-like plant. This sculpture is still safe, in the Baghdad museum today, representing Sumer.

The purpose of a cosmic theater, as Sumer has shown, is to bind cosmos to culture in a play of ideas and art that insures the survival of the culture.

"Then Abraham looked around"—a nightmare must be dispelled, as these words manage to do. Instead of cultural suicide, Abraham's Sumerian origin is saved along with the rest of his history. And E has just made known to us how much that history depends on acknowledging other cultures. That is why the stories of E that precede the Akedah were so mired in Abraham's negotiations with other peoples: the Egyptian, Hagar, and the Philistine, Abimelech.

Waking from the nightmare as readers, Abraham's new cosmic theater has worked through for us what the Sumerian theater was always attempting to do. It is a potentially terrifying truth that we are most dependent upon inheritance—in this instance, for Isaac—and yet it is not *everything*, after all. There is no guarantee Isaac will survive, no sacrificial seal; instead, there is only the theater. The Sumerian statue theater depended upon the movement of time and the closing of eyes: upon feeding, dressing, and putting the gods to bed—in other words, on the internalizing of impermanence. The gods closed their eyes and so did their handlers. Although the gods never died, neither did the death of their handlers enter into the theater. What counted was that the theater endured.

The theater of Abraham's God—a dream theater in E's narrative—will now be revealed as what really matters. Abraham "acted," God will say, but the Lord and his angel remain only voices—they do not cross the boundary into the natural world. Abraham has far more than a voice: he has "seed" that can be "multiplied." We are reminded again of how the covenant depends on human and natural history, and not upon what happens in God's unknowable realm. It all comes down to Abraham as a mortal and historical man: "it was you who listened / and heard my voice." It happened, in other words, in a particular place and time. Abraham is a man with an inner life—a personal god—from Ur, but it will be his physical descendents in the world who embody the Hebraic culture and continue to test the boundary. It is they who are both proof of Abraham's human history and the people for whom that history demands a heightened listening to the past. It is a listening and writing that are worthy of the highest level of art.

The Lord's angel spoke again
calling to Abraham from heaven
By myself I have sworn
says the Lord
as by yourself you have acted—
have not held back even your son
dear to you as an only one—
and for this thing you are immeasurably blessed
and your seed multiplied
immeasurable as the stars in the sky
and as the grains of sand by the sea
For this thing you have done
your descendants will walk freely
through the gates of their enemy
and all the nations of the earth
will feel themselves blessed
one day, knowing
that your descendants thrive
living among them—
for it was you who listened
and heard my voice

Abraham has awoken from the nightmare, and yet he is held within the dream of the cosmic theater of Abraham's God and its covenant of natural inheritance: "your seed multiplied / immeasurable as the stars in the sky / and as the grains of sand by the sea." When Abraham asked Yahweh after his return to Canaan from his first sojourn in Egypt, "what good is prospering when I walk toward my death without children, my inheritance passed down to a son of Damascus, Eliezer, accountant of my house," Yahweh took up the case of this accounting and replied, "Look well, please, at heaven; count the stars—if you can count them. So will be your seed." Yahweh had taken Abraham's

Sumerian sensibility about inheritance into account. Now, this incalculable cosmos requires a dream to contain it.

And still it remains a dream: "your descendants will walk freely/ through the gates of their enemy / and all the nations of the earth / will feel themselves blessed / one day, knowing / that your descendants thrive / living among them." Only in a dream can the nightmares of history, which Abraham's descendants will endure, have such satisfying results. It was especially a dream for E in Samaria, where the northern kingdom of Israel would soon be destroyed by the conquering Assyrians. But Abraham has a real, historical awakening from the dream:

So Abraham returned to his young men
they turned and started out together
for Beersheba
and Abraham stayed there, in Beersheba.

Although Isaac isn't mentioned here, it isn't necessary. It was Abraham alone who was author of this dream. Still within it, Abraham broke the spell of the nightmare when he "looked around" to see the ram. Now, we are outside of the dream altogether when "they turned and started out together." The return to the real world is emphatically a historical place, Beersheba. And from now until his death, he will "stay there," in the real world, to work out the Sumerian-like details of his death and burial.

Two centuries later, with the southern kingdom of Judah destroyed and the Jewish people in exile in Babylon, Isaiah (the third writing prophet to assume that name) renews the dream in great biblical poetry. The memory of Abraham's original covenant continues to ground his dream. Since it was a historical promise of sexual seed and fruitfulness, leading to a future Israel, it now must focus on *cultural* inheritance and survival. Israel has been a nation for many centuries during the time of this Isaiah, and so he expands the meaning of the words with further irony. Israel will be civilization in its fullest sense, Isaiah dreams, including even the eunuchs at the royal court, who have no seed. Even these eunuchs will be accepted into the covenant and "not cut off" (unlike what befell their sexual potency).

Here in Isaiah, the eunuchs become a sublime metaphor for the writers of the Bible, who cannot reproduce their Hebraic culture fruitfully without the aid of art. This is the art that J's Yahweh understood better than the confusing sexuality of human beings—an art of words spoken and written. It was an art documenting the historical as well as the cosmic time of Yahweh's "sabbaths," which are themselves firmly anchored in time by the days of the week and which find their origin in the Sumerian cosmic theater.

To the eunuchs who keep my sabbaths,
who choose the things that please me
and hold fast my covenant,
I will give, in my house and within my walls,
a monument and a name
better than sons and daughters;
I will give them an everlasting name
that shall not be cut off.

The irony that Isaiah displays about monumental "everlasting" names and sexual organs "not cut off" responds to J's original representation of Yahweh's problem with sexual inheritance, starting with getting Sarah pregnant. Inheritance has now superseded the sexual; it requires dramatic acts within a specific culture ("keep my sabbath"). Now, it is the whole civilization, Israel, that stands in for Isaac in the nightmare. Israel will survive, as did Abraham's son, but outside the dream and the covenant there will also be the terrible nightmares of threatened extinction.

EPILOGUE

Death and Burial

DIVINE INTERVENTION

I wanted to write this book in a way that would not require knowledge of Jewish, Christian, or Islamic religion. At the same time, what we assume as "common knowledge" had to be combated. And that was the hard part: to encourage a letting go of stereotypes that are repeated time and again, and which are usually based upon a confusion between what is natural and what is supernatural. Religion and secular culture are usually taught in a way that separates one from the other—perpetuating the misunderstanding between them—so the task became to reconcile them anew. The inevitable tension between religion and culture compels creative thinking, since civilization was founded on their unity. Abraham stands at the crossroads of this tension, suspended between the human and cosmic. His life helps us to recognize how the journey to the future is rooted in Sumerian and Hebraic soil.

To realize why religion is needed at all—and why, on the other hand, we cannot do without art and literature—we must see how diminished our common knowledge has become. Terms such as "spirit," "afterlife," "angels," and even "divine" are used as if their meaning were sufficiently defined by religious knowledge: you either believe in supernatural revelation or you don't. Yet when these meanings are taken for granted and not probed anew, we lose a sense of how the term "divinity," for instance, can represent a realm unknowable to us, beyond space and time. Meanwhile the unknown (that is, something that can one day be known and is not *unknowable*) is too easily taken for granted in scientific theory (as if we will one day know everything that is beyond the human senses). True, we may know what today seems impossible—the exact day and hour of our death, for instance—but by then our lives might have become artificially manipulated.

Meanwhile, the separation between secular culture and religion has to be refocused. The original conception of civilization in Sumer, as we have seen, helps us to do that. The mutual need of religion and culture for each other created a bold imagination when that need was understood—and later, when it was refined into the Hebraic cosmic theater. History was at the core of it, recording a journey to being at home in the landscape and in the universe in the same moment. That was Abraham's journey, out of Ur and into a land turned into a cosmic stage.

Yet it is no longer good enough to think that the Hebrew Bible is "miraculous," on the one hand, or literature with a political agenda on the other. It is an understandable product of human intelligence and art, growing out of a deep history that developed over centuries into ancient Hebraic culture. Built upon earlier ones going back to Sumer, Hebraic culture provided a new sensibility that is found in its first individual, Abraham, as well as in the authors who later shaped his life into episodes of the Bible. That is what we have witnessed in this book. But not long ago, little was known of the writing of the Hebrew Bible and the history that preceded it, resulting in endless confusion of the supernatural with the natural—as if it hardly mattered.

Even now, when God is invoked, the idea of supernatural power is so ingrained in us that we can easily forget how the biblical authors strove to portray the human side—the known side—of the boundary between us and what lies beyond time and space. In the episode of the sacrifice of Isaac, supernatural interference only *appears* to be so, and it is pushed aside in favor of natural events. The illusion was created that God was in control of the entire episode—by virtue of a "test." And yet the audience of the time understood that a test, like a dream, involved a literary trance. And so we must re-learn how the biblical author employs creative stagecraft that goes all the way back to Sumer.

The atmosphere this biblical writer has created of humans controlled by God's will feels uncanny to us because it is the condition of dreaming. Abraham and Isaac move and talk as if in a dream, their bodies beyond their control. Dreaming, as we have seen, was refined into dialogue between man and god in early Sumerian poetry. It was further refined in the Hebraic culture as communication between prophet-poet and the Creator: the author of this portion of Abraham's history was writing during the same period as the first literary prophets, including Isaiah. At the same time, our biblical author, E, had before him the J narrative and its Sumerian sources.

Abraham must finally test both God and covenant in a loaded dream (it appears that God is testing *him*, which is what makes it a nightmare), and we watch the events unfold in a literary spell that encompasses biblical character and reader equally. When Abraham "looked around"—breaking the spell to find a wild ram caught in a thicket—he has awakened naturally, and the covenant that would have been nullified by Isaac's death can now be repeated in its most poetic form.

For this thing you have done
your descendants will walk freely
through the gates of their enemy
and all the nations of the earth
will feel themselves blessed
one day, knowing
that your descendants thrive
living among them—
for it was you who listened
and heard my voice.

The covenant now validates the dream, in the manner of the prophetic dream-communication that was a paradigm for this time. There has been no divine intervention because that is not the expectation of the biblical author or the biblical audience. Instead, they harbor a rational hope for a natural outcome (as the wild ram signifies). The Hebrew debt to Sumer suffuses all that takes place around the writing of this episode: the testing of a covenant with the Creator; the tense diplomacy with nations reflected in the prophets' nightmares of destruction; and the faithfulness to history—to which the known names and places in the episode testify.

Even in Harran, when Abraham was called to leave his father's home he put into play a cosmic drama of Sumer, in which one's personal or household god interacts with the public god. The personal god gives the advice to leave the home, and the public creator-god takes over, promising "a land I will bring you to see."

J was consciously evoking for her Hebraic audience a merging of classical Sumerian rhetoric (the "advice" about leaving home and the "curses" on enemies, which also reminds us that the personal god speaking here was portable) with Hebrew's poetic universalism ("all families of earth [will] see themselves blessed in you") that only a creator-god like Yahweh could promise.

In the same way, the "divine inspiration" that guides the biblical author sifts the *public* sources of history through the author's *personal* inspiration—and in the balance between public and personal the Sumerian cosmos of temple and household gods continues to be acknowledged. Yet some scholars still proclaim "Anonymous" as the true author, citing a lack of physical testimony about the early Hebraic culture that was destroyed. But it is not all that surprising that it could have been lost within a shockingly short period. In our own time, a unique literary culture of authors in the Yiddish language was wiped out in Europe's Holocaust only a little more than half a century ago. It now remains the work of Jewish scholars in the future to keep the Yiddish authors' individual sensibilities alive, just as we seek to restore the humanness of the ancient biblical authors.

In order to anchor ourselves in history today, it's necessary to reimagine biblical inspiration. The attribution of "divine inspiration" simply covers over the history that has been missing—for if it was divine, who cares who the authors really were? It is precisely this "Who cares?" that hides the real caring of open-minded readers. For as we have seen, the earlier civilization of Sumer and the Hebraic one it continued to influence preserved the names of its authors; those authors needed no supernatural license to collaborate poetically with the gods. Moreover, the names of the authors we call J and E were no doubt preserved in their Hebraic culture as well, before it was conquered.

FAITH AND THE IRRATIONAL

The convergence of Abraham's journey with those of the original authors has been part of our story; so too has been the way in which Abraham's journey engages our own modern individuality. Like Abraham, we try in our own way to bridge the divide between secular culture and religion—even if only in the fictional realms of art and literature. That is why it is worth returning to the history of faith. While divine inspiration needs belief to support it, faith is more complicated. In the time of the biblical authors, faith continually *tested* belief. A productive culture arose from the interaction—rather than separation—of faith and skepticism. Today we lack this accommodating interface. In our modern notion of the opposition between church and state, faith is poorly represented by "church." But during the ancient Hebraic civilization, it was faith that probed the border between church and state, relishing and absorbing the exuberant writing at the kings' courts.

We have seen that it is the very uncertainty of where the boundary lies between the natural and the supernatural that necessitates Abraham's covenant with his God. Thus it would be reductive in this context to equate faith with certainty. In the life of Abraham, faith was primarily invested in covenant-making, probing the outer borders of human knowledge with the same art and creativity as science exhibits in the realm of the rational. Long before, faith had created a cosmic theater in which to portray the world beyond us, and by the time of Abraham's negotiation with the representative of that world—Yahweh the Creator—there are twists and turns that can take our breath away.

As we encounter the last chapter in Abraham's life and its realistic, Sumerian-like acceptance of death and covenant, it will be helpful to contrast the survival and meaning of that covenant today. These days we commonly accept the idea that anti-Semitism—the hatred of Abraham's covenant with God—is irrational. It was madness when Germany embraced it in the twentieth century, and it was madness when even the president of Malaysia mouthed it at the United Nations in 2004.

Anti-Semitism remains the realm where permission is given to deny the history of God, including the history of the covenant and its delineation of the unknowable. As we have seen, anti-Semitism even predates the writing of the Bible: it was symbolized by Sodom and Gomorrah then, cities that rejected Yahweh's universal "truth and justice." Yahweh made Abraham a witness to it.

BURIAL

The Hebrew Bible became a foundation for Christianity in the same way as the conquerors of Sumer appropriated Sumerian culture. At the time of Abraham, whose education in Ur would have been thoroughly Sumerian, the actual people of Sumer had become extinct. Those who weren't killed were enslaved and assimilated by their conquerors. But the Sumerian culture remained sacred in memory, as does the Hebrew Bible today for a world far larger than Jewry. As we have seen, Sumerian civilization influenced the historical Abraham of Ur, who enlivened and renewed it in the founding of a Hebraic culture. It was built upon a cherishing of the individual life and the principles of inheritance. And at the end of his own life, Abraham is obsessed with both as he prepares for death.

Abraham wants to die in a specific way, as a Sumerian would, but instead of a house he wishes to be buried in a cave that also commands the field before it, a wild place. It is a new drama that begins with Sarah's death but whose implications look out from the cave upon the entire Earth. When Abraham says

> *"I am a foreigner and an immigrant here"*

the word foreigner stands in for anyone. It is the opposite feeling about the word from that of an anti-Semite, whose identity is built upon contempt for strangers. The latter resents any representation of the cosmos that is not his own, and this resentment corresponds to a denial of wildness, of what it is to be a species and proclaim uniqueness. Although the modern understanding of nature includes a use for everything, the anti-Semitic worldview sets humans apart from nature. The wild ram that saved Isaac's life as well as the covenant between God and man would mean nothing to anti-Semites. Neither does the devotion to human history and historical record, since anti-Semitism is content to project its own fantasies of power over the "inferior races" or "infidels" of this world.

When Sarah dies, it is the human bond with Abraham that is our legacy, human love; it is a supremely natural death. No afterlife is invoked and no triumphant religion. Yahweh has withdrawn, and in his place Abraham is left to negotiate over the survival of his family's history.

> *And Sarah's life enfolded a hundred years and seven and twenty. Sarah died in Kiryat Arba—it is today Hebron—in the land of Canaan. Abraham mourned for Sarah, crying over her. Then Abraham stood and turned from the sight of his dead to the sons of Het, saying "I am a foreigner and an immigrant here. Allow me a field for a tomb among you. May I bury my dead here, out of my sight . . . "*

Hebron will later become the cultural capital of Israel prior to Kings Saul and David, and it is cited by J as historical proof: "it is today Hebron." "Today" is the seventh century BCE, a thousand years later, and this is P's story of the importance of contracts to Abraham, and he is careful to preserve a trace of the human plot ("Abraham mourned for Sarah, crying over her"). We sense what a great love existed between man and wife, perhaps as necessary a foundation for the new culture as any other. It balances the covenant drama of negotiating a burial plot. We have seen the diplomacy worked out before in the X episode, where Abraham and Melchizedek act out the contractual ethic of integrity, showing that it is based upon Yahweh's truth and justice. We see the same here:

> *Abraham took the weight of money of which the sons of Het had heard him speak and counted it out for Ephron. It was four hundred shekels of*

silver, according to the current rate. So Ephron's field in Machpelah, opposite from Mamre, was purchased by Abraham before the witness of the sons of Het. It included the cave that was in the field and every tree, and testimony to it was given at the city gate. So then Abraham buried Sarah, his wife, in the cave of the field of Machpelah, opposite Mamre—which today is Hebron—in the land of Canaan. So that the field and the cave within it were testified to, by the sons of Het, as passing in possession to Abraham.

The end of Abraham's life continues to be a negotiation of an individual's place in the world. To our continual surprise, Abraham's faith remains attached to the real world—to the integrity of a contractual covenant, as in Sumer, rather than a supernatural metaphor about the blessing of his descendants. After the nightmarish negotiation with Yahweh over Isaac's inheritance of the covenant, we re-awake in a real-world predicament: finding a place to be buried. But it has all—life and death—been a negotiation of one kind or another, and in every case it was based on the Sumerian way of establishing a rough equality to both sides.

Abraham has achieved an equal status in each of his negotiations based upon his integrity, which echoes Yahweh's "truth and justice." Just as Abraham's integrity has this cosmic dimension, it is also grounded on Earth, where the future is conceived of in the cultural terms of Abraham passing down his knowledge. A spiritual Abraham or a divine revelation is hardly to be found. We are face to face with real history, and the negotiation with neighbors that Abraham will now undergo helps to establish Hebraic principles. This art of diplomatic negotiation was crucial in the time of J and especially that of E, when prophets and historians alike are engaged in diplomacy based in ethics.

Even in Abraham's death, the Sumerian ethic will be honored: leaving the stage gracefully and not making a fixed monument of one's life. Thus Abraham's "journey" continues in our own history, since we still carry a faith in the written record. Written history is the educational foundation that Abraham bequeathed to Hebraic culture and to us, rooted in the Sumerian contract, the family record, and the problem of inheritance.

OVER THE SHOULDER

What remains to the life of Abraham is obsessed with the historical and documentary: Sarah's death; contracting for a burial place; finding a wife in Harran for Isaac; and listing Abraham's survivors. Finding a wife for Isaac is what we might call a "family contractual drama." Abraham asks his surrogate servant to "Swear for me, by Yahweh" that he will retrace his steps back to "my homeland, my birthplace." We face here Abraham's journey in reverse—and now he is not receiving advice about it from his God. Instead, he concludes the covenant by insuring that the next generation will also be steeped in a Sumerian background.

> *Now Abraham was very old, his better days—thoroughly blessed by Yahweh—behind him.*
>
> *"Please put your hand under my thigh," said Abraham to the senior servant, head of all under his roof. "Swear for me, by Yahweh, God of sky and earth, that you will choose no wife for my son from Canaanite daughters, though I'm settled among them. Instead, visit my homeland, my birthplace, bring out a wife for Isaac, my son."*

He wants no Canaanite influence, yet Abraham has already committed to Canaan when he negotiated burial rights. So he seeks to insure that the private, Sumerian education he gave to Isaac will be passed down to his grandchildren. The servant here is a sharp reminder of Eliezer of Damascus—"accountant of my house"—of whom Abraham complained to Yahweh long ago, the man who would inherit his household if he remained childless. Now, in an ironic reversal, it may be Eliezer or another in a similar position who will insure the inheritance is passed down. And he is painstaking in his task:

> *"What if the woman won't come, following me back to this land?" the servant asked him. "Do I then bring out your son—from here, back to the land you left behind?"*

But does it make sense that Abraham's servant-colleague suggests that Isaac go back to Mesopotamia if necessary? Could an Eliezer be clueless that the future of the covenant is precisely located in Canaan? But this is J's ironic text, and we note how the emphasis falls on the servant's repetition of covenantal language: "bring out" and "left behind." Instead of argument, what Abraham gives his servant is no less than an angel by his side, as we're about to see. It is a Sumerian household god turned into a guardian angel.

And now we become aware of where the angel will appear: in the region of Harran—exactly where Yahweh first advised Abraham in the manner of a Sumerian personal god. Then we hear how Yahweh is recognized by Rebecca and her family: "Come, Yahweh's blessed," says Laban to Abraham's servant. The recognition of Abraham's God here resembles the form used for a Sumerian household god. In Canaan, however, Yahweh had already grown into the "God in the skies" of the covenant. That is how Abraham refers to him now. But Abraham's servant speaks of Yahweh as if, like a household god, his primary concern is family relations—in short, arranged marriages.

> *"Watch yourself," Abraham said to him. "Don't turn to returning, especially my son. Yahweh, God in the skies, who took me out of my father's house, my homeland, who spoke to me, giving his word—'I will give this land to your seed'—will place his angel by your side, until you choose a wife from there, for my son. If she won't follow, won't be beside you, be cleansed of this vow—so long as my son doesn't settle there."*

Having prepared for grandchildren who will be linked to Canaan and to Sumer via Harran, Abraham has fulfilled his journey. The crucial thing now is that he has had a natural life—*and* that he will have a natural death. It is his death that renders him permanently historical, for it is an ordinary and natural death, yet it begins a complex literary process that continues to unfold in commentary and interpretation.

The original story spans millenniums, although the latest date in history at which it arrives is merely the sixth century BCE. The history of Abraham by that time had been solidified in the Hebrew Bible and amplified in legendary midrashic commentary. It will be many centuries until Christianity takes over these Hebrew sources, and then many centuries again before the Islamic interpretation of these same Jewish sources, although neither can any longer distinguish the historical from the legendary.

The covenant between Abraham and his God is also complex: it has been negotiated in many forms, including proclamation, direct conversation, cross-examination, ritual, psychodrama, reinterpretation, and, ultimately, Abraham's test of Yahweh with Isaac. It is also a test of inheritance. Isaac is the heir who must be educated in *two* cultures: that of his father, Abraham, who has come from the world's oldest civilization in Ur, and that of his father's *new* circumstances, an immigrant who will not assimilate in his new land.

So just as Isaac would have read of his heritage in Ur "over the shoulder" of his father, we are having to learn to read over the shoulders of the original authors. Together with their original audience, the authors embody the covenant within the Hebraic culture as it broke with local Canaanite tradition and reimagined the world with Sumerian sources. We can see that the biblical authors themselves inherited a poetic history, yet they shaped it into one that continues to negotiate and separate itself from the world of myth and superstition, where borders are confused. An author like J intended to express a new sensibility, corresponding to Abraham's and linking back to Sumer, one that teaches us to come close and explore the boundary between culture and religion, man and God.

WHY CULTURE AND RELIGION NEED EACH OTHER

Most people keep their faith separate from their objectivity when it comes to the natural world. We believe in science, in exploring the universe, and in understanding the history of human evolution and the origins of life. Most people, in other words, confine the realm of the supernatural to their faith in a supernatural being, or in a soul, or in an unnatural human perfectibility. In this way, we hope to know the difference between the two—natural and supernatural—and where the boundary lies between them. It is the same when it comes to the border between thinking and feeling: most people feel capable of suppressing their feelings and thus sensing a boundary between them and their mental powers.

Perhaps this is as superficial a way of thinking about religion and culture as to separate morality from art. It's a common cliché that religion is more high-minded than aesthetics, but we are all to some degree confused about our wishes and fantasies. Nearly all of our wishes can be thought of as supernatural, in that they ignore the laws of reality, however slightly. The most rational and atheistic among us may wish that they have permanently overcome irrational fears, for instance—and in that way they are thinking magically (or supernaturally) as opposed to realistically. We may wish to overcome poverty, boredom, sexual dysfunction, or tyranny, for instance, and instead of devising a rational plan we may daydream and override reality.

That is why it's important to continue to define the border between the natural and supernatural, as Abraham did. It's a daily struggle for the individual within society, and the best tools that we have are those that civilization has long honed, culture and religion. Each attempts to usurp the boundary of the other; religion wants to create literature and art to commend itself, while culture wants to colonize the realms of ritual, ethics, and prophetic history in order to lend itself moral authority. And so it has been the contention of this book that the origin of civilization lies in exploring the boundary between religion and culture. Abraham's journey, as we have followed it, spans this quest.

Even in a later interpretation from the Kabbalah, two thousand years after the original biblical authors, the renowned Rabbi Isaac Luria is still focused upon the sensibility of Abraham—just as J had been—although tradition had lost all knowledge of the real history.

> "This is the mystical meaning of God's command to Abraham: When he went to the Land of Israel, he caused the sexual principle ("Go forth . . . and I will make you into a great nation") to develop and mature into the level of 'intellectual' consciousness."
>
> —Rabbi Isaac Luria ("the Ari"), Kabbalist of Safed, 16th Century

While mysticism often confuses the supernatural with the natural, here is commentary that shows the need for a cultural basis to Abraham's journey. Sex and intelligence are not mere religious metaphors for the Ari (the "Lion of Learning"); his view of Abraham is that he founded a great nation of learning.

How the Christian religion embellished Abraham's history in the New Testament, and how the Islamic religion adopted its story of Abraham in the Qur'an from Jewish legends, testifies to radically different times. Two thousand years had passed between the time of Abraham and when the New Testament was being written; and it was several centuries later when the Qur'an came into existence. Not only was knowledge of Sumer and Mesopotamian history lost to these later authors but the language and culture of the original Hebraic authors and their audiences were now unknown. The Abraham who emerges in Christian and Islamic literature is thus a mythic figure.

When Paul speaks of Abraham, for example, in the New Testament's Book of Acts, it is not Abraham but his God who acts, turning Abraham into a figure of legend: "He caused to spring from one forefather people of every race, for them to live on the whole surface of the earth." Even today, in Western Judeo-Christian tradition, it's often assumed that Abraham's life is a legend. That's what makes it vital to return to historical sources in order to comprehend our origin. The Abraham of history presented a sensibility not unlike our own; he was a man who *had* to exist precisely because *we* exist in relation to his worldliness. At some point, a man or woman had to reconcile religion and culture. Abraham's life and death represent the first time that religion, governed by the creator-God Yahweh, informed secular culture in stories of truth and justice. And at the same time, a secular Hebraic culture joined religion in constructing a cosmic theater within the narrative art of the Hebrew Bible.

One of the major characters in the life of Abraham was Yahweh, the original God we know today, and I had to uncover ways to represent, first, how Abraham's education prepared him for their encounters, and then, how Abraham understood that a monotheistic Yahweh could dispel the earlier gods. I came to understand that Abraham's history is not a story of religion or theology but rather one whose background is the decline and development of cultures.

And in the foreground, a history is played out of remarkable intimacy between Abraham and his father, Terah (though it is largely implied); between Abraham and his wife, Sarah; between Abraham and his nephew, Lot; and between Abraham and his son, Isaac. The model for all intimacies in the Bible, however, is the one between Abraham and Yahweh, in which God disguises himself first as a father-figure and then as a man, conversing and hammering out with Abraham a covenant of inner and outer worlds.

After his history we find that religion too, like secular culture, need not exist in isolation. It is most alive as a human enterprise within cultural, social, and political contexts. Yet modern scholarship has focused upon restoring the social and political context—at the expense of the cultural. It has asked what the Bible is used for, what its political and moral motives are, but it has scanted its cultural origins. Even the literary studies that narrow the focus on priestly "redactors" of the Bible remystify the text by ignoring Hebraic culture.

The life story of Abraham, a journey of historical self-awareness, led to the founding of a new culture. It was a story that restored the original Sumerian creativity in exploring origins, from the Edenic land of origin, Dilmun, to the exotic wetlands of Sumer in lower Mesopotamia. If we are to be "Abrahamic" today, we might take our fuller knowledge of natural history and make of it a poetic theater where science and religion can come together. However, our contemporary understanding of speciation, as described in the science of biological evolution, hasn't yet found inspiring words to account for human prehistory as well as our future. We have no sign of a contemporary Abraham arriving to catalyze the story, yet once upon a time it happened for the Sumerians. The range of divine and natural beings in their cosmic theater had suggested all species—and then it was lost. But it was kept alive in the Hebraic culture that wrote the history of Abraham. Called out of Ur and Harran, Abraham brought the Creator down to earth and into the ongoing negotiation of our place in the cosmos.

Chronology

BCE

c.33,000 *World's oldest known great art discovered in the Chauvet cave of southern France in 1994. Natural creatures in their landscapes are portrayed, undistorted by supernatural material.*

c.8000 The city of Jericho (pop. 8,000), in Canaan, covers more than ten acres and is completely walled in.

c.4500 The city of Eridu, in Sumer, contains a temple similar to those in the early metropolitan cities known as city-states.

c.4000 Domestication of donkeys and expansion of caravan trade.

c.3500 Prototype of first terraced ziggurat built in Eridu.

c.3300 Uruk (pop. 55,000), the city of King Gilgamesh, is flourishing, along with other Sumerian cities. They are metropolitan, with central temple and civic institutions; public meeting places and art; business and trading sections; markets and harbors; schools and playgrounds; residential and factory quarters; and they are surrounded by small suburbs, farms, orchards, and pastures.

c.3100 First Dynasty of Ur

c.3000 Cuneiform, a complex system of abstract writing, has been invented in Sumer. In the previous millennium, a form of pictographic script was already in use for business, government, and religious communications, as well as personal documents and seals. With the advent of cuneiform, however, the culture explodes, as different dialects and languages can be represented and assimilated. Archives and libraries are expanded for literary texts on tablets, which are translated and transcribed from the earlier writing—and in some cases, oral tradition—as well as being newly composed. The new compositions are commissioned by royal court, temple, and eventually private citizens; the tradition of scribal schools and museums is begun.

c.2500 *Indus civilization in India, with numerous metropolitan cities and hieroglyphic script.*

c.2455 Second Dynasty of Ur.

c.2370 Sargon of Akkad conquers Sumer. Akkad was a Semitic civilization that absorbed Sumerian culture and established the first cohesive empire.

c.2300 Enheduanna, poet and translator, was appointed high priestess in the Temple at Ur.

c.2200 *Minoan civilization begins on the island of Crete.*

c.2112 The Third Dynasty of Ur is founded by Ur-Nammu.

c.2110 The first ziggurats in Ur, Uruk, and other cities.

c.2100 *The Middle Kingdom of Egypt begins. Hieroglyphic writing is newly codified, followed by a proliferation of texts.*

c.2000 Extensive histories of Ur and Sumer are written, of which the Sumerian Kings List survives.

c.1950 *Linear A script, the first Greek writing system, comes into use, but it has not yet been deciphered in our time.*

c.1900 Semitic Amorites immigrate and take over Sumerian-Akkadian cities, including Mari and Babylon. Mari was a cultural capital and center of scholarship; Babylon was a minor trading center.

c.1792 Hammurapi becomes king of Babylon and begins a campaign to unite the former Sumerian and Akkadian empires, turning Babylon into its capital.

The time of Terah, Abraham, Isaac, and their progeny begins in this period. A speculated dating of significant periods in their lives unfolds within the historical context of this book.

c.1750 It is approximately 1750 BCE (Before the Common Era, as history is noted by scholars) when Abraham is born in Ur, once the capital of Sumer and now, in Abraham's day, an already ancient center of classical culture. The early Hebrew Bible, however, written in Jerusalem seven centuries after Abraham's death, does not name dates. This may be for an obvious reason: the first audience of educated readers was familiar with a history of civilization of which we were largely ignorant until recently, when the clay tablets of Sumerian and Akkadian literature were deciphered.

c.1600 Development of old Canaanite alphabet, which will become the basis for writing the Hebrew language in c.1100.

c.1250 Moses and the Israelites who were enslaved come out of Egypt.

c.1000 *Ideogrammatic basis for writing Chinese language begins.*

c.1000 David moves the kingdom of Israel from Hebron to the new capital of Jerusalem.

c.980 Chaldeans occupy Ur.

c.965 David's son, Solomon, expands Israel.

c.928 Israel splits in two; Solomon's son, Rehoboam, becomes king of Judah.

c.920 *The Book of J,* a history of the world that begins with Creation and ends with the death of Moses, is written in Jerusalem at the royal court of Rehoboam. It is one of several historical narratives commissioned by the early Judaic kings, including the early history of Hebrews and Israelites up to Kings Saul and David.

c.810 *The E History* composed for the royal court in Samaria.

c.740 Amos written in Samaria; First Isaiah written in Jerusalem.

c.721 Destruction of Northern Kingdom of Israel and its capital in Samaria by Assyrian empire.

c.586 Destruction of Jerusalem and Judah by Babylonian empire; exile of Jews to Babylon.

c.550 *The P text,* adding to and re-editing the combined narratives of J and E.

Essential Notes in the Margin

HISTORY AND TODAY

It's not uncommon to claim that a new book is the first to do this or that. There are always historical firsts in publishing. For instance, I could say that no previous biography of Abraham has set out to be a full historical portrait, building upon comparative history and literature rather than relying upon religious authority. Preceding books have been satisfied to interpret the legends.

But there is a crucial second sense of "first" that provides *Abraham*'s subtitle. Abraham is the first individual in history for whom we can study more than one ancient culture to achieve a portrait in depth of an ordinary citizen. The distinct cultures of Sumer, Akkad, Babylon, Assyria, Canaan, and Israel are all part of his history. Yet no part of Abraham's life is claimed to be either kingly or divine, as are prior figures. After Abraham, who lived in the eighteenth century BCE, the next individual whose life can be drawn from the perspective of several cultures is the historical Buddha who lived in the sixth century BCE, Shakyamuni. That is a huge jump forward in time.

Abraham's life is our first historical one. In modern times, we know there is no leaving it all behind—no escape from history. Abraham was a man who brought the baggage of civilization with him when he left Mesopotamia. The voice of his God did not ask him to leave it all behind; instead, the God of Abraham asked that what had come before be transformed into a new way of recording history.

—

But the old idea that all our fathers might be Abrahams is beside the point. A historical figure is not an archetype. The point is that we all are Isaacs, male and female, and that the way to survive our fathers is to record their lives—rather than to act them out. If Isaac didn't pass down his father's life, we wouldn't know Abraham. And we wouldn't know Isaac either, since his father would have killed him (figuratively) with the need for obedience. Instead, Isaac saves himself by finding his own way to keep the story alive: he makes his father into a *dreamer.* As a result, the history that is recorded avoids either sentiment or alienation.

Today, it's a tremendous misunderstanding of the dream-story of Isaac's sacrifice that lies behind justifications of suicide bombing by contemporary youngsters. Theological interpretations are almost always wrong when they interpret the text literally, hallowing the notion that there is no right choice to be made between obedience to faith and waking up from a nightmare.

As with the figurative rather than the historical Abraham, many modern scholars think that the appearances of God in the Bible are likewise mythical. These scholars tend to discount the supernatural. But this book attempts a new way of conceptualizing the supernatural in the relationship between religion and culture. A cosmic theater is explained, in which God and humanity share a supernatural stage imposed upon a natural landscape. Thus, we arrive at a new understanding of the original authors of the Bible as spiritual historians as well as poet-scholars.

In this historical view, there is the critical character of the Creator's voice, which begins as the voice of the household god in Ur and evolves into the God of Abraham. The Creator appears in disguise with his messengers, seeking to enter human history through the family and become its source of education in the unfolding of history, both natural and cosmic. Yet the Creator remains in the background of this story. It is always foremost a history of struggling to grow and survive as a family—not only physically but culturally. The cultural uniqueness of Abraham is what throws a natural emphasis on his background in Ur.

There are several variants of "Ur" attached to present-day sites. Urfa in Turkey is one that has taken advantage of that since the Middle Ages. Many of the legends about Abraham and his wanderings were "authenticated" in Muslim tradition at that time, but they in fact date back to much earlier Christian and Jewish legend. Mostly Jewish. There were important Jewish communities on the Arabian peninsula at the time the Qur'an was being written in the seventh century CE and its scribes weighed the Jewish knowledge in their own spiritual scales. Those legends with serious weight in their eyes became part of their foundational history.

But once again, Abraham's first home was described as "Ur of the Chaldees." Yet there were no Chaldeans in Abraham's day or before. The Chaldeans were a new empire that inhabited Ur just a century or so before the Bible was being written, so the purpose of referring to "Ur of the Chaldees" was to highlight the site for the Bible's Hebraic audience. In other words, this part of the Bible was being written in Jerusalem for the educated and literate classes of a few thousand souls surrounding the king's court, and they would have known of their present-day Ur as a capital of contemporary Chaldeans. It would have been clear to them that the site was the same as the ancient Ur of the Sumerians and not any other Ur-like-sounding place, including Uruk, the archaic seat of King Gilgamesh.

Ur is dust in our day—and it was also dust in the Middle Ages, when Urfa was solidifying its legends. Nobody has known where Ur was through thousands of years after Israel's first kings, and not until the early twentieth century was it partially dug up. Found in the digs were hundreds of literary texts that make it quite clear that the legends of Urfa and Islamic tradition, along with Judeo-Christian legend, are apocryphal. There is no evidence of Arabian or Turkish detours for

Abraham; he would have followed a well-traveled path from Ur to Canaan, passing through Damascus.

Archaeologists, who dig into the historical ground, nevertheless have a penchant for avoiding history when it comes to literature. The history of the world was written in cuneiform before the Bible writers began, and it too was a form of digging, incising abstract sculptural forms in clay. Rather than face up to it, many archaeologists assume writing merely recorded oral histories. Since the writers were simply recorders in this view, they were beholden to political or religious agendas: they chose and slanted what they recorded in order to further their aims. Rarely does an archaeologist come along like Leonard Woolley, the excavator of Ur, who takes into account the artistic aims and the dedication to truthfulness of the writers.

The biblical author J, for instance, may have been more interested in Abraham and other biblical figures, but it is Abraham's God who underpins Western civilization and the monotheistic religions of Judaism, Christianity, and Islam. Until now, far more has been contemplated about the God of Abraham than about Abraham's life. Thus, for the human subject and the cosmic one to come together in our own day—as if upon the same stage—a new form of history is required. This form of biography can show how the Bible's first authors witnessed their own history in artistic form: human history and the cosmic realm unfolding as one. The power of artifice in the biblical text comes from the invention of its cosmic theater. To sustain the metaphor, as this biography of Abraham attempts, is to be able to hold religion and culture in mind (rather than merely the topical polemics between them) as if it mattered today.

Are we today the new cultural Babylonians, making endless copies and variations in contemporary books and art? Or are we actually in the process of becoming new Sumerians and Hebrews—our landscape transformed by the science of evolutionary time and our human history deepened by natural history? After Abraham, Earth opened up and the landscape of space became a stage, while the natural unfolding of time was what we counted as history. Within this modern theater today, as the boundaries between space and time disappear again (after Einstein), we are reminded of our first explorers in Sumer and Israel. Each employed written literature and commentary to expand the walls of the temple and place them within our own minds.

—

What we can say in the end is that Abraham was a real person and that he brought a new way of recording history to Canaan. That new way is what I have called a cosmic theater, in which Abraham's God enters human history. After Abraham, the history of heaven and the gods themselves is no longer of interest; humanity takes center stage in its full sexuality and thirst for knowledge. The Creator's problem with sexuality and the way heirs are produced (how is the new religion to be passed on?) becomes humanity's problem with knowledge: how to educate our inheritors. All of this is dramatized on the same stage for the first time, the landscape that will be named Israel.

—

When a scientist or scholar says, "I don't know," they have reached a border. Either they will push it back and the unknown will become known, or they will declare what lies beyond the border as unknowable by the human species and therefore in the realm of religion. And when a clergyman says, "I don't know," he or she has likewise reached the same border from the other side: what is unknowable may very well be possible to know but as yet unknown. Neither science nor religion minds saying "I don't know" in the beginning, for it signals a desired search for knowledge. But neither is usually ready to admit in the end that their way to knowledge is lost, and that the journey ends in "I don't know." There are signs, however, that this admission is growing in strength today, and what that portends is a new encounter with the boundary between natural and supernatural. That is where Abraham found himself in his day, and if we are to learn from it we need to reencounter the biblical cosmic theater with an enlarged vision of human history. We didn't create this world or any of the more than ten million species now alive, including *Homo sapiens.* But if we can continue to imagine a Creator who is both personal and yet unknowable—that is, if we can enter the linguistic drama of the unknowable without losing our place in our reading of the natural world—then we will see ourselves as explorers of the boundary. Such was Abraham of Ur, the figurative last Sumerian and the historical first Jew.

Perhaps the most overlooked cultural event of the twentieth century was the huge revival of spoken and literary Hebrew, to the extent that any Israeli newspaper reader can skim the Hebrew text of three thousand years ago with little difficulty and thus reconnect with Abraham's original heirs: they, too, were readers, though merely a few thousand literate souls.

Selected Bibliographic Notes

Hundreds of books, monographs and articles were consulted in research for this volume. Many took months to track down; for instance, "Donkey Breeding in Sumer," which helped to understand Terah's stopping in Harran. The same holds true for an Italian article of eighty years ago, on the Canaanite culture of Sodom. Something could be said for each of the hundreds of entries, yet the vast majority would remain of academic interest only. So I have selected representative books that range from the important and unique to the typical and predictable, annotating each one.

Abba Eban, *Heritage: Civilization and the Jews.* New York: Simon & Schuster, 1984.

This book was the companion to the most popular history of the Jews composed in the late twentieth century. Eban himself narrates many hours of a film documentary that is distilled into the book, and it's a worthy condensation, beginning in ancient Sumer, "when Jewish history begins." Yet like many before him, Eban fails to separate the culture from the religion. His Sumer reflects a confusion of myth and poetry, as if the Sumerian poets themselves "believed" the archaic myths they used for their poetic art. The same fundamental error is carried over into the writing of the Bible. We are to assume that the biblical writers were fundamentalists at one with their subjects and sources, when actually they took many creative points of view for the sake of both historical and contemporary accuracy. Still, Eban is among the first of world figures to impress us with the richness and depth of Sumerian culture. His Abraham steps out of a Hebraic history that we feel is grounded in world history.

Edward Chiera, *They Wrote on Clay*, edited by George G. Cameron. Chicago: University of Chicago Press, 1938.

This book was posthumously edited from a draft by one of the great explorers of Sumer. It was an attempt to communicate with the educated layperson the grandeur of something that appears to be flat. The best way to describe Chiera's goal in this work is to imagine him as a scientist of the Everglades trying to communicate the richness and power of his seemingly monotonous landscape to an audience accustomed to hearing about Yosemite or Yellowstone. The mountains of Yosemite need only be looked at like a coffee table picture book; the wetlands of the Everglades must be read. Of course there is much more to Yosemite, but the point is we can be impressed without knowing what we are missing. Chiera was in competition for the affections of his potential readers with his own field's equivalent of Yosemite: the Egyptologists, who could count on immediate sympathy by staggering us with a pyramid or mummy. All that Chiera had to show were contracts, letters, and the dirt mounds where they were found. Indeed, Chiera opens his book with a discussion of this dilemma, using well-known Egyptian finds for counterpoint. The method he chooses to resolve the dilemma is ingenious, and when one is through with reading the book, a pyramid or Egyptian tomb will never be thought of again without thinking of Sumerian libraries (such was the preponderance of writing and records on the clay tablets of Sumer and Akkad that they outnumbered all the mud bricks of the Egyptians). In Sumer, a cuneiform tablet was worthy of recording all manner of histories, from temples and courts to shopkeepers and donkey breeding. Even if a Sumerian could not read, he or she knew enough to find someone who could, to inscribe any business in cuneiform on clay. An aspiration for educating their children was made possible for the Sumerians by those two things: clay and cuneiform.

Clay was everywhere, and only a stylus and what was in one's head were needed to inscribe them. Schooling and training were not uniform, but they were at the core of what was respected. What is most valuable in this small book is how it suggests a world in which nearly every event, every cultivation and transaction, was inscribed, catalogued, and annotated, reflecting a hunger for knowledge. The scholarly work of Chiera and others is beginning to be inscribed, too—as well as their primary Sumerian sources—through digitized translations onto the Internet, with copies in several collections (mimicking Sumerian practice). As cuneiform tablets have become readable on Web pages, we may be coming closer to recognizing ourselves as latter-day Sumerians.

Sir Leonard Woolley, *The Sumerians.* New York: Oxford University Press, 1940.

Prior to this book, Woolley, one of the world's foremost archaelogists, wrote several books and monographs on the excavations of Sumer and Akkad and particularly at Ur. Unlike most archaeologists, Woolley was a writer and thinker with a range of irony almost unknown in the world of archaeology and Mesopotamian history. To read him is to understand how Sumerian writers and artists demanded greatness in their work—our first Western conception of what makes great art and literature. However, Woolley does not tell this to us directly; rather, he provides a historical portrait that sweeps across culture and religion—from political history to marriage and divorce. When Woolley reaches "the end of the Sumerians," we understand what a great loss it was. We also understand how Abraham would have been able to assimilate this loss within himself via his scribal education at Ur.

Sir Leonard Woolley, *Abraham: Recent Discoveries and Hebrew Origins.* New York: Charles Scribner's Sons, 1936.

"There are good grounds for believing that the fact of Abraham's existence was vouched for by written documents." No one, including Woolley, has found these specific documents, but the mere assumption of their existence sets Woolley apart from other biblical archaeologists and historians. It is only his lack of familiarity with Hebraic studies that keeps this book from becoming a rudimentary biography of Abraham. We are never close to understanding Abraham's sensibility, particularly his religious creativity. Yet the historical reconstruction of Abraham's Ur remains stunning to this day, even though many details have been updated since Woolley's death. For some reason, this book passed under the radar of biblical scholarship, probably due to Woolley's unconventional creative strengths. Even Abba Eban appears not to have read it, thus missing out on so much of Jewish, Christian, and Islamic prehistory.

Samuel Noah Kramer, *Sumerian Mythology: A Study of Spiritual and Literary Achievement in the Third Millennium B.C.* New York: Harper and Row, 1944 (revised 1961).

Kramer's many books have helped us to realize that the Sumerians were like us. This book extends that comparison to the artistic aspects of their culture. Kramer's translations, in many cases, were the first readable ones. However, it's up to the reader to deduce the literary and spiritual qualities of Sumerian poets, because like many scholars, Kramer has difficulty imagining the Sumerian writer's sensibility and motivation. The great Greek poets and dramatists gave archaic myths new psychological dimensions—they were poets first, not mythmakers. But the Sumerian poets preceded them. Nevertheless, in Kramer's book, it remains hard to separate myth from literature, and that is a great failing. Few books, however, have provided such a wealth of signposts and maps to further study. Kramer has extended Woolley in helping us to face the genius of Sumerian creativity. (In fact, it was Kramer who first stitched together the handful of Sumerian poems about King Gilgamesh that had already been deciphered by the 1930s, when this book originated.)

Jean Bottéro, *Religion in Ancient Mesopotamia* (originally published in French in 1998). Chicago: University of Chicago Press, 2001.

This book purports to be a definitive account of one of the world's oldest known religions and, like Kramer's book, insists on how much like us the Mesopotamians were. Like Woolley and Kramer, Bottéro has a lively mind worth following, even when it seems to be going in the wrong direction. Bottéro provides layers of delineation—up through Babylonian and Assyrian religion—in a way that clarifies our ultimate debt to the Sumerian imagination. However, Bottéro himself does not do enough to interpret the significance of this. Instead, he journeys on, noting the Sumerian influence upon the writing of the Hebrew Bible while failing to consider the authors or their Hebraic culture.

In an earlier book (*The Birth of God: The Bible and the Historian,* 1986 in French) Bottéro suggested how Sumerian inspiration was magnified in Israel. "This very small people succeeded in not only formulating but in solving the supreme problems of religious thought, which those powerful and immortal Babylonians had barely caught sight of." Unfortunately, Bottéro was able to exalt religious thought while separating it from its original creative culture, much in the manner of more conventional scholars.

Jean Bottéro, *The Oldest Cuisine in the World: Cooking in Mesopotamia* (originally published in French in 2002). Chicago: University of Chicago Press, 2004.

From these kitchen recipes, many derived from Sumerian cuneiform tablets, Bottéro enlarges the frame to include the relationship between the art of cooking and the appreciation of a culture and religion. The preparation of food by the Sumerians ranges from intimate dinner parties to the "Table of the Gods." There are drinks and there are "artistic creations." But always at the forefront is the Sumerian and Akkadian culture that is indirectly illuminated by the linking of metaphors of food and eating, living and dying. Thereby, this book recreates a sense of ancient intellectual reality.

Karen Rhea Nemet-Nejat, *Daily Life in Ancient Mesopotamia.* Westport, CT: Greenwood Press, 1998.

This book is a synthesis that ranges from the lowest funerary footstool to archives and libraries. Nemet-Nejat builds up an impressive campus of facts, and it is up to us to determine which classes to take. Date Cultivation or Ghosts of the Dead? In fact, it is the date palms we have most to learn from, though this book will leave that up to you. And then there are the origins of writing, canals and irrigation, foreign trade, and women's roles—all of seemingly equal import and common inspiration. Still, Sumer remains lost. There is little sense of how great the loss is—almost as if we were back in the Middle Ages and had not heard of Athens.

Ephraim A. Speiser, *Genesis: Introduction, Translation, and Notes* (The Anchor Bible). New York: Doubleday, 1962.

Speiser was a student of Chiera's and became that rare hybrid today of archaeologist, linguist, biblical scholar, and literary historian. Consider first one of his early monographs, *Excavations at Tepe Gawra* (University of Pennsylvania Press, 1935). Not only does Speiser communicate the loss of Sumer at the same time as he treasures what has survived, he goes behind Sumer to pre-literate cultures: Tepe Gawra is the "Great Mound," and in its lower layers a whole civilization was reimagined by Speiser. It is based on finds as various as pottery and toilet instruments, frying pans and cylinder seals, amulets and Temple burials. But this culture had not yet begun to write. "The cultures in question are prehistoric largely because they are pre-literate and hence articulate only in terms of material remains." And yet Speiser renders these remains articulate by relating them to the explosion of writing in Sumer. So that when, in his late great work, *Genesis,* Speiser comes to situate parts of the Bible in Sumerian sources, we feel the weight not only of the millenniums of writing that preceded the biblical writers but also the complex pre-literate art and religion receding even further back in time.

To some historians, the Bible is imagined as merely a record of oral history and thus its actual writing is to be safely ignored. This allows these timid souls an added benefit: it avoids giving offense to those of pious religious belief, for whom the writing was orally inspired (literally, *breathed*) by the Creator. For Speiser however, human history itself is sacred, and thus the historical writing of the Bible is crucial to know for all of humanity. As Speiser understood and as his notes for this book bear out, Abraham probably discovered how deep was the loss of Sumer and Harran when he left them behind. It was parallel in some ways to the loss expressed in the classical Sumerian laments Abraham would have known. We can therefore understand his motivation to create a culture that could not be lost—that would be written into history, as the Hebrew Bible has proved. The range of Speiser's learning so far exceeds our contemporary scholars that we are allowed to feel what Abraham feels as his entire ancient world is brought to life.

Most books after Speiser actually retreat from history, shrinking into narrow academic scholarship and linguistic theory that requires little imagination. How the text came to be written is usually of less concern than how it was edited and thus can be homogenized for a multitude of courses. But ancient Hebraic culture and its origins remain repressed, as they were when Speiser rejected the German scholarly notion of impersonal "strands" and treated the J and E portions of the text as living authors with cultural points of view. The culture we are most in need of is the one in which Hebraic authors, like great writers in cultures before them, created a cosmic stage—this time in narrative—upon which man and God interacted, often uncannily, depending on the greatness of the individual author.

When we read Speiser we hear "Go forth from your land and your birthplace and your father's house" as the words and rhetoric of partisan "advice" given by a Sumerian personal god, whose job it was to counsel the household. But the Sumerian household god was also portable, so that Abraham's father's ancestral god was brought from Ur to Harran. It was this god who had originally advised Abraham's father, Terah, to leave for Canaan in the preceding passage. Terah had done so, but he stopped in Harran, the farthest outpost where the authority of a Sumerian god was recognized. This is but one of many openings into history that Speiser has given us and that continues to be ignored by scholars today. Instead, we are offered the reincarnated spirit of Martin Buber, for instance, who is made to represent a primitive oral unity in the text (see Buber entry that follows).

Martin Buber, *On The Bible: Eighteen Studies,* ed. Nahum N. Glatzer from Buber's *Collected Works* in German, 1964. New York: Schocken Books, 1982.

Buber reacted strongly to the leading German biblical scholars who presumed to delve into historical authorship. He felt that they neglected the Jewish or Hebraic sensibility of the authors—or worse, demeaned Hebraic cultural origins. To counter them, Buber insisted on the oral origin of the Bible, of which no archaeological proof existed, confounding the Germans. Yet Buber was ironic here, to the point that his essays on the Bible mostly ignore the oral assertion and concentrate on the Bible's sophisticated literary articulation of Hebraic religion and culture.

But Buber was also a translator of the Hebrew Bible (into German, with Franz Rosenzweig), and he was greatly dissatisfied with the academic biblical scholarship that identified the authors as J, E, and P, among others, but failed to humanize them and their artistic aims. For Buber and other Israeli scholars, the Europeans were too close to dealing with text and culture as if they were dead. But when Buber writes of Abraham, "The man sees, and sees also that he is being seen," the parallel to Buber's contemporary, the British psychologist D. W. Winnicott, is uncanny. Although Winnicott is describing the relationship between mother and infant, "the reciprocity of seeing between God and man," as Buber puts it, marks the same revelation. For once the infant recognizes that its mother is more than the sum of her parts—breasts, eyes, arms, etc.—she achieves a oneness that accounts for the child's radical reconception of itself. And here, in parallel, we enter the realm of what Buber calls reciprocity. In this book, Abraham is the origin of this reconception, and the author J dramatizes this reciprocity in the covenant-making between Yahweh and Abraham.

Apart from Buber's metaphysical insights, however, his essays remain a step behind the illuminations of history that Speiser advanced. For Buber's notion of the written text required him to consider it "unhistorical." The text in Buber's hands becomes numinous, even "a voice," yet at the expense of grasping its surprisingly fertile ancient history. Without ancient Hebraic culture and its writers, Buber nevertheless managed to ally biblical vision with Sumerian origins, each attuned to the cosmic drama of daily life.

Benjamin Mazar, ed., *Patriarchs.* New Brunswick, NJ: Rutgers University Press, 1961, 1970.

Mazar was a student of Speiser's, who is also included in this volume along with colleagues H. L. Ginsberg and Moshe Greenberg. In one breathtaking volume, we are able to compare Sumerian, Ugaritic, Canaanite, Babylonian, and other cultural influences that shaped the lives of Abraham and his offspring. More pertinently, the alphabets of these pre-biblical and other Semitic languages are graphically contrasted, including their cuneiform redactions. Mazar himself brings together Akkadian documents from Mari with Egyptian documents and others to establish the donkey caravan routes that traversed Canaan. He confirms "the spread of the Akkadian language and culture in the Western Fertile Crescent," and he shows how cuneiform-written Akkadian became the lingua franca of trade and diplomacy in the ancient world.

While the historical breadth of this volume is considerable, Mazar and his colleagues neglect to show how the Jerusalem court and the Hebraic culture that was responsible for the Bible were educated and influenced. Nor do we learn how those alive and literate during the patriarchal age were educated. Yet it remains obvious that those alive in these ancient eras would have been students of ancient cultures—no less than these scholars of our own day, thousands of years later.

Jeffrey H. Tigay, *The Evolution of the Gilgamesh Epic.* Philadelphia: University of Pennsylvania Press, 1982.

As evidenced by recent translations, the original Sumerian poems of Gilgamesh have been largely ignored in favor of the later Akkadian reductive epic (in its even later Babylonian rescension). This epic is sometimes taught in universities today as if it was an original poem "authored" by a great Babylonian redactor. Tigay's book would seem to demolish this illusion of an original epic. Instead, Tigay opens up for us the reality of multiple poems and multiple sources. If anything is original, it is the oldest Sumerian written poems of Gilgamesh, which for Tigay cover the years between 2800 and 1700 BCE. Eleven centuries of Sumerian poetry was our greatest heritage and the fact that much of it has not yet been found should rivet our attention.

But it is not for Tigay or any more recent translators to reckon this loss; rather, they all blithely pass on to the redacted Akkadian epic of roughly 1700 BCE—precisely the time when Abraham may have been studying its already ancient but still vital sources. Abraham would have absorbed and internalized the loss of Sumer and the richness of classical Sumerian culture, including the original poems of Gilgamesh for which today we have only fragments (in some cases, barely a few words). Ignoring this great literary loss, Tigay proceeds to examine the various formulations and redactions of the Akkadian and later Babylonian epic. Although but a tiny capsule of the original Sumerian oeuvre, the Babylonian epic has entered our academic canon by virtue of being close to fully documented on clay tablets. The power of Tigay's book is to reveal how this came about and how extensive are the various documents.

Still, we miss the original Sumerian confrontation with archaic myth and the Sumerian poets' sublime distinctions between religion and culture. It is disappointing to find Tigay referring to them as "Sumerian stories" or, in the locution of recent translators, "Sumerian tales." These great poems tamed the wildest of archaic myth and spiritual journeys—creating a historical context for them at the beginning of recorded history. For instance, the character who is called Enkidu in the Babylonian epic is reckoned to have been "a wild man." But for the Sumerian poets he was a man who was born into a *culture*—albeit a nonhuman culture. For us moderns today, and I suspect already by the time of the Babylonian version of Gilgamesh, it had become impossible to even imagine our existence in anything but a human culture.

Andrew George, *The Epic of Gilgamesh: A New Translation: The Babylonian Epic Poem and Other Texts in Akkadian and Sumerian.* New York: Penguin Press, 1999.

One of the great virtues of George's translation is that he surrounds it with some of the Sumerian poems of Gilgamesh that are extant, as well as Babylonian texts ranging from Ugarit to Israel. As a Sumerian and Akkadian scholar, George cannot forget the depth of the Gilgamesh epic's origin in Sumer. And so, as we read the later Gilgamesh epic in George's fertile translation, we're exposed to the vicissitudes of history with a rich seasoning of ellipses the translator employs. While these ellipses and additional reminders of lacunae convey what we may have lost in the Akkadian redaction, they also force us to recall the Sumerian *Bilgames* (Gilgamesh). Among George's incisive intros and appendices, we find this: "new pieces of Gilgamesh continue to appear." We can also hope that new pieces of the Sumerian oeuvre are still to be found or creatively restored and re-imagined by poet-scholars.

N. K. Sandars, *Poems of Heaven and Hell from Ancient Mesopotamia.* New York: Penguin Press, 1971.

When we read these translations of a few Sumerian poems, we begin to understand how Abraham's inner world would have been connected to the cosmos. Even as they are immersed in myth, these poems evince less interest in the afterlife and reveal a greater trust in natural processes and the soul, the latter an analogy for Abraham's inner world. Bilgames or Gilgamesh's quest for "fame"—whether a name, a place, or an immortal soul—will correspond to Abraham's journey-quest for "a place that lasts." These Sumerian poems amount to meditations on the soul and remind us how much we have yet to learn from the literary heritage of Sumer.

Israel Finkelstein and Neil Asher Silberman, *The Bible Unearthed: Archaeology's New Vision of Ancient Israel and the Origin of Its Sacred Texts.* New York: Free Press, 2001.

These authors have set out to turn Martin Buber's world of the Bible upside down. They step on the pedal of historicity and crash through the text as if it were the sound barrier. The biblical authors are reduced to "politicians or historians" with an agenda, thus rendering them voiceless as far as their art, education, or intelligence is concerned.

When, where, and why was the Bible first written? Their theory is one-sided because these authors display no idea of how a great writer conceives of literature. They ask, "Is the Bible true?" Yet what actually is the *truth* in art if not built upon the *humanity* of the author and his or her culture. This book is not really interested in that, nor is it interested in separating myth from reality; rather, it fantasizes upon the political agendas of certain kings and priests in history and assumes the Bible was written as a form of propaganda to further those agendas. Thus this book is able to conclude that the history of Israel was not first written in the time of David and Solomon, but rather was invented by authors of an ideological bent more than two centuries later.

Since there are no written artifacts of the original writing of the Bible for these authors to dig up out of the ground, J does not exist for them. "There is no sign whatsoever of extensive literacy" in her day, according to this book. And yet, since it did not take more than a few thousand literate souls to become the audience for J and E, why should we expect to find their libraries? For some unexplained reason the authors of this book assume that the Bible was originally written for the masses.

The Hebrew kings who are supposed to have rewritten biblical history to serve their political and ideological ends amount to a form of fiction in this book. In Jerusalem and Samaria, the court culture would have first demanded definitive character in their stories of history—and not ideology. They would have embraced Abraham's Sumerian roots rather than merely his local significance. Political agendas would have been attached to the biblical narratives later. Yet Finklestein and Silverman invent "seventh century creators of this national epic" by assuming that they "wove together earlier stories" that had no authors or history of their own. Perhaps only the head of a grandiose academic department today could imagine biblical authors as agendas, their stories "woven" as if by looms rather than humans.

To be generous, an answer might be found to this book's motivation in the literary origin of parts of the Bible. In their own way, the archaeologists behind this book are reacting against contemporary literary critics who presume to dig into the text as if they were credentialed literary archaeologists. This literary digging no doubt goes too far when it discovers artistic tools and linguistic devices used to make the text—allusion, metaphor, and rhetoric among them—without reimagining the sensibilities of those who made the tools. So the longtime antagonists of archaeological and literary scholarship in the field of Bible studies are still at it.

Jonathan N. Tubb, *Canaanites.* London: British Museum Press, 1998.

The author, an archaeologist, has given us a wonderfully ironic book. Probably against his best intentions, he reveals both the pre-biblical, Canaanite origins of Hebraic culture as well as the literary and theological uniqueness of Israel. Tubb appears to think that he is arguing against the Bible as a historical document—an agenda shared by many archaeologists who must make do with words in lieu of artifacts. Yet in fact, the historicity of the Bible is not about documents but rather the origins and development of Hebraic sensibility. To his credit, Tubb acknowledges this when he writes that the source material drawn upon by J "probably included historical texts." However, he is unable to view J as anything more than a historian herself: "the motivation for composition was surely to create a historical 'golden age.'" So our impression is meant to be that J was really not much of a historian but rather given to inspirational fantasy. Thus a faint whiff of anti-Israel feeling permeates this work, as it does among many British and European archaeologists who write about Canaan.

The real motivation for J's written history is cultural: a Hebraic audience who knew how to appreciate the newly literate art of history. Perhaps what is worth learning from this book is how Tubb describes Canaanite artistic traditions, "drawing elements from a variety of sources and countries, and blending them together." In this regard, Israel appears not only to fit right in the land but also to exercise the greatest of restraint in the "blending."

Raphael Kutscher, *Oh Angry Sea (a – ab – ba hu – luh – ha): The History of a Sumerian Congregational Lament.* New Haven: Yale University Press, 1975.

Kutscher connects the Bible, via the Book of Lamentations, to Sumerian laments dating back many centuries earlier. More than that, he traces how the Sumerian genre had "degenerated into a ritual lament full of standardized clichés"—a typical fate of great Sumerian poems in Babylon. Like Tigay, Kutscher elucidates a literary tradition that is built upon great Sumerian poets. We are shown how the composition of "Oh Angry Sea" was motivated by an actual destructive event in Sumer and how it was adapted into the Sumerian cosmic theater "at ceremonies marking the demolition and rebuilding of temples." What is sublime in Kutscher is that he always considers the full Sumerian cosmic theater. For instance, he notes how most city laments, although bearing directly upon the occasion for which they were written, were eventually "scrapped from cultic use and were retained as secular literary works, appreciated for their belletristic values only."

Revealed to us here, for instance, are the poetic ironies of the names for gods in Sumer—for example, "The One Who Feigns Sleep"—in contrast to the later shriveling of serious play in Babylon and Canaan. And at the back of this book are stunning photographs of the actual Sumerian cuneiform tablets that contain the complete text.

Harold Bloom and David Rosenberg, *The Book of J.* New York: Grove Press, 1990, 2005.

It was not the concern of Harold Bloom or myself to identify the bones or genealogy of the Bible's first great writer, J. Rather, by focusing upon her sensibility in almost daily conversation over a period of three years, we attempted to re-create the vitality of the living Hebraic culture in which she worked. I grew increasingly worried about Bloom's obsession with J's "genius," however, to the exclusion of her

Hebraic sources, including the life of Abraham and his family. He was right in the beginning: it was important to establish the fact of the J writer's independent brilliance, for without it the uncanny and thus lasting effect of her work would be difficult to confirm. But I grew concerned about Bloom himself, for he may have been naïve about how much his scholarly colleagues resented his anxiety about genius-hood. Sure enough, many of these scholars attacked him after the book was published, and thereafter my old friend Bloom wanted little more to do with Hebraic sources.

So the idea for this biography of Abraham took root after *The Book of J* was published. It developed out of the continuing need to restore the lost Hebraic culture at the source of our Western heritage. The necessity for this restoration was firmly planted in *The Book of J* and remains accessible there. In the words of Emmanuel Levinas, "To admit the effect of literature on humanity—that is perhaps the ultimate wisdom of the West in which the People of the Book recognizes itself." And in his own way, Bloom argues on behalf of Buber, Scholem, and other Hebrew scholars that the old Germanic biblical scholarship, which solidified the historicity of the Bible and its authors, at the same time negated their humanity by ignoring their literary achievement as well as their sexuality.

Chapter and Verse: On Translating Faithfully

When I was growing up in fifties Detroit there was a philosophy called Existentialism, and, on the periphery of my young ears, it debated the Death of God. It was a dare to divine retribution, I thought. In public, however, the subject was discussed calmly, as if there was an acknowledged boundary of discourse between religion and secular culture. This existential theology embraced a cosmic theater in mind (even if silent, God had to exist), yet it would never establish a public stage that could last.

So in the early 1970s it was my dream as a poet-scholar to recreate that public stage by restoring the authors of the Bible and their first audience. It takes imagining what that audience knew about its authors to envision a cosmic theater. When the Bible was being written, the authors were living representatives of Hebraic culture, known to their audience by name. Those names are long lost, yet when a pious believer today joins the ongoing biblical audience in time, semblances of the authors are still found in the text: Moses and David, for example, among other biblical characters. Most of us, however, need the complexity of history, and ever since Spinoza discussed the original authors (in seventeenth-century Amsterdam) we have turned to the art of historical interpretation.

Yet the newest translations still get by with avoiding the original authors completely. Instead of great writers, the authors are imagined to have been political historians, priests, or prophets. All the evidence about ancient cultures, however, points in another direction. Cultures that preceded the Hebraic one by thousands of years had literate poets and writers at their royal courts, in addition to historians and translators. In each kingdom and in most generations, these writers either added poetic interpretations to their own tradition or restored lost history. Consider the lamentation poems for the great Sumerian cities—in particular those of Ur, Abraham's city. These poems were addressed to the gods in the temple and received intimate performance upon the temple stage when the cities revived.

However, the courts of Hebrew kings asked their writers for history in place of myth. What they got were historical narratives uniting the cosmic (in realistic disguise) with the natural world. These powerful narratives were then combined into the early books of the Hebrew Bible as we now know them, beginning with Genesis. It was then, centuries after the Bible's original writers lived, that the division into chapter and verse began, accompanied by the first translations of the Hebrew Bible into Aramaic in the fifth century BCE. Those translations are lost, but later ones in Aramaic survive from the third century BCE and are known as *targums*, a Hebrew word for translations.

The first translators knew that the scrolls were combined from more than one ancient source and author. To recapture the original poetry, a more abstract use of idiom sparked the imagination of these translators, so that the deity no longer "came down from" heaven but rather "made himself present." The translator into Aramaic, taking on the role of poet-scholar, turned himself into the original poet, allowing the text to come to life again in a modern idiom. In our own day this rarely happens. Religious translators lose the lifeblood of the original by ignoring the art of the authors. On another level, academic translators leave behind the electricity of the original by presenting the text as homogeneous, failing to reimagine its idioms. An art that fits the present moment must always be found anew in order to transform the unique history of the Hebrew Bible into a compelling text. Such an art will place a delicate lens over the past, one that won't allow us to feel as though we have lost the presence of the original authors.

It was as a poet-scholar, therefore, that I made my way back to the written alphabet of the original texts and began to study the Phoenician script. One Jerusalem summer thirty years ago, I found myself in the sublet apartment of Raphael Kutscher, a renowned Assyriologist. His specialized books lined the walls of every room and hallway, and I became obsessed with them. And in discussions with Chaim Rabin, the foremost philologist of ancient Hebrew, I explored the origins of creatively inspired authorship that were later obscured by priestly self-effacement. What I was learning of biblical origins helped turn me from a poet-translator who had studied with rabbi-translators such as Robert Gordis and Harry Orlinsky into a poet-scholar.

And so I discovered for myself that when the scrolls of the original biblical writers, written in the Phoenician alphabet, were translated into the Babylonian alphabet (what we call Hebrew letters today) many ancient idioms were lost. It is a process that afflicts all living languages to some extent, but only in recent years have we built up enough historical context to reexamine the roots of Hebrew. For example, consider that in a few years from now, university students will no longer know why a blueprint was blue. New idioms continue to enter the language: "Make me a Xerox of that." Yet an ancient idiom, comparable to the word blueprint, was often translated directly into the new Hebrew script without comprehension. It was then interpreted according to its assumed meaning: a "blueprint" would become simply a "plan." Many anachronisms like this can be identified in the biblical text today, but we can no longer account for their origin. For this, a poet's knowledge of how idioms are mistranslated is necessary.

A poet also has the advantage of a natural tendency to look backward toward greatness. No matter how far human knowledge advances, great poetry is unlikely to supersede Gilgamesh or Confucius, Homer or Isaiah. Rabbinic scholars are similar in temperament: they look back to the greatness of Abraham and his authors. When they couldn't account for lost sources and idioms, the rabbis created a long tradition of speculative interpretation. Yet today we have more historical sources than any poet or rabbi had in the past. Many of these resources are older than the Bible itself, and some exhibit equal poetic gifts.

But it was not until J, the first major biblical author, that the Hebrew cosmic theater was transformed into a great narrative. There can be little doubt that J, who wrote in the Phoenician script, also read her

Sumerian predecessors in cuneiform. Yet within a century or two after J died, the memory of Sumer was lost. Hebrew authors continued to look back to the famous civilization of "Shinar," yet no one remembered where Shinar was and from where this word for Sumer came. Until the twentieth century, no one knew how to read the cuneiform tablets that were being dug up in Iraq and elsewhere. So when I began to study cuneiform writing, I felt suddenly in the presence of sources that J herself knew. I could envision her as a poet-scholar for her Hebraic audience. More than that, I understood that a poet-scholar must reinvigorate an ancient cosmic stage in danger of being drowned by either religious convention or radical skepticism. In other words, in a time of confusion between natural and supernatural (or unknowable), a new space must be cleared for a boundary that allows their healthy interaction. That is what keeps an audience alert to the intellectual tango of myth with history. The words in J's narrative may reflect roots according to the music of archaic wordplay, and this helps the audience attend to double meanings.

For instance, when the disguised angels come to rescue Lot and his family in Sodom, the incommensurate realms of natural and supernatural become enmeshed. It is two scenes in one that the original audience understood, and the play of idioms was their guide. Today we may not know the meanings and resonance of the older layers of ancient Hebrew, but we can re-echo them in a poetic usage of English idiom. Thus, I attempt to summon up the original poetic play of J, as an excerpt will illustrate. The Bible was not written in the flattened tones of conventional narrative, and neither did it sound stilted or fitted to one scholar or another's theory.

> *"Listen, I have two daughters who have not known a man intimately. Let me bring these out for you:* handle *them as you please. Only leave the visitors* untouched, *bring no* hand *to them: I have brought them under my roof's* wing."

Here is Lot in his existential dread. Although the scene is a natural one, with everyone unaware of the supernatural "visitors," the audience sees two scenes. In one they witness the earthly town of Sodom, and in the other they see through the angels' disguises and experience Lot's dread of their exposure.

The play of language alerts the audience to the doubled scene. To "handle" Lot's daughters is opposed by leaving the angels "untouched," with no "hand" applied to them. But then, the language as I've translated it tells us that Lot considers the angels under his "wing." Unlike a hand, the ordinary cliché for a roof's wing is transmuted here into a reminder that we are also in the realm of angels.

Yet the Sodomites see only the literal scene, where "hand" and "touch" have no higher poetic resonance:

> *"He comes here to share our shelter and already he* hands *down the law. Now you will know . . . a* touch *of our contempt."*

What happens next, however, makes the second scene more vivid to the audience once again, through its wordplay:

> *But from within a* hand stretched out, *brought Lot toward those visitors in the house. Now they shut him in. They blinded them with light: the people at the door, boys as well as graybeards. They would* grope for the door handle *vainly.*

And it is this supernatural scene, superimposed on the literal one, which accounts for the figure of Yahweh's "hand" becoming visible—in the "reaching out" to Lot and his daughters, once they have been secured in the "grasp" of the angels.

> *He wavered; the figures* grasped *his arm, his wife's, the hands of his two daughters—it was Yahweh* reaching out *to them. They brought him out, stopping only outside the city.*

Only when a translator keeps the original audience in mind can the poetics of the original authors be interpreted. Most religious translators overlook the poetry of such scenes as this one in Sodom, while academic translators neglect the creativity of the original Hebraic culture.

But in the best translation traces of the original authors are left visible, as in the rich scale of phrasing that characterizes the King James Version, or in the range of cultural context provided by the Anchor Genesis. I learned much from both.

The King James (1611) testifies to the great literary ambition of the original Hebrew. Add to that E. A. Speiser's Genesis volume in the Anchor Bible (1962), which is framed by concise notes that make the original authors accessible for the first time. "Translations are so much more enjoyable than originals," relates Speiser in typically ironic manner, "because they contain many things that the originals leave out." In other biblical translations, the most significant "leaving out" are the sources and ancient knowledge available to the original audiences. Without this basic context, we cannot expect an accurate translation.

Until recently, however, knowledge about how the text was written was thought to be unimportant. All the attention was on the spiritual "why" of the text: the development of religious thought. Ancient Hebraic culture itself had largely been forgotten. Yet much had changed by the 1960s, when Speiser rejected the German scholarly notion of impersonal "strands" and treated the J and E portions of the text as living authors with cultural imaginations. For generations, cultures had been studied as isolated units, but now the emphasis was to fall on how they intersect and echo one another. In each, there are traditions of individual authorship. Poet-scholars opened a path to some of these in the twentieth century and proved a strong influence in my own early education.

When I was in high school and dreaming of becoming a poet, I encountered the ancient Chinese translations of Arthur Waley. The disarming lucidity of these poems served as a trellis over which Waley draped his commentary, and I was soon charmed by the innovation of his books, which presented poem and commentary together in a new form. Waley was a fresh example of the poet-scholar. Neither a poet who translates nor a scholar who writes poetry, Waley rediscovered a poem as if it were written by an ancient twin, merging his own identity with the original author. He then placed the poem in its original culture with contextual annotation. A few years later, when I began to translate some Hebrew psalms, I also wrapped them in commentary, allowing poems and prose together to tell a single story about the historical day in which the original author wrote. But often I removed my commentary from the text, afraid it distracted from my purely literary ambitions. Unlike Waley's Chinese poems, which were the first translations into English in many cases, my psalms could be contrasted with a host of other versions in English, including many that dripped with pedantry.

Arthur Waley was a pioneer modernist when he brought out his first book in 1918. Looking back in later years, he noted that his combination of the scholar and the poet could only succeed "when scholarship is in a rather rudimentary state, as it was as regards Chinese when I started." In a striking parallel, the field of biblical authorship itself is still brand-new, and although I've been concerned with the original writers since the 1970s, it took much digging far afield to get my bearings. Just as Waley provided the historical context—or literary archaeology—for his Chinese poems by exploring comparative cultural history, I probed related fields, including Sumerian and Canaanite studies, to enlarge the context for biblical authorship.

Of the poets I studied with in youth—Snodgrass, Lowell, Hall, Koch, Schwartz—all but one were literary sons of T. S. Eliot. Yet their life experience was the stage upon which they performed, rarely venturing into serious research. In my own discovering, I found Gertrude Stein closest in spirit (and actual friendship) to Waley. She had immersed herself in a range of studies from linguistic and psychological theory to modern art and American history—and she always began by exploring the origins of each field, as with William James in psychology or Cezanne in modern art. Her studies of the Wright Brothers and of Ulysses S. Grant remain untapped primers on the American sensibility. Although I failed to complete my doctoral thesis on her work, in 1971 I followed a path directly from Stein to the linguistic origins of the Hebrew Bible. That might not seem an obvious direction, but Stein's influence took the form of intrepid insistence upon origins.

Later, I took Israel's Gershom Scholem as my model of the poet-scholar. Scholem often weaved his presentations of poetic Kabbalistic texts into a contextual commentary. So seamless was the effort that he was rarely thought of as a poet at all. Yet my own scholarship led me far from Scholem's academe and back to Waley, who had worked independently. It was then I discovered how Waley came from a Jewish intellectual tradition on both sides of his family, so that it wasn't hard to imagine him as a biblical scholar and interpreter had he lived several generations in the past.

In the years after I published my first translations of Hebrew psalms (*Blues of the Sky,* 1974) I have been arguing for uncovering the lives of the original authors. It's not that they are more important than what they wrote; rather, awareness of them as literate human beings illuminates what was written as no doctrine or literary approach can do by itself. Without the authors, we have no cultural equivalent for divine inspiration—that is, how an individual is wounded and inspired by history, culture, and language.

What is divine inspiration? We have to start with the fundamental questions about truth and justice, good and evil, ecstasy and suffering, with which our original authors struggled. The answers were inspired by reading, hearing of, or translating earlier cultures and traditions, even when they were presumed to be one's own tradition. However fine-tuned by a moral lens, it is due to artistic inspiration that we can still overhear the dialogue between God and man when no witness was present. Maintaining the archaic tradition of divine inspiration required the human creation of a cosmic stage, upon which Earth and the unknowable heavens could be credibly represented and updated. Myth could be reoriented to reality and constrained to history on this stage, as long as it was preserved by artistic inspiration.

As a poet-scholar, I work to restore the cosmic theater enfolding biblical narrative and poetry. Behind it—behind biblical chapter and verse—lies a lost Hebraic culture. A faithful translation should evoke this culture as a presence we feel if not see. It should not look or sound dated or flat but rather be accessible to us as a spirit at play in our own language today. I need to translate and interpret this spirit as a poet inspired by historical processes. Yet as a scholar I have no desire to transcend the human situation; I only wish to explore its boundaries.

Acknowledgments

It's a commonplace that no writer exists without help. More than that, Shifra Asarch, my mother, continued pushing as she asked, during the writing of this book, "Where is Abraham now?" When she was gone, my brother Sanford sustained the loyal interrogation, as well as Bert and Wanda, parents in more than law.

When this book was in its oral phase—still talk—it caught the ear of a superb translator of ideas into facts, Howard Morhaim, who became my literary agent. From Howard's hands to Basic editor and publisher Elizabeth Maguire's, whose loyalty over many years, from first hearing to final draft, proved a writer's best company.

Help with research came from fellow writers Michal Govrin, David Shapiro, and Leonard Michaels. Lenny insisted I write faster but also admitted he was the slowest writer he knew. I could not write fast enough to hear Lenny's response to the finished manuscript, alas.

I received invaluable help in early stages of editing from Peter Guzzardi, who was willing to act the general reader in place of the extraordinary one he is. John Michel's editorial wit and skill opened up reservoirs of rethinking. Andrew Solomon aided early research, stimulated by the affectionate curiosity of Joyce, Mark, and Andrew Davidson. My debt to scholars, rabbis, and teachers is noted in this book's appendix, *Chapter and Verse*. Absorbing the work of many Sumerian translators along the way, I have also ventured my own renditions based upon the cuneiform tablets I studied.

I'm grateful for the listening posts provided by Jed Sekoff, Nancy Milford, Evan Eisenberg, Peter Raven, Prof. Z. Buber, and poets Grace

Schulman in New York, Kent Johnson in Illinois, Harold Schimmel in Israel, and the Canadian guardians of *The Martyrology*, by B. P. Nichol (1944–88), the nine singular books of which keep me going. The literary character Nichol creates of himself is more like Abraham than any other in modern literature. Nichol's authorial consciousness journeys from childhood to death to found and explore a cosmological language, sustaining it within his family drama.

Finally, it is most common to acknowledge one's soul mate, if lucky enough to have found one. Sometimes this mate is first reader and editor, and it is then de rigueur to acknowledge the companion without whom this book would still be a pipedream. But in this instance, the sentiment beggars the facts. Rhonda Rosenberg sat beside me and coauthored the first draft of this book, after contributing her uncanny research skills. If anything, she is the book's spine and I am its far from svelte stomach. Her talent as a writer and thinker is unrivaled by most that I know. As a result, it has become inconceivable to me that Abraham would have passed one night on the road, let alone a lifetime, without the mind of Sarah beside him. And although reputed for her beauty, it was Sarah's brilliant composure that saved their lives in Egypt, in Canaan, and most likely in Ur and Harran. It would be an understatement to say that everything revolved around her, for when she named her son Isaac (cognate to the word for laughter in Hebrew) she recalled her own prompting of Yahweh, also in a laugh, to remember the unlikelihood of his sexual promise.

Index